DETECTIVE FICTION IN A POSTCOLONIAL AND TRANSNATIONAL WORLD

Detective Fiction in a Postcolonial and Transnational World

Edited by

NELS PEARSON
Fairfield University, USA

and

MARC SINGER
Howard University, USA

ASHGATE

Published by
Ashgate Publishing Limited
Wey Court East
Union Road
Farnham
Surrey, GU9 7PT
England

Ashgate Publishing Company
Suite 420
101 Cherry Street
Burlington
VT 05401-4405
USA

www.ashgate.com

British Library Cataloguing in Publication Data
Detective fiction in a postcolonial and transnational world.
1. Detective and mystery stories—History and criticism.
2. Postcolonialism in literature. 3. Politics and literature.
I. Pearson, Nels. II. Singer, Marc.
809.9'33556–dc22

Library of Congress Cataloging-in-Publication Data
Pearson, Nels, 1969–
Detective fiction in a postcolonial and transnational world / Nels Pearson and Marc Singer.
p. cm.
Includes bibliographical references and index.
ISBN 978-0-7546-6848-0 (hardcover : alk. paper)—ISBN 978-0-7546-9642-1 (ebook)
1. Detective and mystery stories—History and criticism. 2. Detective and mystery stories, Commonwealth (English)—History and criticism. 3. Detective and mystery stories, Caribbean (French)—History and criticism. 4. Detective and mystery stories, Latin American—History and criticism. 5. Detective and mystery stories, American—History and criticism. I. Singer, Marc. II. Title.

PN3448.D4P425 2009
809.3'872–dc22

2009011304

ISBN 9780754668480 (hbk)
ISBN 9780754696421 (ebk)

Printed and bound in Great Britain by
TJ International Ltd, Padstow, Cornwall

Contents

Notes on Contributors

Claire Chambers is a Senior Lecturer in English Literature at Leeds Metropolitan University and a specialist in South Asian literature written in English and in literary representations of British Muslims. She takes an interdisciplinary approach to texts, and in her work to date she has been interested in fictional representations of such disciplines as science and technology, anthropology, and history and their imbrication in (neo-) colonialism. She has published widely in such journals as *Postcolonial Text*, *The Journal of Commonwealth Literature*, and *The Journal of Postcolonial Writing*.

Emily S. Davis is Assistant Professor of English at the University of Delaware, where she teaches courses in world literature, literary theory, globalization, and feminist cultural studies. Her research focuses on transnational formations of intimacy in romances by postcolonial women and queer writers. She has published recent articles in *Camera Obscura* and *Genders*.

Robin Truth Goodman is Associate Professor of English at Florida State University. Her publications include *Policing Narratives and the State of Terror* (forthcoming from SUNY Press), *World, Class, Women: Global Literature, Education, and Feminism* (Routledge, 2004), *Strange Love: Or How We Learn to Stop Worrying and Love the Market* (co-written with Kenneth J. Saltman; Rowman & Littlefield, 2002), and *Infertilities: Exploring Fictions of Barren Bodies* (University of Minnesota Press, 2001).

Jason Herbeck is Assistant Professor of French at Boise State University, where he teaches a wide range of French and Francophone language, literature, culture, and theory courses. His research focuses primarily on evolving narrative forms in twentieth-century French and Caribbean literatures, and how these forms relate to expressions and constructions of identity. He has presented papers on lovers' discourse, jazz, philosophical approaches to literature, Caribbean intertextuality, and detective fiction. Some of his articles have appeared in *L'Esprit créateur*, *Dalhousie French Studies*, *The French Review* and *Romanic Review*.

Soo Yeon Kim is a doctoral candidate in the department of English at Texas A&M University, College Station. Her writing has been published, or will be published, in *Doris Lessing Studies*, *The Greenwood Encyclopedia of Asian American Literature*, and *South Central Review*. Kim is currently working on her dissertation, "Ethical Desire: Betrayal in Contemporary British Fiction and Film."

Wendy Knepper is an adjunct lecturer at Brunel University and Research Fellow at the Institute for the Americas, University of London. Previously, she has held appointments as a Visiting Scholar at Harvard University and New York University and taught at the Humboldt University of Berlin. Her research interests in the areas of postcolonial theory and transcultural approaches to literary studies are represented in numerous contributions to journals and essay collections, including recent contributions to *Small Axe* and *PMLA*. Having recently completed a critical study of Patrick Chamoiseau, she is currently at work on a second book-length project, entitled "The Global Imaginary in Contemporary Caribbean Writing."

Raphaël Lambert holds a Ph.D. in English from the University of Wisconsin-Milwaukee. He is an assistant professor at the University of Tsukuba in Japan, where he teaches jazz, the blues, slavery, and Hollywood cinema. His current research focuses on media representations of the transatlantic slave trade. His recent publications and talks include works on Richard Wright's *Native Son*, Percival Everett's *Erasure*, and the theme of the middle passage in poetry, graphic novels, and film.

Maureen Lauder teaches at Michigan State University. She is currently working on a project on desire and narrative in postwar British and American fiction.

Jennifer Lewis is a part-time lecturer at Bath Spa University, where she teaches American and postcolonial literature. Her research interests are in the areas of postcolonial theory, feminist theory, and cultural geography, particularly in relation to twentieth- and twenty-first-century African American writing.

Nels Pearson is Assistant Professor of English at Fairfield University, where he teaches courses in twentieth-century British literature, Irish literature, and modernism. His research focuses on relationships between modernism, empire, and postcolonial studies, and his articles have appeared in such forums as *ELH*, *European Joyce Studies*, *Studies in Scottish Literature*, and *Conradiana*.

Marc Singer is Assistant Professor of English at Howard University. His articles on contemporary literature, narrative theory, and popular culture have appeared in *Critique*, *Post Script*, *JNT: Journal of Narrative Theory*, *Twentieth-Century Literature*, *African American Review*, and the *International Journal of Comic Art*.

Haiqing Sun received her B.A. and M.A. in Spanish from Peking University, and her Ph.D. in Spanish from the University of Southern California. She is Associate Professor of Spanish at Texas Southern University, specializing in contemporary Latin American narrative. She is also one of the Chinese translators of José Echegarray, Gabriela Mistral, Octavio Paz, and Luis Buñuel.

Greg Wright teaches film studies and critical theory at Kalamazoo College. His research focuses primarily on issues of media forms, intertextuality, and adaptation. He earned his Ph.D. in American Literature and Film at Michigan State University in 2007, and his dissertation, "Textual Evolution: Adaptation in Literature, Film, and Culture," synthesizes evolutionary theory with narrative theory in order to explore how texts adapt, mutate, and proliferate over time and space. He has published articles in the *Quarterly Review of Film and Video* and *The Journal of Popular Culture*.

Introduction

Open Cases: Detection, (Post)Modernity, and the State

Nels Pearson and Marc Singer

> How does one tell of murder in a new town?
> Where does one begin?
>
> —Ngugi, *Petals of Blood*

The rationale for scholarly interest in the detective novel has shifted considerably in recent years. Since the 1970s, academics have often regarded detective fiction, like other popular genre fiction, as a set of conventions and formulas that reaffirm a culture's dominant ideology, "confirming existing definitions of the world" and attempting to resolve their tensions or contradictions (Cawelti 35). This approach, which retains some critical currency today, views detective fiction as a paradigm and an implement of the hegemonic processes of the Western nation-state, tantalizing readers with aberrant, irrational criminality while assuring them that society ultimately coheres through a shared commitment to reason and law. For scholars such as Franco Moretti, the detective genre "resolves the deep anxiety of an expanding society" and reassures readers "that society is still a great *organism*: a unitary and knowable body" (143, 145; his emphasis). For more narratologically-minded critics like Peter Brooks, the crime-and-inquest structure of detective fiction typologizes or lays bare "the structure of all narrative" (25).[1] In both of these approaches, the detective novel is reduced to a formulaic, forensically deducible cultural product whose structural conventions reflect knowledge production either

[1] Peter Brooks, extending the arguments of Tzvetan Todorov, makes this observation in *Reading for the Plot* (1984). Todorov had exemplified this approach in "The Typology of Detective Fiction" (1977), wherein external (social, political, economic, cultural) history, if it is considered at all, is taken to have no bearing upon developments in literary history, which proceed only according to the internal logics of form and genre. For Todorov, "history" means only the timetable of structural evolutions within a genre, as is evident when he discusses the development of the suspense novel: "Historically, this form of detective fiction appeared at two moments: it served as transition between the whodunit and the thriller and it existed at the same time as the latter" (51). By interpreting the genre solely as a representative of or test case for formalist and structuralist principles, too much of the past criticism on detective fiction has relegated such concepts as society, law, criminality, or morality to a strictly abstract plane—a realm of generalization made possible in part by the relatively stable status of these terms within the achieved state, and by the desire to universalize these concepts which lies at the foundation of the imperial state.

in the abstract or as a dominant (white, Western, capitalist, and nation-statist) cultural practice. Both the sociological and the narratological approaches consider the form and content of the detective novel to be an open and shut case: a matter of how the genre both creates and resolves epistemological and ideological tensions.

More recent studies of detective and crime fiction, however, have refocused around fundamentally different arguments about how the genre engages structures of knowledge, especially those "external" to the text. Much of the current criticism views the genre as formally diverse, flourishing in multiple cultures, and engaged with the production of knowledge and transformation of consciousness within and across societies. As Christine Matzke and Susanne Mühleisen note,

> The boundaries of the genre have become fuzzier than ever, stretching over a wide range of registers, themes and styles, from pulp fiction to highly literary novels with elements of crime, from cosy mysteries with a sense of closure to fragmented narratives focusing on racial tensions, gender conflicts or the morals of violence. (3)

In his analysis of American crime fiction's complex relationship with race and cultural difference, Andrew Pepper argues that the detective "has always been a liminal, contrary figure," especially in the hard-boiled and black detective traditions (34). For Pepper, the crime novel is hardly a form that doles out social-cognitive coherence or hegemonic affirmation; rather, it is one "riven with ambiguities and contradictions, [...] amenable to antithetical readings, [and] satiated in a logic that is simultaneously reactionary and progressive" (34). When we venture beyond the Anglo-American "clue-puzzle" or "cozy mystery" traditions of abstracted ratiocination, we encounter figures whose investigative practices challenge presumptions of objective policing and deduction—and, potentially, the legal and social orders that are founded upon such presumptions. Stephen Soitos, who focuses exclusively on African American detectives in *The Blues Detective* (1996), argues that such figures provide agency, visibility, or identity to marginalized communities:

> First, [African American writers] made the detectives—both male and female—black, and their blackness an integral ingredient for the success of the investigation. Second, the blues detective's identity is directly connected to community [...] all of them are aware, and make the reader aware, of their place within the fabric of their black society. (29)

For Ralph Rodriguez, who studies adaptations of the genre in Chicano/a literature, the detective novel also offers "a productive form," insofar as it engages the "new discourses of identity, politics, and cultural citizenship that speak to the shifting historical moment in which Chicana/os have found themselves since the demise of the nationalist politics of the Chicana/o movement (ca. 1965–1975)" (2).

This turn of the critical tide—from seeing the detective novel as a reflective or paradigmatic narrative to seeing it as a locally engaged, formally diverse, and discursively productive text—is due partly to the proliferation and diversity of detective fiction in contemporary literature, and partly to a broader movement in studies of popular culture to correct the "modernist mass-cultural theory that [blindly and routinely] ascribes a central meaning to a whole form" and makes sweeping generalizations about "the way[s] popular fiction serves social conformity" (Docker 220). But it is also driven by our increasing awareness of the fact that, from its inception, the detective genre has been intrinsically engaged with epistemological formations that are not simply those of "society" in the abstract—that is, dominant cultural groups and their hegemonic discourse—but those produced in encounters between nations, between races and cultures, and especially between imperial powers and their colonial territories. This study draws upon, and hopes to enhance, both of these critical trends. Our aim is twofold: first, to highlight the increasing number of postcolonial and Asian, Latino/a and black transnational authors who adapt detective and crime fiction conventions, often dispensing with presumed boundaries between high and popular culture; and second, to encourage scholarly conversation, from different critical angles, about the many ways these texts dramatize the challenges of formulating a genuinely democratic approach to knowledge-production, justice, and human rights in a transnational and postcolonial world.

Detection, Race, and Empire

No contemporary critical account can overlook the formative roles that race, nation, and empire have played in the development of detective fiction. From its origins in the nineteenth century to its commercial dominance in the twenty-first, the detective genre has connected the imposition of law and order to colonial, postcolonial, and transnational spaces and communities. As Upamanyu Pablo Mukherjee and Caroline Reitz have demonstrated, nineteenth-century English crime fiction developed in conjunction with the formation of imperial authority, especially in India, drawing upon narratives of colonial governance to formulate its own portrayals of domestic policing. In *Detecting the Nation* (2004), Reitz argues that detective fiction enjoyed a "mutually formative relationship with such narratives as histories of British India, English accounts of the Indian practice of Thuggee, and Kipling's imperial fiction" (xvi) long before it coalesced into its own distinct genre. Stephen Knight, in a survey of crime fiction in three British colonies—Australia, America, and Wales—observes that "Crime fiction is an early, often the first, voice to respond to new social and cultural encounters generated by the colonial situation" (25).

Evidence of colonialism and empire has therefore been legible in the detective genre since its beginnings. From Edgar Allan Poe's "The Murders in the Rue Morgue" (1841), in which C. Auguste Dupin attributes a pair of grisly murders to a racially-encoded Bornese "Ourang-Outang" brought to Paris by a profit-minded sailor, to Arthur Conan Doyle's *A Study in Scarlet* (1887), wherein Sherlock Holmes exposes the murderous revenge of a frontier settler who tracks his fiancée's killers from the deserts of Utah to the gaslit streets of London, the classic detective fiction of the Victorian era suggests that this migrating violence is not a social aberration but a structural feature of empire.[2] Transnational encounters are not always dangerous in this period; they can lead to spiritual reinvigoration for touring Europeans, as when Holmes wanders from Mecca to Tibet following his apparent death at Reichenbach Falls, or to improved local knowledge and more efficient colonial policing, as in Rudyard Kipling's spy novel *Kim* (1901).[3] Beyond these fantasies of Orientalist wisdom and beneficent imperialism, however, classic detective fiction and its close cousin the spy story more typically align mystery conventions with anxieties over contamination, irrationality, and the threat posed to imperial modernity by unassimilated racial and cultural difference. This combination is not only a common fixture, but also—in narratives such as Joseph Conrad's "Heart of Darkness" (1900) and *The Secret Agent* (1907)—one that easily traverses the boundaries of high and popular culture.

Mystery writers in the early twentieth century continued to rely on foreign settings, characters, and menaces, even in the stereotypically English genre of the country house or clue-puzzle story of the interwar years. In 1929 Ronald Knox, a founding member of the Detection Club, issued "A Detective Story Decalogue," which included such tongue-in-cheek prohibitions as "No Chinaman must figure in the story" (201). While Reitz interprets such aphorisms as evidence that "Golden Age writers and subsequent literary critics want to get back to some Edenic version of prewar England untouched by the 'unseemly' and immoderate aspects

---

[2] H.R.F. Keating, himself the author of a series of postcolonial detective novels, has written that America repeatedly figures as a "cauldron of troubles" (56) in Arthur Conan Doyle's Holmes tales, a place of lawlessness and savagery; other mysteries are prompted by the Ku Klux Klan in "The Five Orange Pips" (1891) and by an Apache raid in "The Adventure of the Noble Bachelor" (1892). Jefferson Hope, however, is doubly exoticized, a "savage-looking young fellow" (*Complete Sherlock Holmes* 60) who possesses "a power of sustained vindictiveness, which he may have learned from the Indians amongst whom he had lived" (73). Subsequent crimes originate in India (*The Sign of Four*, 1890, "The Adventure of the Speckled Band," 1892, and "The Adventure of the Crooked Man," 1893) and a fictitious Central American dictatorship ("The Adventure of Wisteria Lodge," 1908). Catherine Wynne has argued that Conan Doyle modeled Professor Moriarty's criminal network on Irish secret societies in England, Ireland, and America, suggesting yet another imperial subtext in the Holmes tales. As Joseph McLaughlin notes, "Holmes's work almost always involves encounters with dangerous foreigners" (57).

[3] Tibetan expatriate writer Jamyang Norbu links both of these narratives in *The Mandala of Sherlock Holmes* (1999), which details the years Holmes spent in Tibet and introduces the detective to Kipling's Bengali spy Hurree Chunder Mookerjee, effectively reuniting classic detective fiction with the spy novel while writing against the imperialist assumptions of both genres.

of imperial rule" (67), Knox's pronouncement also highlights the high incidence of exotic foreigners in the classic period of detective fiction; if "Chinamen" had not already seen frequent use or overuse by 1929, they would not appear in Knox's "prohibitions against using clichéd devices" (Horsley 41). Nevertheless, the clue-puzzle stories continued to use foreign countries and colonial holdings both as sources of mystery and evil and as exotic backdrops for otherwise conventional mysteries of "closed circle societies" (Bargainnier 30) of Englishmen, as in Agatha Christie's *Murder in Mesopotamia* (1936) and *Death on the Nile* (1937)—English country house mysteries lacking only England and the country house.

But just as scholarship regarding the detective genre has shifted from examinations of formal devices to questions of socio-political engagement, interrogation, and transformation, so too, albeit with complexity, has the genre itself. Even as Knox and the Detection Club were codifying the rules of the clue-puzzle mystery, another subgenre was already staking out a radically different set of conventions, including another approach to representing race. In a marked divergence from the English classic detective tradition, American hard-boiled crime fiction defined itself in opposition to the racialist fantasies of imperialism and imperial adventure fiction. Sean McCann observes in *Gumshoe America* (2000) that "the first successful hard-boiled private detective, Carroll John Daly's tellingly named Race Williams, made his debut in a special issue of *Black Mask* dedicated to a fictional debate over the [Ku Klux] Klan—a dispute that Williams entered as an enemy of the Invisible Empire" (40–41). Hard-boiled detective fiction is hardly free of racial and ethnic stereotyping; even a cursory glance at the genre's most acclaimed works will turn up Raymond Chandler's alienated portrayal of Los Angeles's African American Central Avenue in *Farewell, My Lovely* (1940) or the ethnicized gangsters and treasure seekers who populate Dashiell Hammett's *Red Harvest* (1929) and *The Maltese Falcon* (1930). However, McCann argues that "the hard-boiled genre typically neglects to resolve social decay by casting it as a conflict between cultures or races" (69). Hard-boiled detectives inhabit denationalized, multiethnic modern cities but they have accepted and adapted to that lifestyle, in stark contrast to the antimodernist fantasies of exotic adventure fiction and the Klan.

This conversance with a multicultural modernity may be one reason the hard-boiled detective has proven so popular a figure in postcolonial and minority detective fiction. Indeed, the hard-boiled detective novel is not only an example of the depth and duration of the relationship between crime fiction and racial episteme, but one of the sites where the genre challenges that episteme and its alignment with national and imperial ideology. Authors ranging from Chester Himes to Vikram Chandra invoke the hard-boiled detective as a template for their own postcolonial, transnational, or racially marginalized detectives. Some of these investigators, like Himes's Coffin Ed Johnson and Grave Digger Jones or Chandra's Sartaj Singh, expand the detective's role to nationalities and cultural minorities that have been marginalized or exoticized in previous crime fiction. Other investigators comment on and critique the hard-boiled tradition itself; as

Jennifer Lewis observes in her contribution to this volume, Paco Ignacio Taibo II's Héctor Belascoarán Shayne alludes to Brett Halliday's long-running character Mike Shayne, a detective whose origins lie in ethnocentric fantasy. The prevalence of this template perhaps indicates hard-boiled crime fiction's continuing popular and literary capital, but it also suggests that certain features of the hard-boiled detectives—their urbanity and modernity, their ability to cross racial and class lines as easily as they traverse the city, and the tendency of their investigations to broaden out from individual criminal acts to implicate larger social ills—are easily adapted to the cultural critiques common to postcolonial literature. The hard-boiled detective's social mobility has translated to a generic portability that has made the character a recurring type, if also an object of criticism or transformation, in detective fiction around the world.

An equally compelling example of generic transformation aligning with critiques of the genre's earlier imperialist linkages is to be found in the hermeneutic skepticism and generic self-reflexivity of the metaphysical detective story, a comparatively recent subgenre that emerged from the philosophically-minded, avant-garde mystery tales of Jorges Luis Borges, Alain Robbe-Grillet, and other early postmodernists.[4] Sometimes called the anti-detective story, the metaphysical detective story is

> a text that parodies or subverts traditional detective-story conventions—such as narrative closure and the detective's role as surrogate reader—with the intention, or at least the effect, of asking questions about mysteries of being and knowing which transcend the mere machinations of the mystery plot [….] Rather than definitively solving a crime, then, the sleuth finds himself confronting the insoluble mysteries of his own interpretation and his own identity. (Merivale and Sweeney 2)

Although the metaphysical detective story tends to approach these questions as abstracted, ostensibly universal critiques of rationalism and not as localized issues of national or racial identity, many postcolonial writers who have worked in this subgenre have shown that some of the most serious challenges to abstract ratiocination arise within the specific, contested ground of postcolonial and emergent transnational societies.

In this collection, for example, Greg Wright and Jason Herbeck each demonstrate how crime novels of the French Caribbean, particularly the works of Patrick Chamoiseau, locally contextualize the metaphysical detective story's hermeneutic skepticism as they depict the deconstruction of empirical investigation that arises where imperial policing and oral culture collide. For Maureen Lauder and Soo Kim (who study Amitav Ghosh's *The Calcutta Chromosome* and Suki Kim's *The*

---

[4] Although the metaphysical detective story is a late modernist or postmodernist genre, Patricia Merivale and Susan Elizabeth Sweeney trace its origins back to Poe, G.K. Chesterton, and the analytic detective tradition (4).

Interpreter, respectively), the effort to investigate transnational mysteries within centers of multinational capitalism—where a superficial multiculturalism can ironically obscure the disturbing specifics of minority histories—offers an equally poignant historical grounding of the metaphysical detective's inquiry into the nature or attainability of knowledge.

Grounds for the Transient: Postcolonial and Transnational Detectives

To trace the major developments in detective fiction is, then, to recognize a genre that has evolved from seeing transgressions of national and racial boundaries as preconditions for crime to seeing them as keys to its detection and resolution, especially where such solutions include indictments of broader social and political conditions. Most scholarship on this transformation, however, has been limited to the study of detective novels by and about distinct racial or ethnic minority groups. Taken together, these studies suggest a genre in the process of interrogating or defying its own imperial history. And yet, critical study of the international and transnational emergence of the genre from its colonial and race-anxious heritage—that is, study of the shifting discourses of detective fiction as a phenomenon dynamically related to the emergence of postcolonial and transnational cultures on a more global scale—is comparatively undeveloped.

The Post-Colonial Detective (2001), a collection of essays edited by Ed Christian, is a pioneering study in this regard, insofar as it focuses on detective characters who are "indigenous to or settlers in the [postcolonial] countries where they work; they are usually marginalized in some way [...] and their creators' interest usually lies in an exploration of how these detectives' approaches to criminal investigation are influenced by their cultural attitudes" (2). Contributors to Christian's study demonstrate how such detectives engage in a "practical anthropology" that "leads to tolerance of diversity and hybridity [and] to understanding of why people of different cultures act differently than we do" (2). The collection, which focuses primarily on work by white male authors, tends to define postcolonial detectives as cultural informants who work in the "area of overlap [where] the colonizer and the colonized collide" (11), who act as "valuable intermediaries between cultures" (11), and who "combine their indigenous cultural knowledge with western police methods in solving crimes" (3). By relying on fundamental and nationally circumscribed colonizer/colonized and oppressor/oppressed models, the book—which, in Christian's words, does not "resort to explicit theorizing" (8)—overlooks a number of issues that mediate or complicate these binaries, issues that theoretical approaches to race and empire (which tend to be committed to particularity, to the complexity of local histories, and to a rigorous skepticism about utopian multiculturalism) have helped bring to light. These factors—such as persistent neocolonialism, multinational and corporate forms of global policing, individuals and networks of authority that travel across multiple borders, the protean nature of racial or ethnic profiling, and the problems of ascertaining a common ethical language in which to determine and communicate human rights violations—are not only important in any analysis of postcolonial and transnational culture, but also pivotal themes in many contemporary crime novels. Contributors to our collection explore these vital issues from a variety of critical angles and with the aid of relevant theoretical approaches.

More recent, and more in tandem with the objectives of this volume, is Christine Matzke and Susanne Mühleisen's *Postcolonial Postmortems: Crime Fiction from a Transcultural Perspective* (2006). Like Christian and other scholars of contemporary detective fiction, Matzke, Mühleisen, and their contributors demonstrate the active engagement between detectives, their authors, and types or formations of knowledge within postcolonial contexts. However, the scholars of *Postcolonial Postmortems* study a more diverse and expansive body of detective narratives, analyzing the relationship between the forms and discourses of the genre and the ideological and epistemological disputes that arise either in postcolonial settings or when "investigators with a migrant or transcultural background operat[e] across countries and continents" (3). Throughout their collection, detective fiction emerges as a potent and flexible mode for interrogating the imperial histories and racial ideologies that helped spur its own generic development: "postcolonial [crime novels] suggest that power and authority can be investigated through the magnifying glass of other knowledges, against the local or global mainstream, past and present, or against potential projections of a dominant group and a (neo-) imperial West" (5).

This book has similar objectives, offering readers an extension of this important work into the study of new authors and contexts that are not discussed in either of the aforementioned volumes, including more authors of color and non-Anglophone novelists who write about former colonies of France and Spain. These include Patrick Chamoiseau (Martinique), Mario Vargas Llosa (Peru), Vikram Chandra (India), Walter Mosley (black Los Angeles), Suki Kim (Korean American New York), and Latina/o novelists Lucha Corpi, Carolina Garcia-Aguilera, and Marcos M. Villatoro. Unique to this volume, though, is its more targeted interest in stories about investigations that take place at specific intersections of postcolonial and transnational or multicultural life. This collection views the narration of crime and detection in such contexts less as an act that "increasingly transcends, if not invalidates, national boundaries" (Matzke and Mühleisen 8) and more as a confrontation with the disjunctures between real and imagined diversity, between post-national dreams and the realities of being bereft of statehood or collective agency. Indeed, the changes in the writing and reading of detective fiction that we have outlined suggest an important correspondence not with a broadly conceived, increasingly borderless globalization of culture, but with specific concerns and debates about ethics, human rights, and egalitarian statehood that are emerging at the intersection of postcolonial and transnational studies.

In place of static models of culture, transnational cultural studies proposes that cultures are just as frequently "shaped by an intense, continuous, comprehensive interplay between the indigenous and the imported" (Hannerz 5). Responsible studies in the field do not claim, as Arjun Appadurai puts it, "that there are not anywhere relatively stable communities and networks" of culture and economy, but do account for the fact that "the warp of these stabilities is everywhere shot through with the woof of human motion" (231). To understand culture in a global context, Hannerz argues, "[a] clear sense of what penetrates, cuts across, or supersedes boundaries must be at least an important complement to the understanding of whatever may be the internal workings of [...] state apparatuses" (48). Transnational studies thus shares with recent postcolonial theory a need to move beyond nationally circumscribed and center/periphery models of cultural and economic development toward models, and worldviews, that effectively comprehend not just liminal states, but liminal forms of statehood, and that articulate or legitimize multiple trajectories of belonging and identity. The field also recognizes less abstract problems faced by postcolonial and transnational subjects, including one dilemma that is especially pertinent to this collection: laws, human rights, and the assessment of criminal guilt—both as protective and punitive codes—have rarely matched the flexibility of culture, or kept pace with economic developments, across transnational space, or within postcolonial countries where state authorities, agendas, and jurisdictions frequently shift.

Hence, along with the efforts to understand identity and to comprehend culture in less fixed, more fluid and mobile terms, there is an equally strong push to recognize that the nation-state, with its unique ability to secure universal rights and thus, paradoxically, provide individuals the liberty to think and to move freely between their local and global citizenship, remains not only a salient category, but in many cases a goal still to be achieved. It is certainly true, as Homi Bhabha writes, that "the language of rights and obligations, so central to the modern myth of a people, must be questioned on the basis of the anomalous and discriminatory legal and cultural status assigned to migrant, diasporic, and refugee populations[,]" as well as those who are marginalized within or "find themselves on the frontiers between" cultures and nations (175). But it is equally important to observe, as David Chandler does, that "there can be no international law without equal sovereignty, no system of [universal] rights without state-subjects capable of being its bearers" (34). Thus, as Tim Brennan points out, the most equitable mode of globalization might be "*Inter*nationalism," for it "does not quarrel with the principle of *national* sovereignty, [the only] way under modern conditions to secure respect for weaker societies or peoples" (42; his emphasis). Even David Harvey, who is far less sanguine about appeals to universal rights—noting that such appeals have recently served as pretexts for imperialist interventions (178–9)—must agree that "However much we might wish rights to be universal, it is the state that has to enforce them" (180). Although there are numerous significant differences between them, migrant, racially marginalized, multicultural, and postcolonial communities often experience some version of this psychically non-binary, historically non-linear relationship with the political state.

Just as the post-national has been subject to criticism, so too have overly triumphant declarations of the deterritorialization of culture. For many people in emerging postcolonial states, and others who know first-hand the persistence of race-based marginalization, as well as for those building multicultural or transnational communities, pledges of utopian multiculturalism and apotheoses of border-transgression, whether proffered by intellectuals or corporate advertisers, are often empty and counter-productive promises. In this regard, Simon Gikandi cautions us against being "eager to embrace globalization and its images or fictions because of its amorphous character" and worries that

> in their desire to secure the newness of theories of globalization, to posit them as postmodern and postcolonial as it were, many critics and analysts of the phenomenon no longer seem interested in the "Third World" itself as a source of the cultural energies—and the tragedies—that have brought new migrants to the west. […] [They forget that] global culture is a result of the transformations in both "first" and "third Worlds," and especially a transformation of the institutions of knowledge production […] in both zones. (621–3)

As Graham Huggan has similarly argued, to trope the actual experiences of those bereft of statehood or collective agency as we totalize concepts like liminality, migrancy, and hybridity in theories of globalization is to augment "the discrepancy between historical experiences of migration and aestheticized theories of 'migrancy'" and create "a fraught alliance between the allegedly transgressive manoeuvres of postmodern travelling theory and the putatively oppositional politics of postcolonial cultural practice" (117, 120). It is also to lay a weak foundation on which to construct global ethics. Indeed, the more immediate demands are often for valid and recognized national sovereignty, material and economic corollaries to the spoken promises of diversity and tolerance, and transparent, ethical investigations into ethnocentric violence and economic exchanges between ruling elites and first world corporations and governments.

The primary factor that connects the various detectives and detective fictions studied in this volume, then, is not any shared focus on a single type of identity (postcolonial, immigrant, multicultural, or ethnic minority), although each of these experiences are represented in the novels we study. Instead, these stories are united by their common adaptation of the conventions of detective fiction to the cultural work of understanding "transformations of the institutions of knowledge production" at the local level (Gikandi 623)—of representing the interplay of mobility and stability, of identity and justice, that confront peoples and societies who are no longer subjects of the imperial nation-state, who traverse or reside on its borders or margins, or who suffer its politically charged times of transition. The contributors to this collection explore the vexed relationship between detection and statehood, which alternatively creates and vitiates legal and ethical frameworks, and between detection and national, cultural, ethnic, or racial identity, factors which demand that investigators cross borders both external and internal, figurative and literal. Thus, Soo Kim examines the unspoken failures of discourses of multiculturalism and globalization in Suki Kim's *The Interpreter*, in which Suzy Park, a 29-year-old Korean American interpreter in New York City, investigates the unsolved murder of her immigrant parents. Raphaël Lambert traces the fluid racial boundaries of Walter Mosley's *Devil in a Blue Dress*, in which black and white criminals present strikingly similar justifications for their crimes while the biracial Daphne Monet adopts and discards racial identities at will. Haiqing Sun discusses intranational divisions in Mario Vargas Llosa's *Death in the Andes*, in which Corporal Lituma of coastal Peru sees his murder investigation derailed by both the local culture and the Marxist guerrillas of the Andes. Wendy Knepper observes that Romilia Chacón, the Salvadoran American detective in Marcos M. Villatoro's *Home Killings*, conducts a transnational investigation into the flows of trade, culture, and migrant labor that keep the United States in a constant yet fluid relationship with Latin America. And Maureen Lauder presents a transnational reading of Amitav Ghosh's *The Calcutta Chromosome*, in which a database operator named Antar who lives in a New York "emblem[atic] of postcolonial diasporas and transnational consolidations" uncovers evidence of the unexplained disappearance, in Calcutta, of a man who had been investigating the controversial, transnational history of the discovery of a cure for malaria.

As these investigators cross and recross racial, ethnic, and national boundaries, they often discover more than simply the fallibility or arbitrariness of western modes of rationalism. In the course of their work they tend to find, as Soo Kim explains with reference to *The Interpreter*, that a broad multiculturalism or deterritorialized creed of tolerance and diversity is an equally fallible abstraction. Postcolonial and transnational detectives frequently need to balance or to think beyond binaries of West and East, rational and irrational, or universal and local. As Emily S. Davis proposes in her chapter on Michael Ondaatje's *Anil's Ghost*, the postcolonial adaptation of detective conventions has the potential to meet these challenges by generating a productive interplay between modernist and postmodernist discourses—one seeking to interpret social and cognitive processes in universal and hence egalitarian terms, the other to elaborate the experience of marginal, hybrid, subaltern, and effectively stateless subjects into a policy of difference that eradicates the presumptive universality of western rationalism. Moreover, Davis suggests, these competing interpretive frameworks, especially as Ondaatje situates them in Sri Lanka's ongoing civil war, help to dramatize "a tension between materialism and deconstruction that has occupied a central place in postcolonial scholarship." Dealing with similar ideas in her chapter on *The Calcutta Chromosome*, Maureen Lauder studies the ways in which Ghosh's characters "negotiate two forms of knowledge—a Western, rational, scientific epistemology and an Eastern, native, silent epistemology underpinned by the belief that any claim to knowledge is impossible."

The detectives examined in this study variously succeed or fail to develop this nonbinary, transformational approach as they try to negotiate disparities between the theory and practice of international justice and human rights (and hence between transnational ideals, state apparatuses, and local cultures) or to determine equitable codes of policing and punishment when the sovereign state has abandoned its responsibility to provide them. Jennifer Lewis argues, in her chapter on "sympathetic traveling" in Taibo's Héctor Belascoarán Shayne series, that the vicious cycles of neocolonialism, dictatorial verticality, and cathexis of the elite that often go hand in hand with the lack of sovereignty force Taibo's Basque-Irish detective to develop a "horizontal ethics" to determine what potential laws might connect and correct the vast disparities of postcolonial Mexico. In her chapter on Vikram Chandra's "Kama," Claire Chambers focuses on how Chandra's marginalized Sikh policeman, Sartaj Singh, tries to forge an ethical standard of investigative practice that is neither authorized by the state nor influenced by the divisive communal politics and class enclaves of postcolonial Bombay.

In her chapter entitled "The Hunt for the World's Greatest Outlaw," Robin Truth Goodman juxtaposes two radically different narrative accounts of the international policing of Colombia's drug cartels to expose the myriad disparities between police operations and the ways international policing is represented. The first, a journalistic account by Mark Bowden, appropriates features of "true crime," police procedural, and hard-boiled narrative to depict the police as technologically proficient defenders of morality who conspire with paramilitaries in order to overcome the ineffectual Columbian state. The second, Gabriel García Márquez's *News of a Kidnapping*, which incorporates features of the local *reportaje* tradition, is considerably more sensitive to how Colombia's lack of true state sovereignty is implicated in the rise of the cartels, and demonstrates how the drug lords, the police, and the pawns in the cartel hierarchy each reveal the great distance between geopolitical rhetoric and human motives. What hangs in the balance, for García Márquez as for many of the authors and scholars assembled in this collection, is nothing less than the incipient democratic promise of a genuine practice of defending social justice and human rights without replicating the imperial apparatuses that so often deny them.

Whether it is adopted by writers invested in high literary aesthetics such as García Márquez, Amitav Ghosh, or Michael Ondaatje, or practiced by popular but no less ambitious or skillful authors such as Walter Mosley or Vikram Chandra, the detective novel is generically, structurally, and historically suited for creating precisely the kind of dynamic interplay between the modern and postmodern, the material and the metaphysical, the investigation of truth and of investigation itself, that local understanding within a postcolonial and transnational world demands. Thus, many of the chapters in this volume focus on how detectives and adaptations of detective narrative conventions often exploit the rationalism and materialism in crime fiction's history to create productive tension with postmodern themes, social contexts, or formal maneuvers. Other chapters explore how the detective novel's existence within generic and discursive borderlands—between literary and popular culture, between narrative and meta-narrative, between inquest and epistemic critique—highlights the need to perceive ideology even as we deduce criminal guilt, especially when the crime is abetted or supported by institutions that traverse the internal complexity of a state or the external ambiguity of its borders. We have not, then, assembled these studies to propose simple oppositions between a dominant, white, western rationalism and a resistant local or native knowledge. We hope instead that the conversation between these contributors will inspire further study of the ways in which postcolonial and transnational detective fiction encourages serious discussion about how to reconcile the conviction that political identities and methods of deduction are arbitrary, discursive constructs with the conviction that a global code of rights and ethics must believe in the salience of both.

Works Cited

Appadurai, Arjun. "Disjuncture and Difference in the Global Cultural Economy." *The Global Transformations Reader*. Ed. David Held and Anthony McGrew. London: Polity Press, 2000.

Appiah, Kwame Anthony. "Is the Post- in Postmodernism the Post- in Postcolonial?" *Critical Inquiry* 17.2 (1991): 336–57.

Bargainnier, Earl F. *The Gentle Art of Murder: The Detective Fiction of Agatha Christie*. Bowling Green, OH: Bowling Green U Popular P, 1980.

Bhabha, Homi K. *The Location of Culture*. London: Routledge, 1994.

Brennan, Timothy. "Cosmopolitanism and Internationalism." *Debating Cosmopolitics*. Ed. Daniele Archibugi. London: Verso, 2003. 40–50.

Brooks, Peter. *Reading for the Plot: Design and Intention in Narrative*. New York: Knopf, 1984.

Cawelti, John. *Adventure, Mystery, and Romance: Formula Stories as Art and Popular Culture*. Chicago: U of Chicago P, 1976.

Chandler, David. "International Justice." *Debating Cosmopolitics*. Ed. Daniele Archibugi. London: Verso, 2003. 27–39.

Christian, Ed, ed. *The Post-Colonial Detective*. Houndmills, UK: Palgrave, 2001.

Docker, John. *Postmodernism and Popular Culture: A Cultural History*. Cambridge: Cambridge UP, 1994.

Doyle, Arthur Conan. *The Complete Sherlock Holmes*. New York: Doubleday, 1960.

Gikandi, Simon. "Globalization and the Claims of Postcoloniality." *Postcolonialisms: An Anthology of Cultural Theory and Criticism*. Ed. Gaurav Desai and Supriya Nair. New Brunswick: Rutgers UP, 2005. 608–34.

Hannerz, Ulf. *Transnational Connections: Culture, People, Places*. London: Routledge, 1996.

Harvey, David. *A Brief History of Neoliberalism*. Oxford: Oxford UP, 2005.

Horsley, Lee. *Twentieth-Century Crime Fiction*. Oxford: Oxford UP, 2005.

Huggan, Graham. "Unsettled Settlers: Postcolonialism, Travelling Theory and the New Migrant Aesthetics." *Journal of Australian Studies* 68 (2001): 117–27.

Keating, H.R.F. *Sherlock Holmes: The Man and His World.* New York: Scribner's, 1979.

Knight, Stephen. "Crimes Domestic and Crimes Colonial: The Role of Crime Fiction in Developing Postcolonial Consciousness." *Postcolonial Postmortems: Crime Fiction from a Transcultural Perspective.* Ed. Christine Matzke and Susanne Mühleisen. Amsterdam: Rodopi, 2006. 17–33.

Knox, Ronald A. "A Detective Story Decalogue." 1929. Rpt. in *Detective Fiction: A Collection of Critical Essays.* Ed. Robin W. Winks. Woodstock, VT: Countryman Press, 1988. 200–202.

McCann, Sean. *Gumshoe America: Hard-Boiled Crime Fiction and the Rise and Fall of New Deal Liberalism.* Durham, NC: Duke UP, 2000.

McLaughlin, Joseph. *Writing the Urban Jungle: Reading Empire in London from Doyle to Elliot.* Charlottesville: UP of Virginia, 2000.

Matzke, Christine, and Susanne Mühleisen, eds. *Postcolonial Postmortems: Crime Fiction from a Transcultural Perspective.* Amsterdam: Rodopi, 2006.

Merivale, Patricia, and Susan Elizabeth Sweeney, eds. *Detecting Texts: The Metaphysical Detective Story from Poe to Postmodernism.* Philadelphia: U of Pennsylvania P, 1999.

Moretti, Franco. *Signs Taken for Wonders: On the Sociology of Literary Forms.* London: Verso, 2005.

Mukherjee, Upamanyu Pablo. *Crime and Empire: The Colony in Nineteenth-Century Fictions of Crime.* Oxford: Oxford UP, 2003.

Pepper, Andrew. *The Contemporary American Crime Novel: Race, Ethnicity, Gender, Class.* Edinburgh: Edinburgh UP, 2000.

Reitz, Caroline. *Detecting the Nation: Fictions of Detection and the Imperial Venture.* Columbus: Ohio State UP, 2004.

Rodriguez, Ralph. *Brown Gumshoes: Detective Fiction and the Search for Chicana/o Identity.* Austin: U of Texas P, 2005.

Soitos, Stephen F. *The Blues Detective: A Study of African American Detective Fiction.* Amherst: U of Massachussetts P, 1996.

Todorov, Tzvetan. "The Typology of Detective Fiction." *The Poetics of Prose.* Trans. Richard Howell. Ithaca, NY: Cornell UP, 1977. 42–52.

Wynne, Catherine. *The Colonial Conan Doyle: British Imperialism, Irish Nationalism, and the Gothic.* Westport, CT: Greenwood, 2002.

Chapter 1
Investigating Truth, History, and Human Rights in Michael Ondaatje's *Anil's Ghost*

Emily S. Davis

Mystery Fiction, Detective Fiction, and the Problem of the Postcolonial

In his introduction to *The Post-Colonial Detective*, Ed Christian defines the postcolonial detective as follows:

> post-colonial detectives are always indigenous to or settlers in the countries where they work; they are usually marginalized in some way, which affects their ability to work at their full potential; they are always central and sympathetic characters; and their creators' interest usually lies in an exploration of how these detectives' approaches to criminal investigation are influenced by their cultural attitudes. (2)

Although critics have commented on the elements of detective fiction in Michael Ondaatje's 2000 novel *Anil's Ghost*, the novel does not fit neatly within Christian's guidelines as to what texts can be classified as postcolonial detective fiction. For example, the most traditional detective in the novel, Anil, is a diasporic figure who, though born in Sri Lanka, is perceived as an outsider by the other characters. What we could call her dominant "cultural attitude" is her identification with British and U.S. scientific and popular culture discourses, in particular her persistent faith in Enlightenment rationality, rather than any inherently "Sri Lankan" perception of the world. This worldview marginalizes her in interactions with other characters, but it is also a manifestation of her power as the representative of a transnational organization whose decisions will have direct repercussions for characters in a more marginal position than herself.[1] Most importantly, Anil is only one of several protagonists in the novel, none of whom is entirely sympathetic and each of whom brings a different history and method to the novel's story of detection.

The multivalent narrative structure is only one of several postmodern elements in *Anil's Ghost*, including its subversion of traditional detective genre codes and its rejection of metanarratives of universal truth and just punishment (Lyotard),

---

[1] Essentially, my argument here is that while Christian's definition of the postcolonial detective provides a useful starting point, because of its reliance on an "authentic" insider, it cannot account adequately for questions of diaspora and transnational affiliations.

that contribute to the novel's critiques of traditional Western historicism and the concepts of individual responsibility and justice that result from them. Ondaatje's postmodern, multivocal narrative structure challenges the modernist tradition of the lone detective as well as the idea that one can detect a transcendent truth and then enact justice based upon it. In the essay that follows, I will attempt to situate Ondaatje's novel in relation both to scholarship on the histories of crime fiction in Britain and the United States and to Christian's more recent formulation of the postcolonial detective in order to demonstrate how the novel's postmodern style and vexed relationship with questions of truth and justice pose important questions for both detective fiction and postcolonial studies.[2]

The postmodern breakdown of transcendent truth and the inaccessibility of justice is a timely and politically pressing matter in postcolonial countries ravaged by civil war, such as South Africa, Chile, and Rwanda, which have debated these issues in a very public manner through truth commissions in recent years. According to their official web site, the recently formed International Criminal Court has also begun trying cases related to human rights abuses in Uganda and the Democratic Republic of Congo and has opened an investigation regarding Darfur, Sudan. For many of the participants in these commissions and cases, truth without some form of reparative justice has proven unacceptable. This essay aims to explore the ways in which Ondaatje's novel about the ongoing Sri Lankan civil war intervenes in this crucial tension between postmodern and postcolonial challenges to Enlightenment universalism on the one hand and the public need for reparation for past crimes and a workable human rights discourse with which to defend one's life on the other. This opposition represents another version of the standoff between materialism and deconstruction that has occupied a central place in postcolonial theory. As I will discuss, Ondaatje's positioning within this debate has made for a heated and polarized reading of the novel's postcolonial politics. However, I argue that it is the novel's refusal to diffuse the tension between the demands of materialism and postmodernism that makes its approach to detection important for postcolonial studies. At the end of the essay, I return to the truth commissions as a material example of the collective construction of narratives of truth that Ondaatje attempts in *Anil's Ghost.*

Ondaatje's novel utilizes core elements of the detective story as described by narrative critic Carl D. Malmgren. For Malmgren, detective fiction—which he uses to denote the American hard-boiled tradition—is a response to and outgrowth of mystery fiction, the British tradition exemplified by Agatha Christie, which presupposes a "world which has a center, an anchor, a ground" (13). In mystery fiction, "effects can be connected to causes" (13) and signifiers naturally match

---

[2] Wendy Knepper, my co-contributor to this anthology, has written a wonderful essay on the significance of *Anil's Ghost* for postcolonial studies. See "Confession, Autopsy, and the Postcolonial Postmortems of Michael Ondaatje's *Anil's Ghost*" in *Postcolonial Postmortems: Crime Fiction from a Transcultural Perspective*, ed. Christine Matzke and Susanne Mühleisen.

up with signifieds (15). Crimes occur in the past, and this focus on the past "signals [mystery fiction's] commitment to a world which is safe, orderly, and domesticated—a written world, a matter of record" (18). In the modernist universe of mystery fiction, plot is dominant, as the novel's purpose is to reconstruct the crime that has occurred before or at the novel's beginning. Detective fiction, in contrast, operates in a decentered and chaotic universe, in which order cannot be restored by the discovery of truth.[3] By taking the detection process into the "mean streets," the detective novel demonstrates that crime is not an isolated phenomenon associated with disturbed individuals but is part of a larger field of social disorder and inequality. While the detective might be able to unearth the truth about a particular crime, he (or, rarely, she) is frequently unable to bring about justice on an individual scale and is utterly unable to right the wrongs of the social system as a whole.

The lure of righting wrongs is belied by the detective's powerlessness in the face of flawed human institutions. As P.D. James puts it,

> Perhaps this was part of the attraction of [the] job, that the process of detection dignified the individual death, even the death of the least attractive, the most unworthy, mirroring in its obsessive interest in clues and motives man's perennial fascination with the mystery of his own mortality, providing, too, a comforting illusion of a moral universe in which innocence could be avenged, right vindicated, order restored. But nothing was restored, certainly not life, and the only justice vindicated was the uncertain justice of men. (qtd. in Malmgren 42)

Because plot no longer leads in an uncomplicated fashion to resolution, character assumes a greater importance in detective fiction than in mystery. This is what Raymond Chandler points to in "The Simple Art of Murder" when he highlights Dashiell Hammett's devotion to "the grand elucidation of character, which is all the detective story has any right to be about in the first place" (Hammett 236). Detective fiction challenges the centered world of mystery fiction, replacing it with the mean streets of the urban metropolis and transforming the figure of the detective into a modern-day knight whose quest is to unearth the truth of the crime. Thus, while the world of detective fiction is decentered, the detective himself remains a moral center, wanting and able to discover the truth even if he is unable to dispense justice. As a consequence, detective fiction complicates an easy distinction between

[3] Malmgren's understanding of detective fiction as operating in a decentered universe potentially puts him at odds with critics like Franco Moretti, who argues that the detective, as a figure for the state, functions to restore the social order. On this point, the two critics agree. However, Malmgren's focus is more on the post-war hard-boiled American genre that succeeds the texts in Moretti's study. As a result, while Moretti's detectives seek to restore the capitalist order of their day, Malmgren's hard-boiled texts yearn for a social order associated with the pre-war past that is thus unattainable. See Moretti 154–5.

modernism and postmodernism in that it simultaneously decenters the world of its detective and positions him as the truthful center within it.

What Malmgren calls "metafictional detective fiction," however, "continues detective fiction's assault upon the sign by overtly and self-consciously employing murder fiction's generic conventions and codes. Its primary target is a convention that detective fiction inherits from mystery fiction, the sense of closure created by the solution to the crime, the revelation of the truth" (121–2). Metafictional detective fiction, or what Michael Holquist calls "metaphysical" detective fiction (171), challenges the remaining centering element in the detective story: the idea that the detective can uncover the truth about crime, even if there is ultimately nothing he or she can do to avenge it.[4] Here, we enter more fully the realm of postmodernism.

Ondaatje's Cast of Detectives and the Collective Negotiation of Truth

Anil's Ghost follows this metafictional, or metaphysical tradition by using five central characters rather than a single questing detective, thereby undermining the moral or legal authority of any single character. In Ondaatje's novel, a forensic anthropologist named Anil is sent by the Centre for Human Rights in Geneva (under the auspices of the UN) to investigate political killings in her native Sri Lanka, which she had left 15 years before for Britain and eventually the United States. The Sri Lankan government assigns Sarath, an archeologist, to work with her during her six weeks in the country, ostensibly so that the government can keep an eye on her activities. Sarath leads Anil to a historical site containing four skeletons, one of which, she discovers, belongs to someone recently deceased and has been moved to the government site from another location. The rest of the novel revolves around Anil and Sarath's attempt to identify this skeleton, which would give Anil a concrete case of state-sponsored killing with which her organization can indict the Sri Lankan government for human rights abuses. Three other characters become central players in the story: Sarath's brother Gamini, an emergency room doctor; Sarath's mentor Palipana, a discredited archeologist-turned-ascetic; and Ananda, a once-famous religious artist who is now drinking himself to death and working in the gem mines. Representing different disciplinary, class, and philosophical positions, Anil, Sarath, Gamini, Palipana, and Ananda in effect stage a heated debate about the meaning of truth in the postcolonial context of Sri Lanka.

Of the five protagonists, Anil most closely resembles the detective figure of the modernist American literary tradition and the British spy novel. She is the stereotypical hard-boiled loner, isolated from friends, lacking family ties after the

---

[4] Laura Marcus rightly points out that the distinctions between modernist and postmodernist detective fiction are less stable than typologies like Holquist's and those of other scholars such as William Spanos and Stefano Tani might lead us to believe. See Marcus 249–52.

death of her parents several years earlier, and chronically unlucky in love. Instead, Anil throws her energy into her quest for truth through forensic anthropology, spending years traveling to war-torn countries such as Guatemala and Rwanda to identify the bodies of those killed during political upheaval. She arrives in Sri Lanka as a representative of international law to enact justice against the Sri Lankan government, a mission whose urgency and validity she does not question. By naming the four skeletons she and Sarath find at a government archeological dig Tinker, Tailor, Soldier, and Sailor, Anil overtly frames her investigation within the epistemological parameters of thrillers such as John Le Carré's *Tinker, Tailor, Soldier, Spy*, where mistrust of one's colleagues is justified by the fact that anyone can be a spy.[5] Finally, Anil's modernist faith in the universality of truth, particularly through forensic science, marks her as an epistemological outsider in relation to the other Sri Lankan characters, even though it is the country of her birth.

While Anil perceives her role in a way compatible with Malmgren's description of the tradition of detective fiction embodied by earlier figures such as Hammett and Chandler, Sarath and his mentor Palipana present a postmodern challenge to Anil's understanding of truth as scientifically verifiable and inherently desirable by forcing her to situate her fact-finding within the context of Sri Lankan history and politics. During one of his first meetings with Anil, Sarath attempts to complicate her understanding of the conflict, explaining that

> [e]very side was killing and hiding the evidence. Every side. This is an unofficial war, no one wants to alienate the foreign powers. So it's secret gangs and squads. Not like Central America. The government was not the only one doing the killing. You had, and still have three camps of enemies—one in the north, two in the south—using weapons, propaganda, fear, sophisticated posters, censorship. Importing state-of-the-art weapons from the West, or manufacturing homemade weapons. A couple of years ago people just started disappearing. Or bodies kept being found burned beyond recognition. There's no hope of affixing blame. And no one can tell who the victims are. [...] What we've got here is unknown extrajudicial executions mostly. Perhaps by the insurgents, or by the government or the guerrilla separatists. (Ondaatje 17–18)

As Sarath points out, Sri Lanka is not Guatemala, and Anil's tendency to view human rights crimes within a universalizing framework will only impede her investigation. Her response to Sarath's explanation reveals her concern with finding one ultimate perpetrator: "I couldn't tell who was worst. The reports are terrible" (17). For Sarath, the truth is not simply a collection of facts but a narrative woven out of the context clues and material fragments available to the observer. As someone constructing a narrative, the detective must understand what Sarath calls "the archeological surround of a fact" (44). Otherwise, as he warns her,

---

[5] Antoinette Burton notes the reference to Le Carré's novel in her excellent essay "Archive of Bones: *Anil's Ghost* and the Ends of History" (44).

"you'll be like one of those journalists who file reports about flies and scabs while staying at the Galle Face Hotel. That false empathy and blame" (44). Sarath sees his task as reconstructing narrative rather than detecting truth. However, while Sarath challenges Anil's ignorance about the stakes of her political intervention in Sri Lankan politics, he himself has retreated completely from the present violence, burying himself in his work on sixth-century artifacts.

Similarly, Palipana, Sarath's mentor, a once-respected archeologist, has withdrawn from the world into his abandoned monastery in the forest. Like Sarath, Palipana's passion is the past, an important foil to Anil's passionate interest in the present that ignores the impact of the past upon current politics. Palipana had led a movement that opposed Orientalist historiography and had sought to institute a nationalist approach to archeology during the time leading up to and after Sri Lanka's independence in 1948. At the height of his career he was discredited for claiming to have discovered a hidden intertext in the Stone Book at Polonnaruwa, which can only be seen at a particular moment during monsoon season, when the letters cut into the boulder fill with water. The intertext would have called for a revision of the dominant narrative of national history used by Sinhala nationalism. Drawing upon not only his training in textual sources but also his knowledge of local artistic practices such as stonemasonry, "he began to see as truth things that could only be guessed at" (83). Though respected scholars, including some of his former students, accuse him of fabricating his evidence, "[i]n no way did this feel to him like forgery or falsification" (83). Given the fact that the discipline of archeology functions according to Western standards when it comes to proof and evidence, Palipana is shunned not because "he would ever be proved wrong in his theories, but [because] he could not prove he was right. … And so the unprovable truth emerged" (83).[6] Expelled from the intellectual community in which he had been a leader, Palipana himself becomes evidence of the narrative nature of historical fact. When Anil tells him that she has looked him up in the Sinhala encyclopedia before their meeting, he responds, "You're lucky to get hold of an old edition. I'm erased from the new one" (96). Unlike Anil, therefore, Palipana has a much stronger sense of the ways in which so-called facts can be manipulated to serve the interests of those in power.

Sarath's emphasis upon truth as narrative and Palipana's experience of truth as unprovable and even invisible align them with a postmodern understanding of the work of detection that the structure of the book underscores. As in many postmodern texts (*The Crying of Lot 49* is an apt example), Anil's process of detection is constantly thwarted by different groups with investments in different narratives of national history. Indeed, as Antoinette Burton points out, government officials ultimately demand that she prove Sailor's identity by scientifically reading his body but without any of the evidence she needs; as she has been intentionally

---

6 Dipesh Chakrabarty discusses the unsolvable dilemma of postcolonial critics relying on disciplines such as history that are grounded in Western Enlightenment epistemologies in his *Provincializing Europe*.

given the wrong skeleton, she, like Palipana decades earlier, is forced to make claims about truth without evidence (47). In this way, Ondaatje suggests that historical "truth" is especially tenuous in the postcolonial context due not only to the relentless ideological reconstruction of personal and national history involved in colonization and in the nation-building process following independence, but also to the sheer scope of the violent destruction of bodies, texts, and other historical markers. As with characters in Paul Auster novels like *City of Glass*, the characters in *Anil's Ghost* obsessively read the texts in front of them—bodies in particular but also spaces, old buildings, and artifacts—without achieving a definitive reconstruction of the past.

The novel thematizes its solution to the problem of truth through its ongoing trope of reconstructions and recreations. Since we can never get at the thing itself outside of its narrative production within the postmodern world, the different characters dedicate themselves to a self-conscious process of history-making through recreation. Even Anil, who epistemologically rejects the idea of truth as reconstruction, participates in acts of recreation. We learn halfway through the novel, for example, that Anil bought her brother's name from him as a young teenager and literally reinvented herself (67–8). The two other protagonists in the novel, Gamini and Ananda, share a particularly intense physical relationship to the art of reconstruction. Gamini, Sarath's younger brother, is an emergency-room doctor at a government hospital, where he takes speed in order to work around the clock attempting to reconstruct bodies damaged by homemade bombs and imported weapons alike. Ananda, who has turned away from a career painting the sacred eyes on sculptures of the Buddha after his wife's disappearance, has become a miner who drinks himself into a stupor every afternoon after work to shut out the horror of his personal loss. Anil and Sarath, following Palipana's advice, ask Ananda to use his artistic skills to build a facial reconstruction of Sailor's skull, which ends up being the first step on Ananda's road to personal reconstruction.

While Sarath, Palipana, and Anil use material like bodies and architectural remains to reconstruct narratives of the past, Gamini and Ananda's reconstructions work to different ends. Gamini is a figure entirely consumed by the present; more than any other character, he rejects the idea that justice can somehow make the past accountable to the present. Gamini is the one who most overtly identifies Anil's quest for truth as a Western preoccupation that ends for all intents and purposes when she gets on the plane home. During a conversation with Sarath and Anil, Gamini quips,

> American movies, English books—remember how they all end? … The American or the Englishman gets on a plane and leaves. That's it. The camera leaves with him. He looks out of the window at Mombasa or Vietnam or Jakarta, someplace now he can look at through the clouds. The tired hero. A couple of words to the girl beside him. He's going home. So the war, to all purposes, is over. That's enough reality for the West. It's probably the history of the last two hundred years of Western political writing. Go home. Write a book. Hit the circuit. (285–6)

For Gamini, Western concerns with truth and justice lack the attention span to come to terms with places like Sri Lanka. The temptation to view from above, to seek some kind of transcendent objectivity, though, is not just a Western one. The novel ends with Ananda back at work as an eye painter in the employ of the same department of archeology that has likely just coordinated Sarath's murder. While up in the air with his nephew preparing to finish painting the eyes of a new Buddha statue reconstructed after the old one was bombed by hungry villagers seeking jewels to sell for food, Ananda experiences a moment of bliss at hovering above the war-torn world. Like Gamini, who immerses himself in emergency in order to escape his personal war with his brother, Palipana, who retreats to his forest grove outside of civilization, Sarath, who would die for an ancient sculpture but cannot reconcile with his brother or face the death of his wife (157), and Anil, who travels the globe alone at war with herself and fleeing painful loves lost, Ananda is tempted to turn away from the messy world of human loss and communion. However, the novel ends with his nephew bringing him back to earth: "He felt the boy's concerned hand on his. This sweet touch from the world" (307). But what kind of engagement with the world does Ananda's private moment of affection with his nephew imply? Moreover, what are the implications of Ondaatje's postmodern style for the postcolonial questions of truth and justice in the novel?

Early in the novel, Sarath warns Anil that, as an outsider, she cannot understand the complex truths of the Sri Lankan civil war. His challenge to Anil as a Western detective is not just postmodern but postcolonial as well, because he questions the idea that a Western detective using Western methods can reveal the truth about Sailor. Sarath and Palipana's location as Sri Lankan insiders and the ways in which they revise and at times reject Western modes of detection makes them fit more easily within Christian's definition of the postcolonial detective that I quote at the beginning of this essay. Furthermore, their critiques of Anil's project echo those of the Subaltern Studies historians, whose concern is not only that history's truth is elusive, but that its Western-trained seekers ignore the violent implications of their seeking for those around them.[7] Sarath thinks to himself during the investigation that

> for [Anil] the journey was in getting to the truth. But what would the truth bring them into? It was a flame against a sleeping lake of petrol. Sarath had seen truth broken into suitable pieces and used by the foreign press alongside irrelevant photographs. A flippant gesture towards Asia that might lead, as a result of this information, to new vengeance and slaughter. There were dangers in handing truth to an unsafe city around you. (156–7)

[7] While Anil's Western training positions her to speak paternalistically to the global south as the representative of universal truth, as I discuss below, the fact that Palipana is ostracized for challenging the nationalist historical narrative suggests that Western-trained nationalist historiography is equally capable of violence.

Sarath's knowledge of the potential violence of truth, particularly when mishandled by those with insufficient knowledge about the local context, undermines what is supposed to be the novel's detective plot itself—the search for Sailor's identity in order to indict the government. The investigation does eventually produce Sailor's name, Ruwan Kumara, though basically by chance (269). Anil realizes that Kumara must have been a miner while watching Ananda crouch in a way that strains his ankle tendons as he works on his reconstruction. Ananda's reconstructed face itself leads them nowhere, because instead of a realistic depiction of Sailor it reveals itself as a sort of abstract representation of the peace Ananda wishes for his disappeared wife. Moreover, the revelation of Sailor's identity is not the climactic scene of the book. Since the novel does not follow Anil after she gets on her plane, it is unclear what result will come of the discovery other than Sarath's death at the hands of the government.

Even though she has bartered with her brother for her own name, Anil remains obsessed with the idea that names deliver truth, as her quest not only for Sailor's name but also for that of Sarath's wife illustrates. To her mantra that "*One victim can speak for many victims*," (176), that one name can represent the web of relationships among larger collectivities, Gamini warily responds, "*What would you do with a name?*" (252). Although he refuses in this later scene to name Sarath's wife, the woman he loved who became, through suicide, a victim of his private war with his brother, Gamini's retort speaks to the inadequacy of Western detection in the novel. Revealing her name will not bring his lover back, and it will certainly not represent the truth of her identity.

The utter failure of Anil's idea of justice through the revelation of truth begs a key question for postcolonial studies. Is it possible or even desirable to represent questions of postcolonial violence and resistance to it? Several critics have rejected Ondaatje's postmodern use of history on the very grounds on which the novel rejects the Western detective: its reliance on an Enlightenment illusion of objective universality and its inadequate grasp of and commitment to local histories. For the remainder of the essay, I will lay out these critiques as a way to raise broader questions about the relationship between representation and politics as well as the potential political uses of truth and justice in the postcolony.

The Novel as Site of Debate: Questions of Materialism and Postmodernism

One of the most scathing critiques of the novel has been that despite the obsession of its characters with history, it in fact lacks responsible discussion of the historical roots of the conflict in Sri Lanka. In other words, the novel's critique of history has let Ondaatje off the hook when it comes to historical analysis. Kanishka Goonewardena, for example, argues that the novel "only deals with the symptoms of the Sri Lankan crisis, as he paints a picture of the everyday life there in a time of terror." As a result, Goonewardena concludes that "*Anil's Ghost* reads like a story about people dragging a constant flow of dead bodies out of a river that has no hint of what's happening upstream. Who is throwing the bodies in? Why? Is that not worth knowing?" (qtd. in Goldman par. 2). Qadri Ismail argues that while the novel positions itself outside of the different political groups in the Sri Lankan war, its choice of details in fact places it firmly within the camp of Sinhala Buddhist nationalism. As Ismail points out, "all the significant actants in a story about Sri Lanka are Sinhala" (39). He further observes that "all the men have names that resonate deeply within Buddhist iconography" (24), and that the list of the disappeared that appears as an intertext in the novel "contains exclusively Sinhala names" (41). He concludes that the novel dangerously fails to understand its own politics, because the idea that "Sinhala Buddhism may bear some responsibility for Sri Lanka's misery, does not even merit Ondaatje's consideration" (25).[8] Antoinette Burton, who is interested in Ondaatje's use of Palipana as a critic of Western historiography, remarks that "the orientalism of some of the texts on Ondaatje's [bibliography of sources at the end of the novel] is astonishing" (47). She concludes from his use of Orientalist sources that "Ondaatje's critique of History ends up being a re-inscription of western civilization's long romance with it" (50). Margaret Scanlan notes that Ondaatje's postmodern style carries some political risks. "By omitting so much of what we expect from a political novel in the way of public events and historical detail," Scanlan writes, "Ondaatje might risk aestheticizing terror, repeating the modernist gesture of turning away from atrocity to timeless form" (302–3). For Scanlan, the result is worth the risk, because "his distinctive achievement in *Anil's Ghost* is to create a narrative structure that replicates the experience of terror" (303). Of course, this is precisely what Goonewardena found problematic about the book. Whereas Scanlan views Ondaatje's decision to destabilize the reader by withholding historical and cultural markers as a politically responsible move, Goonewardena and Ismail are clearly not convinced of the progressive politics of his artistic decision. Finally, as Burton's critique demonstrates, Ondaatje may be offering a postmodern deconstruction of Western metanarratives, ironically, by grounding himself in Orientalist scholarship.

The critiques of Ondaatje's novel are emblematic of a tension between materialism and deconstruction that has occupied a central place in postcolonial scholarship. While prominent scholars such as Homi Bhabha have embraced deconstruction as a way to demonstrate the inherent instability of colonial discourse, Arif Dirlik, Aijaz Ahmad, and others have argued that postmodernism's focus on deconstructing master narratives has played into the hands of a globalizing capitalism that finds a decentered universe easier to manage than one in which groups can organize around agreed-upon understandings of the truth of oppression and the need for justice.[9] At stake in this tension between materialism and

---

8 Qadri Ismail, "A Flippant Gesture Towards Sri Lanka: A Review of Michael Ondaatje's *Anil's Ghost*," *Pravada* 6.9 (2000). Qtd. in Goldman, par. 3.

9 For example, Dirlik summarizes his position as follows: "The rendering of all problems into problems of language or representation may open up new critical possibilities,

postmodernism are not only strategies of social change but our relationship with the past as well. It remains open to debate whether confronting the past can offer us truth and the possibility and meaning of justice. Where one is situated within this debate greatly influences one's reading of Ondaatje's novel and its author. In a materialist reading, his postmodern refusal of materialist analysis, as well as his identity as a diasporic Sri Lankan Burgher (mixed-race colonial bourgeoisie), make it difficult to locate him as a postcolonial author because he fails to exhibit an explicit political commitment to the people about whom he is writing.[10] With regard to the novel, Anil, as a diasporic character, is not embedded enough within the local context to qualify as a postcolonial detective, at least according to Christian's definition. In a postmodern reading, however, Ondaatje's rejection of the UN as the arbiter for political action is an important statement about the West's disingenuous claims to objectivity when it comes to intervening in postcolonial conflicts. Further, his exposure of history as narrative construction rather than essential truth is one of the crucial tasks of postcolonial scholarship. Ondaatje's postmodern refusal to submit a unified narrative judgment about the Sri Lankan civil war can be read not simply as a manifestation of his privileged position as a wealthy diasporic writer, but more fundamentally as the predicament facing Sri Lanka. As Sarath had explained to Anil, "Every side was killing and hiding the evidence. […] There's no hope of affixing blame. […] and there are no purely just or unjust factions involved" (17–18). Thus, the conflict is itself postmodern.

---

but without reference to a world beyond language, where some are better placed than others by virtue of structures of power to utilize language to their ends, it also limits criticism within a world of discursive economy with its own internal rules, substituting this world for the world of political economy of which it serves as a simulacrum. In its problematization of the question of agency, its scrambling of positivistic categories, its insistence on the constructedness of culture, and its revelations concerning the diffusion of power in social and institutional discourses, postmodernism has opened up new possibilities in the understanding and analysis of power. At the same time, the celebration of 'deconstruction' in so much of postmodern theorizing confounds deconstruction at the level of theory or representation with the abolition of power in everyday life, with sometimes bizarre consequences, representing the operations of power as problems of textuality, while denying the possibility of subjectivities that may be essential to the struggle against power. Postmodernism's own metanarratives of contingency and de-subjectivization may render it not just into the 'cultural logic of late capitalism,' but a mystification of contemporary configurations of power" (187–8). See also Ahmad.

[10] In other words, for many materialist critics, including Ahmad, postcolonial identity entails a sense of political responsibility. The 'postcolonial' is not simply a descriptor but an intellectual and political position of resistance to colonialism in all its forms. For a recent discussion of whether postcolonial studies has been successful in preserving this resistant stance within the academy, see Patricia Yaeger's "Editor's Column: The End of Postcolonial Theory? A Roundtable with Sunil Agnani, Fernando Coronil, Gaurav Desai, Mamadou Diouf, Simon Gikandi, Susie Tharu, and Jennifer Wenzel" in the May 2007 issue of *PMLA*.

This framing of the tension between the demands of materialism and postmodernism makes the novel's approach to detection relevant to postcolonial studies. As Ania Loomba wisely argues, "It is possible to make the case for a productive synthesis [between the demands of materialism and postmodernism]: we can abandon the grand narratives which once dominated the writing of history without also abandoning all analysis of relationships between different forces in society" (240). Loomba contests the claim that scholars of postcolonialism cannot "ride two horses at the same time" (253), suggesting instead that they follow Gyan Prakash's call to "hang on to two horses, inconstantly" (qtd. in Loomba 253).[11] In the context of this heated theoretical debate it becomes possible to talk about Ondaatje's book as not simply a postmodern novel about the breakdown of signs, but a postcolonial detective story that approaches questions of truth and justice in a form that has become increasingly pertinent in the last several years to countries ravaged by postcolonial violence. Ultimately, *Anil's Ghost* requires us to approach the social questions of truth, justice, and crime that are omnipresent in the postcolonial context in relation to the question of postmodernism's challenge to master narratives. If truth is subjective and violence endemic rather than comfortably locatable in a few bad apples, what can one do about the massive problem of postcolonial violence?

Whereas the detective novel presents the dark underbelly of society, *Anil's Ghost* takes the idea a step further, positing society itself as a dark underbelly from which there is no escape. In Ondaatje's novel, there is no character who is not in some way implicated in crime. Gamini has had an affair with his brother's wife; Sarath has passively observed as a man is abducted right in front of him; Palipana has used his historiography in support of a nationalism that works toward ever more violent ends; Ananda reconstructs the statue at the end of the novel in the employ of the same government office that has murdered Sarath; and Anil has given in to the violence of passion and stabbed her married lover. The collective guilt of the five protagonists in the novel reflects the larger political conflict in which, as Sarath has emphasized, everyone has blood on their hands. Ondaatje makes it clear that, when crime can no longer be accounted for by concepts of individual guilt and punishment and exists not only as a past incident but as an ongoing and epidemic problem, questions of crime and justice must be addressed within a different framework than that of even the detective novel's mean streets.[12]

---

[11] For a more detailed discussion of Ondaatje's work in the context of the tension between postmodernist and materialist approaches to postcolonial literary criticism, see Banerjee.

[12] According to Moretti, this is indeed "the nightmare of detective fiction": the idea "that guilt might be impersonal, and therefore collective and social" (135).

Collective Truths and the TRCs

It is at this level of collective crime that the truth and reconciliation commissions in Chile, South Africa, Peru, and now Rwanda have attempted to operate. As Anil's failure as an outsider to understand the stakes of her investigation indicates, questions of truth and justice cannot simply be administered from outside by organizations such as the UN. Samuel Makinda points out that "the West does not see 'rescue' as a matter of affirming that certain things ought not to be done to human beings, and that certain things ought to always be done for them. Instead it, in part, regards intervention as a matter of ensuring that human rights abuses in certain parts of the world are not allowed to disturb global order or threaten the tranquility of life in the West" (qtd. in Derrickson 143). The danger of Anil's investigation is that her personal sense of justice and her growing reattachment to the country of her birth cannot be separated from the mandate of the organization whose bidding she has been sent to do, a mandate not necessarily designed with the best interests of the Sri Lankan people foremost in mind. But this danger is why it is particularly important that Ondaatje situates Anil in a web of characters with which she must constantly negotiate the meaning of her mission. By creating a novel in which not one but five different protagonists with different motivations and beliefs about truth and justice work collectively, Ondaatje aligns himself much more closely with the consensus-driven detection process of the truth commissions.

Ondaatje's construction of a group of investigators who understand the narrative, reconstructive nature of truth points us toward the work of the different truth commissions, which have been wrestling very publicly with these questions about crime and justice. That is not to say that they are a perfect model for conflict resolution in an era of deconstructing master narratives of history, but simply that they are examples of spaces in which the theoretical tensions I lay out above are being negotiated as public policy in postcolonial settings. The structure of the commissions has varied. In South Africa, there was no structure for enacting justice in the traditional legal sense, as those who testified were granted amnesty. In cases like Chile, tribunals decided whether those who admitted to past wrongdoing would be prosecuted for their crimes. All of the commissions have prioritized reconstructing the truth about historical crimes. As many survivors of the disappeared have said, finding the truth about a loved one's disappearance is deeply significant. When it comes to the unnamed skeletons of political violence, names *do* matter. Those without them are forced to make up stories, as Ananda does for his disappeared wife, Sirissa. For some survivors, reconstructing their loved ones' stories has been the only way to gain closure.

At the same time, many have also protested that the failure to prosecute those who murdered their family members will forever deny them closure. Only reparation, they argue, can bring about reconciliation. Roberta Bacic, who worked at the National Corporation of Reparation and Reconciliation in Chile, writes that "the wife of a detained disappeared peasant once told me: 'Let me tell you quite honestly, truth without justice is not truth; it only means the acknowledgement of what has happened'" (20). These survivors often direct their calls for justice to organizations exactly like the one Anil represents, hoping that an international consensus about human rights will make it possible to pursue the justice denied them by postcolonial states that "cannot be relied upon to prosecute those responsible for previous human rights violations, because violence has usually been perpetrated by the state and its institutions, including the justice department" (24). While Sarath tells Anil that "[t]here's no hope of affixing blame. And no one can tell who the victims are" (17), survivors in the postcolony continue to demand sophisticated engagement with questions of truth and justice.

Thus, the tension evident in the response to Ondaatje's book is important to foreground in considering the possible politics of a postcolonial detective. To simply deploy Western ideologies of truth and justice is to betray the complexities of local histories. However, to say that the postmodern dismantling of master narratives prevents pursuing questions of social justice and human rights in a way that is meaningful to populations devastated by political violence is no less a betrayal. Ondaatje presents us with a cast of detectives to probe one of the crucial dilemmas of our time. As with the metafictional detective novel, he declines to present us with a rational universe in which crimes can be solved through reliance on the coherence of signs. However, Ondaatje's deconstruction of the politics of Western truth maintains a space for a collective negotiation of history, truth, and justice in Sri Lanka. And, most importantly, Sarath's sacrifice, Gamini's reunification with his brother, and Ananda's return to artistic reconstruction and "the sweet touch of the world" present a profound refusal of an aesthetics of transcendence and a politics of individual despair in the face of horrific violence.

Works Cited

Ahmad, Aijaz. *In Theory, Classes, Nations, Literatures*. London: Verso, 1992.

Bacic, Roberta. "Dealing with the Past: Chile—Human Rights and Human Wrongs," *Race and Class* 44.1 (2002): 17–31.

Banerjee, Mita. *The Chutneyfication of History: Salman Rushdie, Michael Ondaatje, Bharati Mukherjee, and the Postcolonial Debate*. Heidelberg: Universitätsverlag C. Winter, 2002.

Burton, Antoinette. "Archive of Bones: *Anil's Ghost* and the Ends of History." *Journal of Commonwealth Literature* 38.1 (2003): 39–56.

Chakrabarty, Dipesh. *Provincializing Europe: Postcolonial Thought and Historical Difference*. Princeton, NJ: Princeton UP, 2000.

Chandler, Raymond. "The Simple Art of Murder." *The Art of the Mystery Story: A Collection of Critical Essays*. Ed. Howard Haycraft. New York: Simon and Schuster, 1946. 1–22.

Christian, Ed. "Introducing the Post-Colonial Detective: Putting Marginality to Work." *The Post-Colonial Detective*, ed. Ed Christian. New York: Palgrave, 2001. 1–16.

Derrickson, Teresa. "Will the 'Un-truth' Set You Free? A Critical Look at Global Human Rights Discourse in Michael Ondaatje's *Anil's Ghost*." *Literature, Interpretation, Theory* 15.2 (2004): 131–52.

Dirlik, Arif. "The Postmodernization of Production and Its Organization: Flexible Production, Work and Culture." *The Postcolonial Aura: Third World Criticism in the Age of Global Capitalism*. Boulder: Westview, 1997. 52–83.

Goldman, Marlene. "Representations of Buddhism in Ondaatje's *Anil's Ghost*." *CLCWeb: Comparative Literature and Culture* 6.3 (2004): 14 pars. 18 Mar. 2005. <http://clcwebjournal.lib.purdue.edu/clcweb04-3/goldman04.html>.

Goonewardena, Kanishka. "*Anil's Ghost*: History/Politics/Ideology." Paper presentation. Congress of the Humanities and Social Sciences. Université Lavla, Québec, Canada, 24–6 May 2001.

"Hearing Schedule and Transcripts." *International Criminal Court*. 15 April 2007. <http://www.icc-cpi.int/cases/Hearing_Schedule.html>.

Holquist, Michael. "Whodunit and Other Questions: Metaphysical Detective Stories in Postwar Fiction." *The Poetics of Murder: Detective Fiction and Literary Theory*. Ed. Glenn W. Most and William W. Stowe. San Diego: Harcourt Brace Jovanovich, 1983. 149–74.

Ismail, Qadri. "A Flippant Gesture Towards Sir Lanka: A Review of Michael Ondaatje's *Anil's Ghost*." *Pravada* 6.9 (2000): 24–9.

James, P.D. *Devices and Desires*. New York: Knopf, 1990.

Knepper, Wendy. "Confession, Autopsy, and the Postcolonial Postmortems of Michael Ondaatje's *Anil's Ghost*." *Postcolonial Postmortems: Crime Fiction from a Transcultural Perspective*. Ed. Christine Matzke and Susanne Mühleisen. Amsterdam: Rodopi, 2006. 37–57.

Le Carré, John. *Tinker, Tailor, Soldier, Spy*. New York: Random House, 1974.

Loomba, Ania. *Colonialism/Postcolonialism*. New York: Routledge, 1998.

Lyotard, Jean-François. *The Postmodern Condition: A Report on Knowledge*. 1979. Trans. Geoff Bennington and Brian Massumi. Minneapolis: U of Minnesota P, 1999.

Makinda, Samuel M. "Human Rights, Humanitarianism, and Transformation in the Global Community." *Global Governance* 7.3 (2001): 343–62.

Malmgren, Carl D. *Anatomy of Murder: Mystery, Detective, and Crime Fiction*. Bowling Green, OH: Bowling Green State U Popular P, 2001.

Marcus, Laura. "Detective and Literary Fiction." *The Cambridge Companion to Crime Fiction*. Ed. Martin Priestman. Cambridge: Cambridge UP, 2003. 245–67.

Moretti, Franco. "Clues." *Signs Taken for Wonders: Essays in the Sociology of Literary Forms*. London: Verso, 1997. 130–56.

Ondaatje, Michael. *Anil's Ghost*. New York: Vintage, 2000.

Prakash, Gyan. "Can the Subaltern Ride? A Reply to O'Hanlan and Washbrook." *Comparative Studies in Society and History* 34.1 (1992): 168–84.

Scanlan, Margaret. "*Anil's Ghost* and Terrorism's Time." *Studies in the Novel* 36.3 (2004): 302–18.

Spanos, William. "The Detective and the Boundary." *Early Postmodernism: Foundational Essays*. Ed. Paul A. Bove. Durham, NC: Duke UP, 1995. 17–39.

Tani, Stefano. "The Dismemberment of the Detective." *Diogenes* 120 (1982): 22–41.

Yaeger, Patricia. "Editor's Column: The End of Postcolonial Theory? A Roundtable with Sunil Agnani, Fernando Coronil, Gaurav Desai, Mamadou Diouf, Simon Gikandi, Susie Tharu, and Jennifer Wenzel." *PMLA* 122.3 (2007): 633–51.

Chapter 2
Postcolonial *Noir*: Vikram Chandra's "Kama"

Claire Chambers

Introduction: India and Crime Fiction

Western crime fiction, whether it belongs to the classic, Golden Age, hard-boiled, police procedural or feminist variants, has tended to revolve around a quest for truth. As Gary Day writes:

> generally speaking, the detective story promotes the idea that things can be known—a crime is committed and the detective, through deduction or action or both, finds out who is responsible. (Day 40)

Day points out that the detective novel is a rationalist form that rests on the premise that it is possible to know "facts" about the world. Critics have discussed the ideological implications of the classic crime novel in particular, noting that the genre germinated within Western societies that, as Foucault has shown, were becoming increasingly geared towards surveillance and discipline (Porter 123–4). The genre affirms values of scientific reason, logic, and teleology, and the Enlightenment idea that society is progressing towards a perfectible point. They tend to suggest that everything can be known through empirical deduction; thus most crime novels have conclusive endings in which the villain is unmasked.[1]

Several recent critics have argued further that crime fiction is a genre that developed during the high noon of the British empire and that, as well as promoting ratiocinative principles, it is also centrally preoccupied by issues of race, nationality, and empire. Caroline Reitz, for instance, contends that Victorian detective narratives should not be read, as many critics have assumed, primarily as domestic fictions, but as narratives which "refashioned Englishness as an imperial instead of an insular identity" (xxv). Focusing specifically on nineteenth-century representations of Britain's most important colony, Upamanyu Pablo Mukherjee suggests that these construct India as "an essentially anarchic and

---

[1] As Dennis Porter has observed, it is significant that the trial and sentencing of fictional criminals are almost always posited as taking place after the ending of crime novels, signalling a shift in Western societies away from public punishment and towards surveillance (Porter 122–3).

criminal country" (vi) in order both to justify but also, on occasion, to interrogate imperialist activities. Not only in the British genteel country house tradition of writers like Agatha Christie, but also the hard-boiled American private eye thriller of writers such as Raymond Chandler, the detective is almost always white, and people of other races tend to be villains or people who disrupt the white detective hero's quest for the truth (see Bailey xii).

In the British strand of crime fiction, a fascination with India is notable in such "classic" novels as Wilkie Collins's *The Moonstone* (1869) and Sir Arthur Conan Doyle's *The Sign of Four* (1890). Although Collins is arguably more critical than Doyle of British imperialism (see Reed, Sutherland, and Wynne), India nonetheless functions in both novels as an exoticized locus, replete with treasure, dangerous adversaries, and mysterious curses. It might be assumed that since the demise of their empire in the 1940s, British crime writers would lose interest in the former colonies as settings for mysteries. However, at least two British-based authors, H.R.F. Keating and Leslie Forbes, have recently produced novels, broadly situated within the whodunit and thriller subgenres respectively, set in Bombay. Notwithstanding their attempts to avoid the exoticism inherent in earlier depictions of India, I would suggest that neither writer entirely escapes charges of stereotyping the country and its peoples.[2]

Yet, particularly since the period of rapid decolonization of most European colonies that occurred immediately after the Second World War, an increasing body of what may be termed postcolonial crime novels and stories is being produced.[3]

2 In his 1964 novel *The Perfect Murder* the highly-respected whodunit writer H.R.F. Keating introduced a detective based in Bombay. Inspector Ghote proved so popular a figure that he has appeared in more than 20 of Keating's novels. Although Keating only set foot in India for the first time after having written several of the novels in the series, the critic Meera Tamaya argues that his painstaking research means that he is commendably aware of social and political currents in India, capturing well the rhythms of Bombay life and speech (Tamaya 19–23). Despite this, I submit that Keating's novels should still be categorized as quintessentially British whodunits (as is suggested in his ironic title, *The Body in the Billiard Room*), providing gentle stories about the triumph of the underdog. Arguably, they project India as being in some ways a more innocent place than post-imperial Britain, where old-fashioned courtesies and respect for hierarchy still exist, and problems can be overcome. More recently, the British-based journalist and travel writer Leslie Forbes produced a wearingly self-referential thriller, also set in the subcontinent and entitled *Bombay Ice* (1998). This novel provides a rather sensationalized depiction of Bombay, abounding in *hijras* (hermaphrodites), gangsters, film stars and slum-dwellers.

3 The term "postcolonial" is of course a highly contested one (see, for example, Dirlik, McClintock and Zeleza), and in using it I do not wish to suggest either a complacency that colonialism is safely a thing of the past, nor that writers from postcolonial countries are preoccupied with empire and its aftermath at the expense of other concerns. As Matzke and Mühleisen rightly point out, colonialism "is not the sole point of reference for the literatures produced in these societies, but may be one among many other experiences" (9). However, in this chapter I hope to indicate that, when it is combined with a clear

Writers such as Jamyang Norbu and Satyajit Ray rewrite the classic crime novel, overturning the genre's usual stereotypical representations of formerly-colonized countries.[4] In addition to Norbu's English-language novel and Ray's short stories (most of which are readily available in English translation from the Bengali), there is also of course a profusion of postcolonial detective texts in other languages. In the subcontinent, detective fiction has long been popular, particularly in the south Indian state of Tamil Nadu.[5] From the 1940s onwards, writers such as Devan, Vaduvoor Duraiswamy Iyengar, and Tamil Vanan worked in a thriving pulp magazine culture more or less coterminous with American magazines such as *Black Mask*. They created detectives in the classic mold who were idiosyncratic and eccentric, but with exceptional powers of deduction and/or bravery. However, they also brought distinctively Indian concerns to the genre. For instance, Iyengar's detective Digambara Swamiyar is a *sanyasi*, or Hindu religious mendicant, turned private eye (see Gangadhar).

Vikram Chandra's "Kama" and Hard-Boiled Detective Fiction

"Kama," a long short story from Vikram Chandra's collection *Love and Longing in Bombay* (1997), has yet to receive attention as an example of postcolonial crime fiction.[6] Yet, along with several other writers not usually associated with crime fiction, he adapts and subverts some of the genre's conventions in order to

---

sense of historical context, a postcolonial reading strategy is useful both in allowing us to understand Chandra's representations of decolonization as a cultural phenomenon, and also in encouraging the exploration of links with theories of postmodernism.

4 The Tibetan writer Jamyang Norbu took the famous explanation Arthur Conan Doyle gave for resurrecting Sherlock Holmes after his supposed demise at the Reichenbach Falls—that he had instead been traveling in Tibet and India—and wrote a novel imaginatively rendering Holmes's experiences in those countries. He positions Holmes as having his Western rational certainties destabilized by encounters with Eastern mystical thought in what may be regarded as an example of postcolonial "writing back" (see Ashcroft et al). In his "Feluda stories," the Bengali film-maker and writer Satyajit Ray also rewrites and parodies the world of the Great Detective (see Mathur).

5 Apparently Urdu crime fiction (*jasusi navelin*) also flourished between the two world wars and thereafter (see Daechsel), and such figures as Ibne Safi and Izhar Asar were prolific writers of popular crime novels. As someone with only a basic understanding of Urdu and no other Indian languages, I cannot claim more than the most rudimentary knowledge of the subcontinent's pulp traditions. However, I look forward to reading the studies that will no doubt soon be produced by regional-language experts (Francesca Orsini's recent article is a useful initial intervention and Christina Oesterheld is also working in the area).

6 Most of the existing scholarship on Chandra focuses on his first novel, *Red Earth and Pouring Rain* (1995). Of the few articles that deal with *Love and Longing in Bombay*, Christopher Rollason's provides perhaps the best introduction to the collection, but does not discuss "Kama" in much detail.

challenge its assumption of a good/evil dichotomy, and its unspoken complicity with (neo-) colonial law enforcement institutions.[7] Despite, or perhaps because, of the earlier, rather Orientalist, attempts by British writers to represent India in crime fiction, Chandra rejects the conventions of the classic or whodunit subgenres, creating instead a fascinating reworking of the hard-boiled detective genre. This is an unusual choice because, as the preceding discussion suggests, most crime writers using an Indian setting have tended to draw on British generic traditions. However, in rewriting the hard-boiled novel from an Indian perspective, Chandra recognizes, along with many writers of color and feminist writers, that the hard-boiled subgenre's supposed claims to transgressiveness provide fertile ground for interrogation (for discussion of the dubiousness of the association of thriller writing with radicalism, see Reddy, *Traces* 15; Horsley 198).

The collection from which the story comes is based on the premise of oral story-telling, as the old man, Subramaniam, regales his young companions at the Fisherman's Rest pub with a series of yarns. "Kama" is the only detective story within the generically diverse collection, which also includes a comedy of manners, a ghost story, and a piece of romantic fiction. Yet Chandra has published a subsequent story, "Eternal Don," which figures the same protagonist, Inspector Sartaj Singh, as he states that the character was "hard for me to let go of" (Mahoney). This story has been developed into a novel, entitled *Sacred Games*, signaling Chandra's ongoing interest in what he has termed the "gangster-and-policemen book" (Alexandru 14).

Chandra incorporates postcolonial and postmodernist concerns into a broadly hard-boiled structure in order to raise questions about epistemology and ontology, theories of knowing and being. In *Postmodernist Fiction*, Brian McHale claims that detective fiction is "the epistemological genre *par excellence*" (9), a genre that poses questions about the limitations of knowledge and the existence of different worldviews emanating from contrasting environments. McHale is less convincing when he asserts that this interest in epistemology is peculiar to modernism, whereas postmodernism is primarily associated with ontology. As he himself acknowledges (11), epistemological and ontological concerns are interpenetrative and not so easily separable. In addition, postmodernist writers are arguably as much interested in knowledge as in existence, as is evidenced by the attention paid by such writers as Salman Rushdie and Graham Swift to narrative constructions of history, and by Amitav Ghosh's multivocal experimentation with anthropology in *In an Antique Land* (see Chambers, "Anthropology"). As such, in the second half of this paper I will draw upon Patricia Merivale and Susan Elizabeth Sweeney's concept of metaphysical detective fiction, or "fiction with a flamboyant yet decidedly complex relationship to the detective story, and a kinship

[7] Other postcolonial writers who have been interpreted as experimenting with crime fiction practices include Margaret Atwood ("Murder in the Dark"; *Alias Grace*); Michael Ondaatje (*Anil's Ghost*); Romesh Gunesekera (*The Sandglass*); and Sally Morgan (for discussion of her *My Place* as a type of detective narrative, see West).

to modernist and postmodernist fiction in general" (1), to stress the variegated literary antecedents and dense philosophical concerns of "Kama."

Chandra's story centers on the attempts of the marginalized Sikh, Sartaj Singh, to conduct police work amid the divisive communalist politics of postcolonial Bombay and the disorienting break-up of his marriage. Like his American hard-boiled forebears, Chandra describes the "mean streets" of an urban milieu, but demonstrates that the legacies of colonialism make it almost impossible for a detective in late-1990s Bombay to remain an unsullied "white knight" (see Chandler, *Simple*). To briefly summarize the plot: "Kama" charts a police investigation into the murder of a businessman, Chetanbhai Patel, who has ostensibly been killed for his Rolex watch. A local drunkard and vagrant, Ghorpade, is found in possession of the watch, and is arrested in what appears to be an open-and-shut case. Yet from an early stage in the investigation, the officer in charge, Sartaj Singh, is not satisfied that Ghorpade is guilty. He slowly learns that Chetanbhai, the well-liked family man, had a secret life: in the years prior to his murder, he and his wife frequented a seedy hotel in Colaba district in which they liaised with women and couples whom they met through classified advertisements. In the throes of a painful divorce, Sartaj has an affinity for Chetanbhai's sensual behavior and extravagant tastes. Yet the businessman's son, Kshitij, increasingly repels Sartaj, as the detective discovers his involvement with a right-wing Hindu extremist group, the *Rakshaks*, or Protectors. He comes to suspect that Kshitij murdered his father because his ascetic religious beliefs meant that he despised his father's *shaukeen* (which loosely translates as "voluptuary") behavior.

As this outline suggests, there are many reasons to situate Chandra's short story both within and outside the hard-boiled subgenre. "Kama" is set in an appropriately urban milieu: Bombay, now known as Mumbai, is the world's most populous city, and is as notorious for its slums, pollution, and gangsterism as for its thriving film industry and commercial successes.[8] As with many of the most memorable hard-boiled settings—Hammett's San Francisco, Chandler's Los Angeles, Paretsky's Chicago—Bombay is a city with a prominent waterfront, in this case the Arabian Sea. Water frequently acts as a repository of secrets in the hard-boiled novel; accordingly, Chetanbhai's body is discovered half-submerged in a monsoon-flooded ditch, and monsoon moisture is constantly emphasized, suggesting that the detective has to wade through murky waters in tackling his investigation. This is a city in which, when one peels away the glamorous façade, it becomes apparent that corruption flourishes, organized crime and gangsters abound, and the moneyed classes rule the show. When Sartaj confronts Kshitij and his fellow

[8] In 1995, Bombay was officially renamed Mumbai as part of a pro-Marathi program instituted by the ruling Shiv Sena party. Given Chandra's evident dislike of Shiv Senaite chauvinism as manifested in his thinly-veiled parody of the *Rakshaks*, and given that he only uses the term "Mumbai" once in the whole collection (see Rollason), I will follow the "Bombay" usage throughout this paper. For more information on the city, see Hansen, Patel and Thorner, and Mehta.

Rakshak members, for instance, he is acutely aware that he is impotent to arrest them, as such right-wing political groups operate within the law, despite their evidently violent practices (145). Bombay's polarized class divisions are evinced in the contrast between the squalor of a dump "covered with a thick layer of paper, bones, and things liquified and rotted" (107), in which slum children search for plastic bags, and the opulence of the Chief Inspector of Police, Parulkar's, house, the garden of which "actually had a tree in it" (110).

As this last quotation suggests, "Kama" is written in a sometimes spare style, abounding with the one-liners, vivid similes, and unexpected juxtapositions that are so characteristic of the hard-boiled novel. To take just one further example, when Sartaj interviews the Jankidases, a married couple who publish the magazine in which Chetanbhai placed his advertisements, he describes them as inhabiting "as perfect a scene of domestic tranquillity as Sartaj had ever seen. He broke it with some satisfaction" (130). Apart from the third-person narrative perspective, this wisecrack could come straight from the pages of *Farewell, My Lovely*. Although, as we shall see, Sartaj himself is only ambivalently a hard-boiled detective, other characters self-consciously style themselves according to the "tough guy" model. Sartaj's young brother-in-law, Rahul, despite being a rich student with a penchant for Benetton clothing, in his speech affects "a terseness which he had picked up from watching at least one American film a day on laser disc" (91). America's cultural hegemony is also indicated in the strong resemblance that Sartaj's colleague Suman Moitra bears to U.S. feminist detectives such as Paretsky's V.I. Warshawski, given that she is known only by her surname and can match any of her male colleagues for intelligence, toughness, and foul language.

When we are first introduced to Sartaj his characterization also appears commensurate with the tradition of the streetwise, survivalist detective. He is described in an impersonal and detached tone as "an inspector in Zone 13 and used to bodies" (77), his familiarity with corpses allowing him to remain unperturbed even when Chetanbhai's body is revealed to have been eaten away by rats. Sartaj follows stereotypical police procedures, as when he searches Chetanbhai's room along a grid pattern (99) and acts with his colleague Katekar as part of a "good cop, bad cop" routine while interrogating Ghorpade (96–7).[9] In many ways, he is shown to be both physically and mentally hardened, authorizing severe physical punishment for suspects (106; 148–9) and cynically using "half-knowledge and insinuations" (148) to manipulate witnesses into making confessions. Furthermore, he has to some extent succumbed to the corruption that is shown to be endemic in postcolonial Bombay. Although his wife's wealth has allowed him the luxury of refusing monetary bribes, Sartaj nonetheless admits to himself that he has accepted other sweeteners, such as train or restaurant reservations and discounts in clothing stores (149–50).

---

[9] The grid pattern search method was first highlighted in fiction in Poe's "The Purloined Letter."

A far-reaching legacy of the British Empire is the legal and policing structure that it bequeathed to its former dominions. Conservative historians portray this as one of Britain's greatest gifts to the colonies (see Griffiths). Other critics argue that the British-style policing system has proved to be a poisoned chalice. David Arnold makes the following compelling argument about the continuities that exist between the colonial and postcolonial police forces:

> Although created to serve colonial needs, the police passed largely unchanged into Indian hands and have remained of central importance to the political fortunes of Independent India. A colonial institution, designed to uphold colonial rule, and control over which was jealously guarded, the police became a mainstay of post-colonial state power. (Arnold 2)

Ed Christian tacitly reinforces this argument when he writes that the postcolonial detective "risks recolonizing the people" (Christian 11). Because the detective has continuities with the colonizing power, he—both in fiction and in the "real" India, the detective is almost always male—is involved in oppressing his own people and upholding colonial or neocolonial values (Christian 12). Postcolonial crime novels often present a detective who is marginalized within his own society, and who is trying to forge an ethics of investigative practice in the non-Western world.

Accordingly, as the story unfolds, it becomes increasingly clear that the characterization of Sartaj is more complex than this initial portrayal of an unsentimental investigator would suggest. Whereas most hard-boiled detectives work independently, Sartaj is a policeman, who acts as part of a team with colleagues and receives orders from superiors. Indeed, in other ways he is also less isolated than the American hard-boiled detectives. Like most detectives from the classic period through to the police procedural, Sartaj is single, yet this comes not out of choice but as a result of a separation which has left him broken-hearted. Far from being a macho womanizer like Sam Spade, Philip Marlowe, and Mike Hammer, he is depicted as being a slightly effeminate dandy, who cries over memories of his ex-wife (118). He is also depicted as having a close relationship with his mother and friends. Friendships and communitarian links are important to the multicultural detective (see, for example, Plummer 265), just as they are for most feminist detectives (Reddy, *Sisters* 103–12; Pykett 58–60), marking their difference from the Western, individualist, male norm.

Notwithstanding these connections, Sartaj is in other aspects lonelier than his American literary antecedents. Policemen, as Arnold suggests, are regarded as outsiders by most Indians, and this is confirmed in "Kama" when Sartaj's usually recalcitrant subordinate, Katekar, recounts going on a religious journey and telling none of his fellow pilgrims of his profession, for fear of rejection (154). It is also worth noting that Katekar reports that the trip to the holy site of Pandharpur had the additional unexpected result of curing his chronic backache for at least a while. In implied accordance with Fanon's ideas in *The Wretched of the Earth*, Chandra introduces at various points in the text an "atmosphere of myth and magic"

(Fanon 43) to suggest that other forces may be at work than mere logic and material evidence. This has the effect of problematizing both the institution of the police and the assumptions and very workings of the law itself. In most crime fiction, while the police may be lampooned or depicted as bumbling and corrupt, the validity of the law is ultimately upheld, but in "Kama" notions of legality and justice are interrogated. In an internal monologue, Sartaj muses, "I arrested a man for a crime he didn't commit, and that man is dead, and life is very long, and investigation is one way to get through it, but to call it justice is only half the truth" (150). Here the detective acknowledges that his work functions more as a distraction from existential despair than for the benefit of his community. His police-work is partly to blame for the rift that develops between Sartaj and Megha, and when she finds out that he beats suspects she tells him that she hates his world. He recalls wanting to tell her: "it's your world also, but I am thirty-one years old and I live in the parts you don't want to see. I live there for you" (151). This anguished assertion suggests that for all its manifold deficiencies, policing is a necessary evil, with which all bourgeois people are implicated even if they choose not to admit it.

As a member of the minority Sikh religious community as well as a despised policeman, Sartaj is doubly marginalized. His turban, *kara* (metal bracelet) and swaggering walk are conspicuous markers of his alterity, meaning that he is "not very good at shadowing" (141). He experiences prejudice at work as a result of his religion, which is particularly apparent when his boss, Parulkar, warns him against treating the powerful Kshitij as a murder suspect:

> "These are delicate times, Sartaj," Parulkar said. "Pushing too hard, without sufficient reason, on that family could lead to, let us say, sensitivities." What he meant was that for an outsider, a Sikh, to push a little was to push a lot. It was true, even though the Patels were Gujaratis and so outsiders themselves. There were outsiders and outsiders. To say, I was born in Bombay, was very much beside the point. (110)

Here Chandra alludes to the commonplace that fragmented, cosmopolitan Bombay—not unlike America—is a locale in which few people are truly indigenous. As the reference to "outsiders and outsiders" illustrates, however, not all of the city's settlers are of equal standing, and members of visible minority groups are expected to keep their heads down or suffer the consequences. Only Sartaj's personal vanity prevents him for a long time from seeing that Kshitij, as a member of the *Rakshaks*, goes further than Parulkar's coded rebuke, despising him "for his beard, for his turban" (144). Sartaj also finds himself excluded from the domestic sphere. During a marital argument, his ex-wife Megha once accuses him of looking like a terrorist, a remark which, in the context of the often violent movement of the 1980s and 1990s for a separate Sikh homeland of Khalistan (see Jeffrey), leaves Sartaj feeling "desolate and foreign" (95).

Class is an additional factor that contributes towards the breakdown of his marriage. Although Sartaj is a middle-class Sikh who comes from a long line of policemen dating back to colonial times (79), his family pedigree is eclipsed by Megha's impeccable class and caste credentials. When Parulkar puts pressure on Sartaj to sign the divorce papers, as his superior belongs to the same social circle as Megha's family, Sartaj feels "a rush of hatred for the rich [...] for their confidence, their calm, [and the way] they thought everything could be *managed*" (111). His reluctance to sign the papers stems equally from a cultural aversion to divorce:

> In his whole life he had never known anyone who had been divorced. He had never known anybody whose parents had been divorced. He couldn't remember a friend who had known anybody who had been divorced. Divorce was something that strange people did in the pages of *Society* magazine. (100)

Like the reference to a religious worldview discussed earlier in relation to Katekar's pilgrimage, this quotation again suggests an alternative worldview that challenges the assumptions of the Western crime novel.

"Kama" and the Metaphysical Detective Novel

This brings me to another way of interpreting "Kama": from within the framework of what has been termed the metaphysical detective novel.[10] According to Merivale and Sweeney, who provide the most recent and rigorous analysis of the metaphysical detective story, this is a text "that parodies or subverts traditional detective-story conventions—such as narrative closure and the detective's role as surrogate reader—with the intention, or at least the effect, of asking questions about mysteries of being and knowing which transcend the mere machinations of the mystery plot" (2). This suggestive comment resonates with many of "Kama's" preoccupations and devices. It would certainly be true to state that the story subverts the crime fiction practice—particularly common in the classic tradition, but also present, although more ambiguously so, even in seemingly open-ended *noir* novels—of providing narrative closure. The novella does not have a single neat ending and, despite leading the reader to believe that Kshitij has committed the murder, it stops short of providing a definitive solution to the crime. The final paragraph of the story describes the detective disappearing into a bustling, labyrinthine Bombay cityscape, the case unsatisfactorily concluded with Kshitij and his friends roaming free and possibly plotting vengeance against

[10] I prefer this term to the designation "anti-detective novel," finding it inappropriate to Chandra, who is far from being resistant to the popular genre as this would suggest, and to "postmodern crime novel," which is too unproblematic a definition of a text that may also be interpreted as also owing debts to the realist and modernist modes. For discussion of these and other possible terms, see Merivale and Sweeney 2–4.

Sartaj. The paragraph includes the telling words, "Sartaj knew that nothing was finished," (161) a notion reinforced by the fact that the story then opens out to the Subramaniam framing narrative.

Prior to this "conclusion" is another possible ending: the final point of the investigation, which involves Sartaj traveling to the countryside to interrogate Kshitij's mother about the circumstances of her husband's murder. Once there, Sartaj's logical certainties are confounded by the widow's rambling narrative, in a passage which is worth quoting at length:

> She spoke fast in a Kutchi he didn't completely understand, but he understood that there was [...] no solution so simple as a bad man, only a series of fragments, dinner at the Khyber with her husband and her son, their honeymoon long ago in Khandala [...] Somehow it had happened. Not somehow but anyhow. Things happened, Sartaj thought, one after the other, and what we want from it is a kind of shape, a case report. [...] "I understand," Sartaj said, and understood nothing. (157–8)

If, as Merivale and Sweeney suggest, the metaphysical detective story parodies or destabilizes the crime fiction convention that the detective is analogous to the reader, then here both detective and reader are confronted by language's inadequacy and the limitations of particular modes of interpretation. Sartaj recognizes in this passage that the policeman's job is to force random, incomplete, and fissured testimonials into coherent "case reports," but that essential truths are lost in the process of writing down these fragments. The detective recognizes problems associated with knowing and being: he "understood nothing" and is uncomfortably aware that his search for a villain on whom to pin the crime obfuscates the complexities of personality and the possibility that there may be varying degrees of guilt.

This lack of certainties is dramatized elsewhere in the story, such as the passage in which Rahul (who, as has already been noted, assumes hard-boiled mannerisms and speech patterns) takes Sartaj to a bar called The Hideout. This bar is hyperreal in Baudrillard's sense of a state of being whereby reality dissolves and reproductions or simulacra stand in for the real (see Poster). It is a simulacrum of a gangster's den, complete with cave-like walls, waiters in leather jackets and *faux* "roughneck tin mugs" (94). Sartaj reminisces about arresting an actual criminal on that street, and Rahul imagines him to have been a "bad guy," but Sartaj recalls details such as the man's name, and his quiet assertion that he had five children, and knows that despite his greed there can be no such simple conclusion (94). Real felons are more complex than the caricatures of villainy to be found in the hyperreal Hideout.

Identity is thus placed under scrutiny in "Kama." Whereas in mainstream detective novels death provides the main source of mystery, in the metaphysical detective novel life is the fundamental enigma to be solved. Through the process of his inquiries, Sartaj begins to question his own identity. In addition to being compelled, by the prejudice of those around him, to consider his religious affiliations, he also questions the career he has chosen. At various moments in the text, we are presented with the notion that the police officer is a role to be assumed and cast off: for instance, both he and his colleague Katekar assume particular expressions and stances when they interrogate suspects (96; 147). Sartaj questions whether he wants to continue being a policeman, as he finds it difficult to inure himself from the obvious distaste people have for his position (102–3). Yet he comes to realize that what he once thought was only a performance is now impossible to shake off, and that he has become "completely and deep in the bone [...] a policeman like his father, and his father before him" (143). The reference to Sartaj's forefathers reminds that it was during colonial rule that the repressive state apparatus of the police was established. This contributes towards the loneliness Sartaj experiences and his sense of being cut off from most of his compatriots in postcolonial Bombay.

Physical form is just as fragmented as psychological identity in Chandra's narrative. In the mainstream hard-boiled novel, descriptions tend pithily to sum up a person's appearance, as in Hammett's famous description of Sam Spade as a "blond satan" (1) and Chandler/Marlowe's references, in a single scene from *Farewell, My Lovely*, to "[t]he tall beautiful man," "[t]he dark woman," and "the man with the moustache" (140). In "Kama," on the other hand, description becomes increasingly fractured and, while the focus remains corporeal, it is on metonymic body parts, with allusions to "the strangeness of the hand that lay like a knurled brown slab in his lap" (117), "the backs of his thighs in sleep" (140), and "fragments of faces" (91). Fragments are of course a model of knowledge much vaunted by postmodernist thinkers, who privilege a broken, honeycomb structure over monolithic forms (see Cunningham 60). Yet they are also championed by such postcolonial thinkers as Salman Rushdie, who suggests that histories and memories are inevitably broken, incomplete, and fissured, but that this can be cause for celebration as well as regret (12). Derek Walcott also embraces *disjecta membra*, providing an eloquent refutation of those historical accounts which, he argues, have unfairly dismissed Caribbean culture as unfinished, deficient, mimicking. Against this background, it is possible to discern that Chandra's interest in the part at the expense of the whole in "Kama" is a deliberate political strategy aimed at countering the smooth certainties of Western crime fiction. Like a kaleidoscope which contains tiny broken shards of glass that together make a beautiful pattern, so a fragmentary vision of events, Chandra suggests, may be more meaningful than one that attempts to hide the cracks.

Like Rushdie and Walcott, Chandra celebrates the collage-like fragments of the environment he portrays, which is particularly noticeable in the following passage:

> He [Sartaj] leaned against a wall and scanned the layered many-coloured mess of movie posters and political slogans, dominated by the latest broadside bearing the crossed spears of a right political party. He read all this with the concentration of an archeologist smoothing away layers of ancient dust. (81)

This image of a palimpsest of posters echoes a similar depiction of a "riot" of fly-posters adorning aged London walls in Amitav Ghosh's *The Shadow Lines* (100), and evokes comparable ideas about the "layered" nature of cultures and histories in the city. The fact that the image is papyraceous is also significant, as I would suggest that this is a story all about stories, texts, and documents. Many illicit texts are featured in "Kama," including the *Kama Sutra*, *Rakshak* pamphlets inciting political hatred, the clandestine Jankidas advertisements, and the divorce papers that Sartaj hides away without signing. Central clues within the story such as the *Apsara* (statue of a heavenly dancer) which Sartaj discovers to have been thrown in a swamp, and the sexy polaroids of his parents that Kshitij dreads being discovered by his fellow *Rakshaks*, may also be interpreted as kinds of hidden text. Like the reader or the "archeologist," it is the policeman's job to piece together such textual fragments into a coherent whole. This self-referential concern with "embedded text[s]," "the meaning of prior texts, and the nature of reading" is of course characteristic of the metaphysical detective novel more broadly, which, as Merivale and Sweeney point out (8; 7), has a central epistemological concern with the limitations of knowledge.

Conclusion

This essay began with a brief sketch of classic crime fiction's preoccupation with race and empire, before moving on to suggest that Chandra rejects the classic or whodunit subgenres, playing instead with the conventions of the hard-boiled detective novel. "Kama" encompasses both postcolonial and postmodern concerns within its neo-*noir* composition in order to interrogate questions of knowing and being. Chandra's recently published novel featuring Sartaj Singh, *Sacred Games*, similarly has at its core this continuing interest in ontological and epistemological issues, and in the multi-layered nature of protean Bombay. In interview, Chandra indicates that in the later text the question of the existence of God "hangs over the entire narrative," going on to suggest that the novel as a structured form, with the controlling yet shadowy "consciousness" that is assumed to stand behind it, suggests "a coherent form to the universe" (Chambers, "Interview" 45–6). In this essay, I have demonstrated that these same metaphysical questions about existence, erudition, and language's purchase on reality are also centrally highlighted in "Kama."

Works Cited

Alexandru, Maria-Sabina. "'Virtual Reality on Infinite Bandwidth': Vikram Chandra Interviewed by Maria-Sabina Alexandru." *Journal of Commonwealth Literature* 40.2 (2005): 5–21.

Arnold, David. *Police Power and Colonial Rule: Madras 1859–1947*. Delhi: Oxford UP, 1986.

Ashcroft, Bill, Gareth Griffiths, and Helen Tiffin. *The Empire Writes Back: The Theory and Practice of Post-Colonial Literatures*. London: Routledge, 1989.

Atwood, Margaret. *Murder in the Dark: Short Fictions and Prose Poems*. London: Cape, 1984.

——. *Alias Grace*. London: Bloomsbury, 1996.

Bailey, Frankie Y. *Out of the Woodpile: Black Characters in Crime and Detective Fiction*. New York: Greenwood, 1991.

Chambers, Claire. "Anthropology as Cultural Translation: Amitav Ghosh's *In An Antique Land*." *Postcolonial Text* 2.3 (2006): 1–19. <http://journals.sfu.ca/pocol/index.php/pct/article/view/489/320>.

——. "An Interview with Vikram Chandra." *Wasafiri* 23.1 (2008): 45–8.

Chandler, Raymond. *Farewell, My Lovely*. London: Penguin, 1985 [1940].

——. *The Simple Art of Murder*. Boston: Houghton Mifflin, 1950.

Chandra, Vikram. *Red Earth and Pouring Rain*. London: Faber, 1995.

——. "Kama." *Love and Longing in Bombay: Stories*. Boston: Little, Brown, 1997. 75–161.

——. "Eternal Don." *New Yorker* (23 and 30 June 1997): 130–41.

——. *Sacred Games*. London: Faber, 2006.

Christian, Ed. "Introducing the Post-Colonial Detective: Putting Marginality to Work." *The Post-Colonial Detective*. Ed. Ed Christian. Basingstoke: Palgrave, 2001. 1–16.

Collins, Wilkie. *The Moonstone*. London: Penguin, 1994 [1868].

Cunningham, Valentine. *Reading After Theory*. Oxford: Blackwell, 2001.

Daechsel, Markus. "Paper Abstract: Of Poisoned Ice-Cream and Rubber Sea-Monsters: Some Reflections About Urdu Detective Fiction and the Making of Modernist Identities Among the Colonial Service Stratum of Interwar Lahore." *16th European Conference on Modern South Asian Studies*. 6–9 September 2000. <http://www.sociology.-ed.ac.uk/sas/conf16/panel45.htm>.

Day, Gary. "Investigating the Investigator: Hammett's Continental Op." *American Crime Fiction: Studies in the Genre*. Ed. Brian Docherty. London: Macmillan, 1988. 39–53.

Dirlik, Arif. "The Postcolonial Aura: Third World Criticism in the Age of Global Capitalism." *Critical Inquiry* 20 (Winter 1994): 328–56.

Doyle, Arthur Conan. *The Sign of Four*. London: Pan, 1975 [1890].

Fanon, Frantz. *The Wretched of the Earth*. Preface Jean-Paul Sartre; trans. Constance Farrington. Harmondsworth: Penguin, 1967 [1961]

Forbes, Leslie. *Bombay Ice*. London: Phoenix, 1998.

Gangadhar, V. "Of Detectives and Square Tomatoes." *Rediff.* 21 June 1997. <http://www.rediff.com/style/-jun/21gang.htm>.

——. "The Case of the Poetic Detective." *Rediff.* 6 November 1997. <http://www.rediff.com/style/nov/06gang.htm>.

Ghosh, Amitav. *The Shadow Lines.* Delhi: Oxford UP, 1995 [1989].

——. *In an Antique Land.* London: Granta, 1992.

Griffiths, Sir Percival. *To Guard My People: The History of the Indian Police.* London: Ernest Benn, 1971.

Gunesekera, Romesh. *The Sandglass*. London: Granta, 1998.

Hammett, Dashiell. *The Maltese Falcon.* London: Orion, 2002 [1930].

Hansen, Thomas Blom. *Wages of Violence: Naming and Identity in Postcolonial Bombay*. Princeton: Princeton UP, 2001.

Horsley, Lee. *Twentieth-Century Crime Fiction*. Oxford: Oxford UP, 2005.

Jeffrey, Robin. *What's Happening to India?: Punjab, Ethnic Conflict, and the Test for Federalism*. New York: Holmes and Meier, 1994.

Keating, H.R.F. *The Body in the Billiard Room*. Harmondsworth: Viking, 1987.

McClintock, Anne. "The Angel of Progress: Pitfalls of the Term 'Post-Colonialism.'" *Colonial Discourse and Post-Colonial Theory*. Eds. Patrick Williams and Laura Chrisman. Hemel Hempstead: Harvester Wheatsheaf, 1993. 291–304.

McHale, Brian. *Postmodernist Fiction*. London: Routledge, 1996 [1987].

Mahoney, Kevin Patrick. "Interview with Vikram Chandra." *Author Trek.* 1998. <http://www.authortrek.com/-vikram-chandra.html>.

Mathur, Suchitra. "Holmes's Indian Reincarnation: A Study in Postcolonial Transposition." *Postcolonial Postmortems: Crime Fiction from a Transcultural Perspective*. Eds. Christine Matzke and Susanne Mühleisen. Amsterdam: Rodopi, 2006. 87–108.

Matzke, Christine and Susanne Mühleisen, "Postcolonial Postmortems: Issues and Perspectives." *Postcolonial Postmortems: Crime Fiction from a Transcultural Perspective*. Eds. Christine Matzke and Susanne Mühleisen. Amsterdam: Rodopi, 2006. 1–16.

Mehta, Suketu. *Maximum City: Bombay Lost and Found.* London: Headline Review, 2005.

Merivale, Patricia, and Susan Elizabeth Sweeney. "The Game's Afoot: On the Trail of the Metaphysical Detective Story." *Detecting Texts: The Metaphysical Detective Story from Poe to Postmodernism*. Eds. Patricia Merivale and Susan Elizabeth Sweeney. Philadelphia: U of Pennsylvania P, 1999. 1–24.

Morgan, Sally. *My Place.* London: Virago, 1988.

Mukherjee, Upamanyu Pablo. *Crime and Empire: The Colony in Nineteenth-Century Fictions of Crime*. Oxford: Oxford UP, 2003.

Norbu, Jamyang. *The Mandala of Sherlock Holmes: The Missing Years*. London: John Murray, 2002 [1999].

Ondaatje, Michael. *Anil's Ghost.* London: Bloomsbury, 2000.

Orsini, Francesca. "Detective Novels: A Commercial Genre in Nineteenth-Century North India." *India's Literary History: Essays on the Nineteenth Century*. Eds. Stuart Blackburn and Vasudha Dalmia. New Delhi: Permanent Black, 2004. 435–82.

Paretsky, Sara. *Deadlock*. London: Penguin, 1987 [1984].

Patel, Sujata and Alice Thorner, eds. *Bombay: Mosaic of Modern Culture*. Bombay: Oxford UP, 1995.

Plummer, Patricia. "Transcultural British Crime Fiction: Mike Phillips's Sam Dean Novels." *Postcolonial Postmortems: Crime Fiction from a Transcultural Perspective*. Eds. Christine Matzke and Susanne Mühleisen. Amsterdam: Rodopi, 2006. 255–70.

Poe, Edgar Allan. "The Purloined Letter." *Tales of Mystery and Imagination*. Ware: Wordsworth, 1993 [1841]. 203–27.

Porter, Dennis. *The Pursuit of Crime: Art and Ideology in Detective Fiction*. New Haven: Yale UP, 1981.

Poster, Mark. Ed. *Jean Baudrillard: Selected Writings*. Stanford: Stanford UP, 2001.

Pykett, Lyn. "Investigating Women: The Female Sleuth After Feminism." *Watching the Detectives: Essays on Crime Fiction*. Eds. Ian A. Bell and Graham Daldry. New York: St Martin's, 1990. 48–67.

Ray, Satyajit. *The Adventures of Feluda*. Delhi: Penguin, 1989.

Reddy, Maureen T. *Sisters in Crime: Feminism and the Crime Novel*. New York: Continuum, 1988.

——. *Traces, Codes, and Clues: Reading Race in Crime Fiction*. Piscataway: Rutgers UP, 2003.

Reed, John R. "The Stories of *The Moonstone*." *Wilkie Collins to the Forefront: Some Reassessments*. Eds. Nelson Smith and R.C. Terry. New York: AMS, 1995. 91–100.

Reitz, Caroline. *Detecting the Nation: Fictions of Detection and the Imperial Venture*. Columbus: Ohio State UP, 2004.

Rollason, Christopher. "Translating a Transcultural Text—Problems and Strategies: On the Spanish Translation of Vikram Chandra's *Love And Longing In Bombay*." *Fourth Congress of the European Society For Translation Studies*, 26–29 September 2004. <http://www.seikilos.com.ar/LoveAndLonging.html>.

Rushdie, Salman. "Imaginary Homelands." *Imaginary Homelands*. London: Granta, 1991. 9–21.

Sutherland, John. "Introduction." *The Moonstone*. Ed John Sutherland. Oxford: Oxford UP, 1999. vii–xxix.

Tamaya, Meera. "Keating's Inspector Ghote: Post-Colonial Detective?" *The Post-Colonial Detective*. Ed. Ed Christian. Basingstoke: Palgrave, 2001. 17–36.

Walcott, Derek. *The Antilles: Fragments of Epic Memory*. New York: Farrar, Straus and Giroux, 1993.

West, Russell. "Uncovering Collective Crimes: Sally Morgan's *My Place* as Australian Indigenous Detective Narrative." *Sleuthing Ethnicity: The Detective in Multiethnic Crime Fiction*. Eds. Dorothea Fischer-Hornung and Monika Mueller. Madison: Fairleigh Dickinson UP, 2003. 280–96.

Wynne, Catherine. *The Colonial Conan Doyle: British Imperialism, Irish Nationalism, and the Gothic*. Westport, CT: Greenwood, 2002.

Zeleza, Paul Tiyambe. "Fictions of the Postcolonial." *Toronto Review of Contemporary Writing Abroad* 15.2 (Winter 1997): 19–29.

Chapter 3
Postcolonial Epistemologies: Transcending Boundaries and Re-inscribing Difference in *The Calcutta Chromosome*

Maureen Lauder

Detective stories are all about the retroactive formation of a narrative: who did what to whom, and why? The classic detective—à la Holmes or Dupin—is the master of this narrative, an unparalleled reader of people and clues, seeing meaning and causality where the layman sees only randomness and chance. At the story's end, the detective has, one way or another, conveyed to us a new narrative of just what happened and for what reasons. In Amitav Ghosh's *The Calcutta Chromosome*, however, none of the various detective figures provide such a neat summative narrative. Instead, *The Calcutta Chromosome* puts forth the notion of an epistemological quantum leap, in which the detective who discovers is also discovered, and the detective's knowledge becomes something epistemologically other. Consequently, the novel lays out numerous threads and mysteries and, instead of bringing them all together, brings them *near* one another. Rather than summing up and filling in the blanks for the reader, answering the whodunit, the novel lays the groundwork for the reader's own quantum leap, a sudden understanding and insight as to what might have happened and what the novel's mysteries might be about. The epistemology and conventions of the classic detective story serve to bring us to the brink of this leap—but they cannot accompany us across.

In its lack of a clearly articulated solution to a mystery, *The Calcutta Chromosome* defies a prominent convention of the detective genre, but the novel is nonetheless deeply indebted to the traditions of detective fiction. Instead of one mystery, there are several (each one nebulous, shifting, and ill-defined)—as well as several detectives, several time periods, and several settings. In the frame narrative, the mystery concerns a bureaucrat named Antar, who, happening upon some evidence concerning a former co-worker's disappearance, launches his own investigation. The disappearance of the co-worker, a man named Murugan, is itself part of the story of another investigation, that of Murugan's quest to discover what the Calcutta chromosome is, how it works, and who controls it.[1] Though

[1] Murugan is an amateur science historian, specializing in the history of malaria research—in particular, the work of one Ronald Ross, a British officer in the Indian Medical Service and a 1902 Nobel prizewinner for his work on the malaria parasite. In the course of

Murugan is one of several investigatory figures, he is in many respects the most central: his investigations—which range from archival research to old-fashioned gumshoe detection (eavesdropping, skulking in shadows, tailing people, and the like)—touch on each of the novel's other characters and tie together happenings and clues on multiple continents and from more than one historical period.

Murugan's range of knowledge and investigatory facility outstrip that of anyone else in the novel. With insight that would do Sherlock Holmes proud, for example, Murugan can extrapolate, from an uncatalogued letter in a Baltimore archive, that, almost a century earlier, two malaria researchers who never met must have both had contact with a mysterious Indian man whom Murugan believes is one of the keys to the Calcutta chromosome. Murugan moreover serves as the detective-narrator for many of the novel's other investigatory characters: even as he continues along the trajectory of his inquiry, one of his primary roles in the novel is to explain—both to other characters and to the reader—how all his research fits together and what conclusions he has drawn. In spite of his role as a central conduit of knowledge, however, Murugan also remains a continual reminder of how much is unknown and unknowable. Rather than creating knowledge, Murugan serves as a vector for a knowledge that some other entity wishes to transmit. Due to his very status as a conduit, Murugan is denied access to the knowledge he seeks.

The Calcutta chromosome, Murugan theorizes, is not really a chromosome at all, but some kind of biological marker, one that permits the interpersonal transmission of personality. In other words, the Calcutta chromosome bestows a sort of immortality, one that preserves personality and voice rather than identity and subjectivity. In the postcolonial, transnational, relentlessly globalized world of the novel's present, the Calcutta chromosome is what comes next: a mode of human existence no longer rooted in the boundaries and separations necessary to individuality and nationhood, and thus one that transcends the legacies of colonialism. Murugan has come to realize, however, that his investigation is no way autonomous. Clues are laid for him, key witnesses provided at pivotal moments, and crucial documents are placed in his possession at just the right times. (The uncatalogued archival letter, for example, fortuitously falls out of a packet of lab notes "as if it had been left there to wait for me" (118) and vanishes before Murugan can get permission to photocopy it.) Murugan's knowledge—and thus the narrative he creates from that knowledge—is being orchestrated. Instead of the masterful detective who knows despite the criminal's attempts to prevent his

---

his investigations, Murugan becomes convinced that there exists a secret history of malaria research. He believes that Ross's research was guided in a particular direction in order to further the work of a group of Indians who had discovered the existence of a biological marker (which Murugan calls the Calcutta chromosome) that, when properly manipulated, allows for the transmission of personality traits. Murugan comes to believe that the Calcutta chromosome is manipulated by the alteration of knowledge; therefore information about the Calcutta chromosome can be gleaned by examining what has been altered (in this case, the course of malaria research).

knowledge, Murugan knows because he is allowed to: "Someone's trying to get us to make some connections," he tells Urmila, a young woman he meets in the course of his investigation. "[T]hey're trying to tell us something; something they don't want to put together themselves, so that when we get to the end we'll have a whole new story" (214).

Even more damning to Murugan's mastery of the situation, however, is his encroaching realization that he is precluded from knowing and recognizing the Calcutta chromosome simply by virtue of who and what he is: an Indian man steeped in a Western, scientific epistemological framework that insists that all things are at least theoretically knowable. What Murugan seeks is invisible to him precisely because he believes he knows what he is looking for. "[I]f there really is such a thing as the Calcutta chromosome," Murugan finally concludes, "only a person like Mangala, someone who's completely out of the loop scientifically, would be able to find it" (247). The primary detective of *The Calcutta Chromosome*, then, does not truly direct his own investigation. More importantly, his detective-ness actually prevents his access to the knowledge he seeks. In place of the masterful detective of the classic detective story, whose keen eye, analytic acumen, and scientific detachment allow him to construct an objective narrative and body of knowledge, *The Calcutta Chromosome* provides multiple detective figures (including Murugan and Antar, as well as, somewhat more peripherally, a number of others), each of whom holds a piece of a puzzle that Murugan is being shown how to solve.

This multiplicity of detective figures, none of whom achieves any particularly firm solutions, is perhaps not altogether surprising, since *The Calcutta Chromosome* is hardly a pure detective novel; it is just as much thriller or historical novel or science fiction. But this generic mixing—and the presence of many conventions of detective fiction among them—is crucial to the novel's project. Like its genre, *The Calcutta Chromosome*'s setting is fluid and shifting. The action shifts from colonial India to New York and Calcutta in 1995, to a near-future New York City. This future New York stands as an emblem of postcolonial diasporas and transnational consolidations. All the characters we meet there come from former colonies and occupied territories, drawn to New York by the promise of good jobs and American visas, preserving pockets of their old cultures amidst the high-tech, international communities in which they work. The political and economic landscape of this future world are only hazily sketched in, but its primary feature is the International Water Council, a worldwide, presumably non-profit group—created in part through the absorption of a multitude of smaller independent agencies—with employees of every nationality and an office (and concomitant bureaucratic apparatus) in every corner of the world.

In both genre and setting, then, *The Calcutta Chromosome* enacts a fluidity and permeability of the borders and boundaries that exist between the spaces of east and west, past and present, individual and nation. All the novel's characters move repeatedly through and between these borders, but the boundaries themselves remain largely intact. In New York, Antar is always marked and identified (by himself and others) as Egyptian, and he himself always categorizes other people according to their nationality. In Calcutta, despite his Indian origin, Murugan always stands out, indelibly marked by his long tenure in the United States. The boundaries between these spaces may be permeable, but they nonetheless reinscribe the differences that the characters negotiate while traversing these borders.

Murugan's understanding of the Calcutta chromosome points the way to an erasure of boundaries, an alternative space that lies beyond the epistemological quantum leap, where the borders that create and consolidate the individual vanish—and where, by extension, the divisions upon which nation and empire (whether colonial or capitalist) depend are effaced. The Western rational epistemology of detection that Murugan brings to bear on the subject of the Calcutta chromosome enables the novel's theorization of this alternative space, for Murugan sketches in its contours via his investigation. When Murugan comes up hard against the limits of what Western epistemology can know, however, this theorization is confounded. Because he knows in the wrong way, Murugan cannot access this alternative space—and therefore neither can the reader. The novel thus relies heavily on the conventions of the detective genre to posit the alternative space, but the limitations of this speculation are contained in the very epistemological framework and internal contradictions that permit the endeavor in the first place.[2]

The Epistemology of the Border

In most cases, the detective genre proposes that there is a solution to every mystery: it takes only the right gaze to look beneath the surface and reveal the significance of innocuous details and the motives underlying actions. The classic detective is an embodied version of the objective Cartesian gaze, fundamentally indebted to Western Enlightenment values of rationality and objectivity. As Karen Jacobs points out, however, this embodiment (and the subject position that underlies it) ultimately undoes the illusion of objectivity and epistemological certainty implied by the detective's gaze. To solve the crime, the detective requires not an objective gaze, but the correct gaze—one that is aligned with its object (the criminal) in order to better predict the criminal's next move; the detective, moreover, must observe and correctly interpret the right clues. Conveyed through and dependent on the detective-as-subject, knowledge in detective fiction is thus "contingent rather than omniscient," and the "intimately proximate, interested gaze"—rather than an

[2] I use (somewhat unsatisfactorily) the term "alternative" or "other" space to differentiate it from the more common "third space," which is generally used to describe the space *between* two terms of a binary. Both the name and the conception of the third space declare its dependence from and negotiation of the binary relation. While Ghosh routinely depicts liminal spaces that might be described as third spaces (particularly in *In An Antique Land*), my reading of *The Calcutta Chromosome* focuses on its attempts to create a space that transcends binaries and borders without explicitly negotiating or implicitly relying on the presence of those borders for its own existence.

objective one—emerges as the only one that can solve the crime (50–51). Though the formula of the classic detective story stresses knowability, Jacobs's analysis of the detective's gaze hints at the uncertainty of knowledge that haunts the form.

It makes sense then, that *The Calcutta Chromosome*, a novel about what can be known and by whom, would end up looking in some respects quite a lot like a detective novel. The characters in *The Calcutta Chromosome* negotiate two forms of knowledge— a Western, rational, scientific epistemology and an Eastern, native, silent epistemology underpinned by the belief that any claim to knowledge is impossible. The detectives of *The Calcutta Chromosome*—all men steeped in the belief that enough investigation will ultimately yield concrete knowledge—act out the internal epistemological contradictions of the detective. They are men in search of answers who, to varying degrees, come to realize that answers of any sort are radically contingent and often ineffable.

This explicit handling of questions of knowledge and unknowability is fairly common to postcolonial detective fiction: as Patricia Linton points out, the weaknesses and uncertainties of Western epistemologies and methodologies are often highlighted in their collision with other ways of knowing and other methods of investigation. In their struggle with this collision, Ghosh's characters suggest the possibility of transcending or exceeding the boundaries delineated by the contradictions between the knowable and the unknowable. In *The Calcutta Chromosome*, moreover, Ghosh attempts to create a space and knowledge that lie not only outside the binaries of knowledge/nonknowledge and West/East, but that also exist without reference to such binaries.

Ghosh's interest in fluidity and syncretism dates back almost to the beginning of his career as a writer and anthropologist. In 1993's *In An Antique Land*, a reworking of his doctoral thesis, Ghosh explores this interest in terms of the relationship between the scientific knowledge he tries to accrue via ethnographic and archival research and the knowledge gleaned through the complex, intersubjective relationships he forms with the inhabitants of the small Egyptian village where he lives while gathering data. In Neelam Srivastava's view, both the structure and content of *In An Antique Land* take up a project of syncretism, a blending of nationalities, languages, religions, and cultures that takes place across both space and time. Though both medieval and modern cultures are marked by a surprising intensity of travel and cultural exchange, Srivastava notes that by the end of *In An Antique Land*, "[s]yncretism is being erased in favor of cultural separateness" (61) and that "'the remains of those small, indistinguishable, intertwined histories, Indian and Egyptian, Muslim and Jewish, Hindu and Muslim, had been partitioned long ago'" (*Antique Land* 339, qtd. in Srivastava 61).

Ghosh associates this partitioning with the influence of Western thought and empire:

> In 1509 AD, the fate of that ancient trading culture was sealed in a naval engagement that was sadly, perhaps pathetically, evocative of its ethos: a transcontinental fleet [...] was attacked and defeated by a Portuguese force off

> the shores of Diu, in Gujarat. As always, the determination of a small, united band of soldiers triumphed easily over the rich confusions that accompany a culture of accommodation and compromise. (*Antique Land* 288)

Almost five hundred years later, Ghosh sees the results of this new world order, founded on division rather than porosity, when he is unable to explain to an Egyptian official why he, an Indian studying Arab culture, is interested in viewing the tomb of a Jewish holy man. Upon his return to the United States, Ghosh discovers that the official's "understanding of the map of modern knowledge was much more thorough than mine" (341–2). Ghosh finds that the information he seeks is not filed under the category of "religion" but that "that tomb, and others like it, had long ago been wished away from those shelves, in the process of shaping them to suit the patterns of the Western academy" (342). Ghosh locates his information filed under the headings of "folklore" and "anthropology," just as the Egyptian official, who had dismissed the locals' beliefs as "superstition," had suggested.

Ghosh thus discovers that in his own ethnography, much as he tries to create a world in which "India and Egypt are found to be culturally connected without the need for a European reference point" (Srivastava 48), he continues to run up against the divisions and boundaries imposed by modern nation-states and Western epistemology, which sees knowledge as something to be divided into disciplines and meted out by experts. The institutional categorization of the holy man as folklore rather than religion enacts Joseph Priestly's 1767 edict to "subdivide the business, that every man may have an opportunity of seeing everything that relates to his own favorite pursuit; and all the various branches of philosophy would find their account in this amicable separation" (69). Much as Ghosh tries to subvert this division of knowledge, he is unable to do so and ultimately finds himself "caught straddling a border" rather than transcending or disabling it (*Antique Land* 340).

Border Crossings

Ghosh's depiction of the historical and social fluidity of his subject matter is reminiscent of Homi Bhabha's notion of liminality. Bhabha is interested in the "between" spaces for the same reasons that Ghosh is: both see in the confluence of multiple identities, times, and spaces a possibility for something that Bhabha terms the "beyond." This beyond is a future performed in its interaction with the present, one in which the discontinuities and disjunctions of present life are made visible. In Bhabha's view, the epistemological limits of Western hegemonic thought are also a boundary between it and "a range of other dissonant, even dissident histories and voices." It is in this boundary—which Bhabha (following Heidegger) characterizes as a bridge or passage that "gathers" and "crosses"—that the third space of *In An Antique Land* is actualized: the continual criss-crossing of borders and boundaries that Ghosh details in his text mirrors Bhabha's description of the repetitive, iterative back-and-forth movement across the "bridge" between the present moment and the beyond. Both Ghosh and Bhabha emphasize the multiplicity of voices and histories that cross this border, but for both, it is a multiplicity that exists in motion between only two things: the Western and the non-Western, the now and the beyond. They do indeed theorize a third space, but it is a third space that exists within and because of a binary. Bhabha's conception of the liminal space is thus contingent on movement between two other spaces, while Ghosh finds himself "straddling a border," one foot planted in the Western world, one in the non-Western, not quite able to inhabit the "between" of the boundary itself.

Theories of transnationality have worked to explode this binary by emphasizing—as does Ghosh, in *In An Antique Land*—all the different ways that people, goods, and ideas cross multiple boundaries. Ulf Hannerz has developed the notion of the "global ecumene" to highlight the multifarious interconnections and exchanges he sees occurring in both large cities and remote locations (7), while Masao Miyoshi has discussed the rise of the transnational corporation in terms of its putative separation from the modern nation-state. Transnational corporations are in many respects borderless; rather than being based in its country of origin, a transnational is "adrift and mobile, ready to settle anywhere and exploit any state including its own, as long as the affiliation serves its own interest" (736). Such a corporation draws its executives from countries all over the world, increasingly asking its employees to exchange national loyalty for corporate loyalty (741). This transnational class of executives—who come from all corners of the world, who routinely cross borders and traverse the globe, who interact daily with coworkers from around the world, who may retain less and less allegiance to their countries and cultures of origins, and who inhabit the most multicultural and cosmopolitan cities in the world—seem to exemplify the kind of international citizen that Ghosh depicts in *In An Antique Land*, while sidestepping the binaries that Ghosh finds himself reduced to. This transnational world, which forecasts the fall of the nation-state, retains elements of both a borderless singularity (one capitalist community, rather than hundreds of nations) and the multiplicity of locations (each corporation embedded in various ways in hundreds of localities, forming a truly global network) that in Ghosh and Bhabha end up crumpled into the binaries of East and West, colonized and colonizer.

This sense of simultaneous singularity and multiplicity is evident in the future New York of *The Calcutta Chromosome*. Ghosh's description of the International Water Council suggests a political structure that operates on a global level to allocate a global resource, and the international character of the Water Council's staff suggests the transnational class—a single, unified group composed of a multicultural range of individuals—described by Miyoshi. This sense of a singular, global political will (or at least bureaucracy) is belied by the continued emphasis that the novel's characters place on national origin and local custom. The novel identifies all its characters by their nationality and frequently makes note of oddities of dialect or pronunciation. Similarly, the narrator makes frequent mention of dress style, distinguishing carefully between those who wear Western dress and those who retain or adopt attire typical of their homelands. Antar, who has lived for years in the United States, takes a daily walk to Penn Station to get a cup of tea made in a traditional Egyptian style. The emphasis on origin is echoed by the Water Council itself, which provides Antar with a computer "programmed to simulate 'localization'" (14) by speaking to him in the rural dialect of his natal village. Even as the social world of *The Calcutta Chromosome* moves toward transnationality, then, national difference is reified.[3]

Because transnational corporations are vested only in their own profitability, rather than in benefiting any particular locality or community, Miyoshi considers them to be engines of colonialism, extending their own power and reach at the expense of local and national resources and populations (749–50). And many theorists have noted the ways in which the current trend toward both cultural and economic globalization can reinscribe the uneven power relationships that characterized the colonial (Huggan 30–31). Thus, *The Calcutta Chromosome*—which envisions something awfully similar to a globalized, transnational society (albeit one in which the biggest organization, the Water Council, plays an apparently custodial role)—is haunted by the specter of colonialism. Indeed, much of *The Calcutta Chromosome*'s action takes place in the colonial India of the nineteenth century, the same era that Murugan is desperately studying for traces of the Calcutta chromosome. As his rendition of historical events makes evident, Murugan is highly aware of—and contemptuous of—the colonial enterprise from which emerged the scientific advances that he investigates. This awareness is given an additional twist as he begins to realize that—although he was born in Calcutta—his Western training has precluded his participation in the native body of knowledge that surrounds the Calcutta chromosome.

To the degree that the future depicted in *The Calcutta Chromosome* is one in which the problems of race and nation are still fraught, Ghosh still has not achieved what he first attempted in *In An Antique Land*—the transcendence of the boundary. As Ulf Hannerz suggests, "there is a certain irony in the tendency of the term 'transnational' to draw attention to what it negates—that is, to the continued significance of the national" (6). Ghosh's transnational future, like ours, depends too much upon the boundaries that it claims to overcome. Much of *The Calcutta Chromosome*'s project, then, is to imagine what might come after the transnational. What would a world without borders look like?

---

[3] Miyoshi suggests that this reification of difference—in the form of multiculturalism, cultural studies, and postcolonial studies—is a product of transnationality itself, an instrument that "conceal[s] liberal self-deception" and enables us to ignore the environmental and economic havoc wreaked by transnational corporations. "By allowing ourselves to get absorbed into the discourse on 'postcoloniality' or even post-Marxism, we are fully collaborating with the hegemonic ideology, which looks, as usual, like no ideology at all" (751).

The Epistemology of the Detective

The Calcutta Chromosome takes borders and partitions fully into account before attempting to move beyond them. Thus, Western knowledge is depicted as categorically discrete, relying on science and rationalism to extend its reach. The possibility for the multiple layers of detection at work in *The Calcutta Chromosome* (Murugan's scholarly investigations into the work of Ronnie Ross, a nineteenth-century malaria researcher; Ross's research on the malaria parasite; Antar's investigation into Murugan's disappearance; as well as several smaller investigations conducted by an assortment of characters) depends of course on just the sort of Western epistemology that classic detective fiction is founded on—that is, the notion that things can be known and that this knowledge can be rationally acquired and articulated. Classic detective fiction presents a mystery and proposes a solution, its very form promising to provide a resolution that is both comprehensible and logical (Linton 17). Postcolonial or multicultural detective fiction, however, often uses knowledge and knowability against the reader as well. Postcolonial detectives perform the traditional function of guiding the reader to knowledge (that is, knowledge of the mystery's solution as well as an understanding of the logic and circumstances surrounding that solution) even as the narratives themselves resist cultural hegemony by denying the mainstream reader access to an understanding of certain aspects of a minority culture (Linton).

The Calcutta Chromosome utilizes a similar epistemological resistance while attempting to refigure the binary of Western and non Western knowledge into something else—a space that is other rather than between. *The Calcutta Chromosome* is ultimately more about indeterminacy and unknowability than anything else. Murugan—a scientist and scholar who, in the best tradition of Western academia, has tried to consolidate a scholarly reputation by selecting a field of expertise and carving out a highly specific niche of knowledge—is perhaps the novel's best example of the deployment of Western epistemology. However, Murugan has come to believe that, by interfering with Ross's work, a mysterious group of native Indians, led by a woman named Mangala, has controlled the direction of malarial research. According to Murugan, this group—operating under the assumption that to know something is necessarily to change it—has used Ross's research to provoke a mutation in the malaria bug, which would allow them to control the interpersonal transfer of personality traits via malarial infection.

Murugan contends that this group has been laying clues for him, inexorably working toward another mutation that will provoke a quantum leap forward into what will presumably be a new mode of being and knowing. This quantum leap, Murugan claims, would be an "escape from the tyranny of knowledge" (303). In contrast to the determinability projected by both Western science and the very form of detective fiction, Ghosh here proposes a native, Eastern knowledge—consolidated and conveyed by Mangala—turned against itself, one which would change even in the moment of discovery and thus remain ultimately unknowable.

As with *In An Antique Land*, then, *Calcutta*'s purveyors of Western epistemology are counterbalanced by a native investigation and knowledge that is directed toward and works through Western science. Just as Ghosh undergoes the ethnographic gaze of his own subjects, who interrogate him about his own religion and culture, so too do Murugan and Ross engage in both the Western scientific process and in the production of "Eastern" knowledge.[4]

Ghosh envisions this knowledge as a "counter-science," one whose founding principle would be to dispute the assertion of knowledge. This counter-science would rely on silence, "because to communicate, to put ideas into language, would be to establish a claim to *know*" (*Calcutta* 103). Murugan, who provides the bulk of the text's description of the counter-science, posits that its creators began

> with the idea that knowledge is self-contradictory; maybe they believed that to know something is to change it, therefore in knowing something, you've already changed what you think you know so you don't really know it at all: you only know its history. Maybe they thought knowledge couldn't begin without acknowledging the impossibility of knowledge. (104)

Murugan describes here a knowledge that can *only* exist in the past; it has no present existence. This conception of knowledge recalls Edward Said's description of Orientalism. Like Murugan's knowledge, which produces only a history of itself, Said's Orientalism is a mode of discourse that produces the Orient as its object of inquiry. Thus, to study the discourse of Orientalism is to study the history of the West's representation of the East:

> [G]roups of texts, types of texts, even textual genres, acquire mass, density, and referential power among themselves and thereafter in the culture at large […] Orientalism responded more to the culture that produced it than to its putative object, which was also produced by the West. (20, 22)

Ultimately, Said raises the same question that Ghosh poses in both *In An Antique Land* and in *The Calcutta Chromosome*. As Said puts it, one must "ask how one can study other cultures and peoples from a libertarian, or a non-repressive and non-manipulative, perspective. But then one would have to rethink the whole complex problem of knowledge and power" (24).

---

[4] Unlike *In An Antique Land*, however, *The Calcutta Chromosome* envisions these two epistemological modes being exceeded by the "quantum leap," which would turn knowledge against itself and create something else.

The Tyranny of Knowledge

In *In An Antique Land,* Ghosh tries to answer this question by "developing the ethnographic genre in the direction of a narrative and intersubjective cultural account" (Srivastava 46). In *The Calcutta Chromosome*, Ghosh expands on the generic mixing and interwoven narrative structure of *In An Antique Land* by adding silence as a source of power. The character Mangala, who maintains her power through her silence and her refusal to represent herself, is a servant in the laboratory of one D.D. Cunningham, who is, like Ronnie Ross, a member of the Indian Medical Service at the end of the nineteenth century. Cunningham's attitude toward Mangala is patronizingly benevolent: although "a quicker pair of hands and eyes [he] had never seen," Cunningham believes that Mangala is "a little touched": "She's not all there, you see," he tells a young visitor to his lab, "her mind's been wasted—by disease, or licentiousness, or who knows what?" (145–6). Cunningham positions himself as the final arbiter of knowledge in his laboratory: he has deliberately selected assistants that he believes to be uneducated and trained them himself, for that way "[o]ne is spared the task of imparting much that is useless and unnecessary" (145). Moreover, Cunningham situates himself as the authority on the personalities and capabilities of those who serve under him, congratulating himself on his luck in finding such an able assistant in Mangala, even as he constructs her as uneducated, provincial, slightly mad, and mentally deficient.

Mangala makes it all the easier for Cunningham to do so, as she rarely speaks—particularly not to the white men whom she serves. However, Elijah Farley, the visitor to Cunningham's lab, senses that Mangala controls much more knowledge than she lets on:

> His mind began to spill over with questions: how had a woman, and an illiterate one at that, acquired such expertise? And how had she succeeded in keeping it secret from Cunningham? […] The more he reflected on it, the more convinced he became that she was keeping something from him; that had she wished she could have shown him what he was looking for, Laveran's parasite; and that she had chosen to deny it to him because, for some unfathomable reason, she had judged him unworthy. (143)

Farley's apprehension of Mangala's knowledge and authority is facilitated by her silence.[5] Mangala speaks directly to Farley only once, but he frequently catches

---

5 This silence is both verbal and narrative. Mangala speaks very rarely and only once is her actual speech recorded in the text: generally her conversations are described by a distant observer (such as Farley) who can say little more than that Mangala is talking to someone. What we know of Mangala, then, comes almost exclusively from what other people observe of her. Mangala is also the only major character who is depicted solely from an external perspective. Some characters are portrayed via a third-person omniscient narrator that clearly has access to their internal thoughts and feeling. Other characters'

her staring at him, silently angry and intense. Where Cunningham reads Mangala's silence as stupidity and her stare as a native servant's naïvely defensive attachment to her workplace, Farley finds her silence ominous in its suggestion of a knowledge that is ultimately inaccessible to him. He finds himself both afraid and unable to articulate the nature of his fear: "Yet he could find no name for what it was that faced him and why he feared it. And this in turn became his very fear, that he could not name what he knew he must confront" (146–7). In refusing to counter, or even acknowledge, Cunningham's misapprehensions about her, Mangala declines to represent herself and becomes, for Farley at least, unrepresentable. She comes to occupy a site of power and authority that has as much to do with how little Farley knows and understands her as it does with how much Mangala herself knows and understands. Mangala thus serves as Ghosh's answer to Said's question about the representation of the native by redefining both knowledge and power.

This question of representing another, and the role silence plays in this representation, has, of course, been a fundamental focus of postcolonial studies. Rey Chow, for example, examines the role of the native woman in terms of her silence, suggesting that the effort to give the native speech is rooted in a desire to make her "more like us." The speaking native thereby becomes a part of a "subject constitution firmly inscribed in Anglo-American liberal humanism" (128). *In An Antique Land*, by situating individual subjectivities as its primary subject and organizing principle, performs a similar gesture, remaining "bound up in the notion of a universal humanity" (Dixon 4) and relying on humanism as "one of [its] ethical underpinnings" (Srivastava 60). While one might very plausibly argue that Ghosh remains committed to the idea of "universal humanity," *The Calcutta Chromosome* takes the idea one step further, by beginning the subsumption of the individual into the collective. In effecting the "quantum leap" to a new form of knowledge, the characters of *The Calcutta Chromosome* also transcend subjectivity and individuality, becoming part of a group mind that takes the form of a borderless conglomeration of disembodied voices. Here Mangala plays her greatest role, for she is the facilitator of this subsumption.[6]

Serving as the locus around which the native knowledge coalesces, Mangala directs the group of "counter-scientists" that Murugan identifies at the novel's

---

internal states are reconstructed through references to letters, diaries, or conversations. In either situation, the narrative's representation of most characters takes into account their internal beliefs about themselves and their place in the world. Mangala, however, is not accorded this kind of direct depiction by the narrative: her presence is recorded only by those characters that come in contact with her. Mangala never speaks about herself, nor does the third-person narrator ever make her an object of direct inquiry. We thus have neither access to her interiority nor any idea how she might choose to represent herself.

6 Mangala's silence-as-resistance is similar to the resistance staged by the texts Patricia Linton describes, which remain silent to readers on certain culturally-inflected whys and wherefores. However, where Linton depicts the restriction of *access* to knowledge, Mangala refutes (silently) the very notion of knowledge.

beginning. Mangala enforces the silence and organizes the manipulation of others—primarily Western-trained scientists such as Ross and Murugan—to incite desired changes in knowledge. Ross, for example, is led to his discoveries regarding malaria because, Murugan claims, Mangala wished to further her own plans by provoking a mutation in the malaria vector. In a very real sense then, Mangala—though she is never given voice to represent herself—controls both the West's scientific knowledge and what it knows of her. Thus, any representation we receive is one that she has permitted—and while this might not be considered complete agency, it is much more than is usually accorded the silent native.

Mangala's goal, again as deciphered and conveyed by Murugan, is a form of immortality. She has discovered a method whereby she can use malaria to transmit her own personality into another's body. Although the novel remains vague about her success, it appears that she accomplishes this transmission at least twice in the course of the narrative, appearing once as an Armenian woman named Mrs. Aratounian and later as Tara, an Indian immigrant in New York. Ghosh puts forth here a notion of transcendence—both of the body and of subjectivity. Although we are denied any narrative that gives us insight into the type of subjectivity that Mangala/Mrs. Aratounian/Tara might possess, Murugan is insistent on the point that it is personality traits—rather than anything that might be considered a "universal humanity"—that are transmitted.

Humanity, at least as it is understood in Western culture, is deeply bound up with borders and boundaries. The human rights rhetoric upon which post-Enlightenment Western societies are founded turns on the preservation of borders: individuality and subjectivity hinge on establishing and maintaining the boundaries between self and other, self and world. Referring to the process of transmission as "a technology for interpersonal transference" (*Calcutta* 106), Murugan explicitly links the result of this procedure to voice:

> Same stimulus, different response: he says tamatar and you say tamatim. Now think, what if the 'im' and the 'ar' could be switched between you and him? What would you have then? You'd have him speaking in your voice, or the other way around. You wouldn't know whose voice it was. And isn't that the scariest thing there is, Ant? To hear something said, and not to know who's saying it? Not to know who's speaking? For if you don't know who's saying something, you don't know why they're saying it either. (107)

To Murugan's mind, then, what Mangala has achieved is not necessarily silence, but the disembodiment of her voice. In place of the silent native, represented only by others, Mangala stands as a native who may choose not to be represented or who might represent herself in what seems to be the voice of another. This position imbues her with tremendous power, for, as Murugan points out, people fear not knowing who speaks or why. Mangala's "interpersonal transference," then, has the power to divest of its location the voice of the ethnographer, the colonizer, the scientist. Unlike individuality and subjectivity, which are always housed in a body and therefore always subject to discipline and control, personality traits and voice can—in Mangala's world at least—be dislocated and disembodied. Because voice is no longer rooted in a particular subject or individual, it transcends and escapes the boundaries and binaries that render it so fraught with questions of agency and control. In a world of dislocated voices, who is speaking ceases to matter: it matters only what is said.

In *The Calcutta Chromosome,* then, the uncertainty of knowledge that haunts the detective genre is made literal: if we do not know who is speaking or acting, we cannot know the criminal, understand motive, or predict actions. And in disconnecting voice from subject position, Mangala begins to break down some of the most strongly perceived divisions between East and West, self and other. In doing so, she also begets a translation from the purely individual to the communal. In addition to references to "crossing over," which Mangala and her followers apparently use to designate interpersonal transference, there are also references to being "taken across," intimations that others can access some sort of group mentality. When Antar is "taken across," for example, the narrator describes voices, not only near Antar but *in* him, and a sense of communion with a large group:

> But now there was … Tara's voice whispering: "Keep watching; we're here; we're all with you."
>
> There were voices everywhere now, in his room, in his head, in his ears, it was as though a crowd of people was in the room with him. They were saying: "We're with you; you're not alone; we'll help you across." (*Calcutta* 306)

Antar seems to experience here a sense of belonging that has an unusual valence: he is accessing not a group of people, but a group of voices, and these voices seem to express a remarkable sense of all-inclusiveness. In light of Mangala's divesture of the link between voice, body, and mind, it appears that Antar may have gained access to something that does transcend the normal boundaries of subjectivity and individuality.

The irony, of course, is that the outlines of the "circle of the initiates" of Silence, that "ineluctable, ever-elusive mistress of the unspoken," are only visible by way of those who have knowledge of it yet have been excluded (*Calcutta* 123). Murugan and the writer Phulboni both know of and understand the existence of the society of Silence in a way that no other characters do. Yet they are both irrevocably excluded from the Silence because they themselves serve as vectors of knowledge, rather than its object. Phulboni's stories help bring together the characters of Urmila, Sonali, and Murugan, which in turn enables Murugan to put all the pieces together and tell everyone just what they need to know. Antar, in contrast, has "escaped the tyranny of knowledge." In his case, knowledge has been turned on itself and Mangala and her followers have "create[d] a single perfect moment of discovery when the person who discovers is also that which is discovered" (303). At the very moment when Antar understands the possibility of "going across," he is recognized by the Silence as one who can go across. When Antar crosses the boundary, he becomes part of the Silence and yet, as part of the Silence, is filled by voices. And presumably in the course of this crossing is effected the "quantum leap," in which Western knowledge and Eastern non-knowledge are turned against themselves and become something epistemologically other.

For Murugan, however, who is merely the instrument by which the Silence is revealed to Antar, the Silence remains silent, and Murugan is trapped on the wrong side of the dividing line. Just as Murugan is both the vector and the point of failure of information, so too is he both the vector and the point of failure for Ghosh's project. Via Mangala, Ghosh is remarkably successful in envisioning and conveying a voice that is neither granted nor denied agency and in crafting a representation of a native that is neither a creation of nor a reaction to an implied ethnography. Because the character of Mangala herself refigures subjectivity, voice, and knowledge, she successfully evades many of the traps into which postcolonial characters often fall. Mangala thus effectively serves as a figure for an *other* space that is neither colonial nor native, neither a stereotype nor a reaction against stereotype, neither a voice that is silenced nor a voice that must speak with the conqueror's words. Mangala does not represent a between or a liminality: she represents something else, something that depends on neither the colonial nor the native for its existence. So too is her knowledge something other: in the moment of the quantum leap, native knowledge and Western knowledge cease to have any relation to the way Antar and the circle know. But, as close to success as Ghosh skates with Mangala, he cannot quite transcend the same boundaries that she does. The figure of Murugan stands in for all those divides that can never be fully erased, for it is only by virtue of him, and his exclusion from Mangala's Silence, that we readers have any access at all to Ghosh's vision of the alternate space.

Thus Murugan becomes as well the figure for the impossible, paradoxical situation of the detective and the detective novel. Founded in a Western epistemological mode grounded in Enlightenment reason and Cartesian objectivity, the detective nonetheless operates by trying to occupy the criminal's subject position and by creating (instead of discovering) knowledge through interpretation rather than empirical investigation (Jacobs 50–51). The detective is thus forced to walk simultaneously in worlds of certainty and indeterminacy. But as Ghosh demonstrates in *The Calcutta Chromosome*, in a postcolonial world—which struggles to represent without reinscribing the borders upon which colonial thought depends—the paradox of the detective may point the way, however ephemerally, toward something other.

Works Cited

Bhabha, Homi K. *The Location of Culture*. London: Routledge, 1994.

Chow, Rey. "Where Have All the Natives Gone?" *Contemporary Postcolonial Theory: A Reader.* Ed. Padmini Mongia. London: Arnold, 1996. 122–46.

Dixon, Robert. "'Travelling in the West': The Writing of Amitav Ghosh." *Journal of Commonwealth Literature* 31.1 (1996): 3–24.

Ghosh, Amitav. *The Calcutta Chromosome.* New York: Avon, 1995.

——. *In An Antique Land.* New York: Knopf, 1993.

Hannerz, Ulf. *Transnational Connections: Culture, People, Places*. London: Routledge, 1996.

Huggan, Graham. "Postcolonialism, Globalization, and the Rise of (Trans)cultural Studies." *Towards a Transcultural Future: Literature and Society in a 'Post'-Colonial World.* Cross/Cultures. 77. Ed. Geoffrey V. Davis, Peter H. Marsden, Bénédict Ledent, and Marc Delrez. ASNEL Papers 9.1. Amsterdam: Rodopi, 2004. 27–35.

Jacobs, Karen. *The Eye's Mind: Literary Modernism and Visual Culture*. Ithaca: Cornell UP, 2001.

Linton, Patricia. "The Detective Novel as a Resistant Text: Alter-Ideology in Linda Hogan's *Mean Spirit*." *Multicultural Detective Fiction: Murder from the "Other" Side*. Ed. Adrienne Johnson Gosselin. New York: Garland, 1999.

Miyoshi, Masao. "A Borderless World? From Colonialism to Transnationality and the Decline of the Nation-State" *Critical Inquiry* 19.4 (1993): 726–51.

Priestly, Joseph. "The Organization of Scientific Research." *The Portable Enlightenment Reader*. Ed. Isaac Kramnick. New York: Penguin, 1995.

Said, Edward W. *Orientalism*. New York: Vintage, 1978.

Srivastava, Neelam. "Amitav Ghosh's Ethnographic Fictions: Intertextual Links between *In An Antique Land* and His Doctoral Thesis." *Journal of Commonwealth Literature* 36.2 (2001): 45–64.

Chapter 4
Detective Narrative Typology: Going Undercover in the French Caribbean

Jason Herbeck

> Mince alors! Voici qu'on était en plein polar, moi qui avais horreur de ce type de bouquins.
>
> —Raphaël Confiant, *La Baignoire de Joséphine*

Caribbean literature of French expression is certainly not lacking in terms of mystery and intrigue. Quite to the contrary, murders, disappearances, kidnappings, poisonings, larceny, and countless other acts of an illicit nature abound in the region's works. Furthermore, while verging on the commonplace, the ever-enigmatic richness of such activity—ranging from the petty crime evoked in passing to that which, front and center, serves as the plot's driving force—is not just as soon forgotten. Faced with circumstances that resist clear interpretation or rationale, protagonists and readers alike find themselves compelled to question the sum of their observations and to seek out additional clues in anticipation of better understanding the evidence before them. Far from constituting mere *ad hoc* musings or avenues of inquiry, many of the ensuing investigations are thus replete with a veritable detective, witnesses, testimonies, alibis and—often, but not always—a guilty party. Curiously, however, such abundance of unmistakable traits has not led to the emergence of the detective novel as a readily-identifiable genre in the French Caribbean.[1] Although publishers have not hesitated to promote texts' crime-novel features—touting, for example, the makings of an "unbridled detective novel," an "erotico-detective plot" or an investigation that goes "from interrogation to interrogation"[2]—the French-Caribbean detective narrative remains by and large an undercover operation that has yet to be officially recognized.

---

1 Some French-Caribbean novels involving mysterious deaths or occurrences that some or all characters attempt to unravel include Jacques Roumain's early *Gouverneurs de la rosée* (1946) and Édouard Glissant's *La Lézarde* (1958), as well as Patrick Chamoiseau's *Solibo magnifique* (1988), Raphaël Confiant's *Le Meurtre du Samedi-Gloria* (1997) and *La Dernière Java de Mama Josépha* (1999), Gisèle Pineau's *Chair piment* (2002), Ernest Pépin's *L'Homme-au-baton* (1997), Évelyne Trouillot's *Rosalie l'Infâme* (2003), Gary Victor's *Les Cloches de la Brésilienne* (2006) and Maryse Condé's *Traversée de la Mangrove* (1989) and *La Belle Créole* (2003).

2 Cf., respectively, the back cover of Raphaël Confiant's *La Dernière Java de Mama Josépha*, Services Documentaires Multimédia's synopsis of Ernest Pépin's *L'Homme-au-baton* and the back cover of Patrick Chamoiseau's *Solibo magnifique* (my translations).

At first glance, the status of the African detective novel appears faced with a similar case of anonymity, given that the emergence of roughly 40 detective writers on the book scene has gone all but unnoticed by critics (Moudileno 71). On the other hand, as Lydie Moudileno remarks in her study of francophone African literatures published between 1980 and 1990, the publication of these authors' works has in great part been undertaken by branches of French and African publishing houses specifically devoted to the detective novel such as "Polars noirs" by l'Harmattan, Gallimard's "Série noire," "Serpent à Plumes noir," and "NEA polar" by Nouvelles Éditions Africaines (71). Consequently, lack of critical acclaim or interest has not resulted in the works being divested of the genre's recognizable packaging—the impossible-to-miss black cover with title figuring prominently in yellow or white print on the spine and front cover.

Gérard Genette refers to this *generic* packaging as the *publisher's peritext* and describes it in detail in *Paratexts: Thresholds of Interpretation* as:

> the whole zone of the peritext that is the direct and principal (but not exclusive) responsibility of the publisher (or perhaps, to be more abstract but also more exact, of the *publishing house*)—that is, the zone that exists merely by the fact that a book is published and possibly republished and offered to the public in one or several more or less varied presentations. (16)[3]

Interestingly, French suspense novels are not as easily identified. For instance, René Frégni's *On ne s'endort jamais seul* [*One never goes to sleep alone*, 2001] has been camouflaged under the ubiquitous white Folio edition. Furthermore, other francophone detective narratives such as Moroccan Driss Chraïbi's *Une Enquête au pays* [*The Flutes of Death*, 1981] fail to receive the black jacket, whereas English, American, Russian, and Dutch authors in particular are housed comfortably (in translation) in the colors.

Rather than lament the detective novel's absence as a recognized and recognizable genre on the French-Caribbean book scene, the goal of this article is to better understand this absence in light of detective typology and the varied ways in which French-Caribbean texts seemingly challenge or call into question

---

[3] In the introduction to *Paratexts*, Genette explains: "A paratextual element, at least if it consists of a message that has taken on material form, necessarily has a *location* that can be situated in relation to the location of the text itself: around the text and either within the same volume or at a more respectful (or more prudent) distance. Within the same volume are such elements as the title or the preface and sometimes elements inserted into the interstices of the text, such as chapter titles or certain notes. I will give the name *peritext* to this first spatial category [...]. The distanced elements are all those messages that, at least originally, are located outside the book, generally with the help of the media (interviews, conversations) or under cover of private communications (letters, diaries, and others). This second category is what, for lack of a better word, I call epitext [...]. In other words, for those who are keen on formulae, *paratext = peritext + epitext*" (4–5).

key elements or structures of this most universal of narrative paradigms. Whereas critics such as Leah D. Hewitt have suggested that certain Antillean novels including Maryse Condé's *Traversée de la Mangrove* [*Crossing the Mangrove*, 1989] and Patrick Chamoiseau's *Solibo magnifique* [*Solibo Magnificent*, 1988] mimic the detective novel genre, the current study proposes to examine not only the manner in which Caribbean texts diverge from standard detective norms on narrative terms (thus placing them *technically* outside the genre) but the potential interpretations and implications of these divergences on a cultural, historical, political and (post)colonial level. To this end, I will first juxtapose the prototypical detective narrative with both traditional and non-traditional detective novels from France, Belgium, England, and the French-Caribbean before focusing on one Caribbean novel in particular, Patrick Chamoiseau's 1997 *L'Esclave vieil homme et le molosse* [*The Old Slave and the Watchdog*]. As I will demonstrate, Chamoiseau's text, while at first glance the furthest removed from traditional detective norms of the novels I discuss, may ultimately offer the most intriguing case study for the very reason that, in content and structure alike, it identifies itself *after the fact* as an intentionally *undercover* detective novel of epic proportions.

Of Detective Fiction and Typology: Traditions and Transformations

Since the mid-nineteenth century, when Edgar Allan Poe's "The Murders in the Rue Morgue" (1841) marked what is generally considered to be the birth of detective fiction, the detective genre has experienced considerable growth not only in terms of its popularity and appeal but with respect to an ever-evolving number of sub-genres. In accentuating the distinguishing characteristics of three such categories in *The Poetics of Prose*, Tzvetan Todorov recognizes the *roman à énigme* (or *roman policier classique*), the *roman noir* and the *roman à suspense* (or *roman à victimes*).[4] Claire Gorrara succinctly summarizes their primary distinctions as follows:

> The *roman policier classique*, in the mold of Agatha Christie, tends to highlight the analytical and/or logical processes of deduction. [...] The mystery or puzzle element of the crime predominates and the reader is encouraged to align him/herself with the detective who restores social order through exercising his superior intellect. The *roman noir*, in contrast, privileges the social milieux in which the investigation takes place. The disorder and violence of contemporary

---

[4] *The Poetics of Prose* was first published in 1971. While other variations of the detective novel—such as the police procedural and the metaphysical detective story—already existed at the time, they were not yet readily recognized as sub-genres *per se*. Because the very genre of detective fiction, let alone its sub-genres, has arguably not yet found an identifiable (peritextual) niche in the French Caribbean, I will for the purpose of this study focus primarily on the (over-arching) genre itself and its distinctive narrative typology.

> society is integral to a narrative which explores the social, political, and economic conditions which produce criminality. Unlike the retroactive and retrospective narration of the *roman policier classique*, the *roman noir* situates its detective figure in the midst of things, searching to understand a sequence of events which often result in unsatisfactory or provisional conclusions. A third form of detective writing, the *roman à suspense*, combines elements of the previous two genres but is defined by the importance given to the victim of crime, commonly the focalizer of the text. (314)

When the *roman noir*—initially an American import brought to France by Gallimard's *Serie Noire* in 1945[5]—began to struggle in the late 1960s, the off-shoot *néo-polar*, or neo-detective novel, provided a needed rejuvenation of sorts in the 1970s and 1980s. Politically militant and unabashedly engaged, the *néo-polar* offered an invigorated critique of social corruption and, as Jean-Pierre Deloux explains, cast characters that had not previously been associated with the genre: "broke, marginal, marginalized, unemployed, rejected by society, outraged etc., everything designates them as serving the role of scapegoat and propitiatory victim of the very society that excludes them."[6] Jean-Patrick Manchette, the oft-designated father of the *néo-polar*, furthermore expressed a literary preoccupation in his later novels:

> After *Nada* [1972], I concerned myself less and less with "content" and focused more and more on writing detective novels that were self-destructive, that are excessive, in other words that try to be to the classic detective novel, to the American detective novel what, all things considered, Don Quixote was to tales of chivalry.[7]

Echoing this literary trend in her discussion of the *néo-polar*'s relative success among African writers, Moudileno notes:

> The *néo-polar* is different from other detective novels to the extent that it is marked by explicit ideological preoccupations (Evrard, Lits) and by particular attention paid to the literary qualities of the narrative. A genre practiced with success today in France, it is emulated by African authors who write on the cusp between the detective novel and the literary, thus confirming the global phenomenon of the past twenty years during which the border between the two has tended to blur. (Manchette) (73, my translation)

5 Cf. Gorrara's article on the *roman noir* in post-1968 France.

6 "Le Noir new-look," *Magazine littéraire*, no. 194 (April 1984). Quoted in Gorrara 321.

7 Quoted in Gorrara 321 (my translation).

In this regard, given the considerable scope and tenor of French-Caribbean novels' characters, the resulting in-depth exploration of social injustice and/or corruption, and the largely "undercover" detective narrative status the works have maintained (they are after all sold as *literary* works), many of these novels can arguably be categorized as *néo-polars*.[8] However, it should be stressed that in both theory and practice, and in spite of its evolution over time, the detective genre has for the most part adhered to a rather stringent narratological morphology. Thus, in discussing the divisions that can be identified with respect to detective writing, Gorrara nonetheless notes: "critics have emphasized the features common to these three genres in terms of structural constraints and character types" (314).

Few studies of detective narrative structure enter into as much detail as those of Tzvetan Todorov and Gérard Genette. According to Todorov in his essay "The Typology of Detective Fiction," a simple yet fundamental duality governs all works of the genre. In fact, "the whodunit par excellence is not the one which transgresses the rules of the genre, but the one which conforms to them" (43). In such works, a dual narrative is formed when the crime is committed, at which point the second of the two narratives (the story of the investigation) sets out to compile information on the first (that of the crime). Once the investigation has pieced together the elements of the crime story, events in the past relevant to and including the crime can effectively be understood, the guilty party identified and the narrative—its task accomplished—thereby comes to an end. For this reason, Todorov affirms that the crime story is absent yet real, whereas the investigation is present but insufficient (46). Furthermore, since the investigation can technically only begin once a crime has been both committed and discovered, it is significant that in their purest form the two stories do not overlap in space or time. Structurally, traditional detective typology may therefore be represented by the following simple graphic, the elements in **bold type** representing the actual (printed) text:

(crime story) **[investigation story]**

As I have suggested, the detective novel is certainly not unrepresented in the French Caribbean. Thus, if *L'Esclave vieil homme et le molosse* presents evident inconsistencies with certain narratological protocols relative to the genre, other works of the region find these conventions more visibly intact from the start. Martinican Raphaël Confiant's *Le Meurtre du Samedi-Gloria* [*The Murder on Holy Saturday*, 1997], for instance, opens with Carmélise's gruesome discovery of Romule Beausoleil, one of Fort-de-France's most renowned wrestling champions, whose lifeless body has fallen prey overnight to the city's ravenous mongrels. As the title of the novel indicates, Beausoleil's body is found the morning of Holy Saturday, and inspector Dorval and his deputy Hilarion are soon afterwards

[8] Todorov writes: "to 'improve upon' detective fiction is to write 'literature,' not detective fiction" (43). For a discussion of detective fiction's supposedly inferior, "throw-away" status, cf. Uri Eizenweig's *Le Récit impossible* (80–81).

combing what prove to be the poorest and most dangerous neighborhoods of Martinique's capital in search of clues. In this sense, Dorval stands in stark contrast to fictional predecessors such as French crime writer Émile Gaboriau's formidable Inspecteur Lecoq of the late nineteenth century or Belgian Georges Simenon's Commissaire Maigret who tirelessly traversed France and beyond from the late 1920s to the early 1970s. While the latter sleuths were clearly admired by their contemporaries to the point of holding sway in various social circles, Dorval's 15 years of professional training in a police station in Paris's 14th arrondissement afford him little if any respect among his peers or the residents of Fort-de-France's lower-class neighborhoods. Nonetheless, when his colleagues shirk cases that would require setting foot in these less-than-desirable parts of town, Dorval—curious to rediscover his native Martinique—accepts them without hesitation.

The cultural, historical, linguistic, economic, and even political richness that Dorval's investigation divulges serves to highlight the seemingly inherent violence and corruption in Martinique's lower-class *quartiers*. This "privileged" perspective of social milieux thereby gives *Le Meurtre du Samedi-Gloria* the steadfast qualities of a *roman noir* and, indeed, Dorval soon finds himself struggling in the midst of such disorder, as much in search of his own bearings as he is Romule Beausoleil's assassin. If at length *why* Dorval arrives at determining the guilty party poses considerable problems in terms of detective narrative norms, it should be remarked that Confiant's novel ultimately adheres to the *how* in terms of detective narrative typology: at the novel's end, the murder having been explained, the assassin is duly named and taken into police custody.[9]

Of course, as with any imposed format or structure, the often dogmatic components that allow a work to be housed within a given genre also represent potential obstacles in terms of plot and character development. Whether they be restrictions of a typological nature or those that pertain specifically to the sleuth and criminal—such as those found among S.S. Van Dine's 20 golden rules (1928) or those reformulated in 1964 by Boileau and Narcejac—authors find themselves forever searching for ways to pique the curiosity and astonishment of readers while nontheless heeding conventional "fair-play." As a result, the parameters of detective fiction are often tested, as rules governing the genre are bent or virtually skirted in an attempt to keep readers wondering *whodunit?*

Some attempts have succeeded better than others. While Gaston Leroux's 1907 *Mystère de la chambre jaune* [*The Mystery of the Yellow Room*] remains to this day a detective classic for its clever unraveling of a seemingly impossible-to-solve "locked room" crime, in the case of Agatha Christie's *The Murder of Roger Ackroyd* (1926), for instance, the author's choice of narrator as murderer proved fatal for the book itself—at least in terms of the critical reception it received by readers loyal to the genre. None other than French literary theorist Gérard Genette

---

[9] For a detailed analysis of *Le Meurtre du Samedi-Gloria* as detective narrative, cf. Jason Herbeck's "Raphaël Confiant's *Le Meurtre du Samedi-Gloria*: Crime and Testimony".

declared the novel a "trick," suggesting that the paraliptic text constituted "an omission of essential information that the murderer's focalization should have included" (1983: 45, my translation).[10] In his essay "Introduction to the Structural Analysis of Narratives," Roland Barthes likens the novel to "cheating" due to the "blatant[ly]" deceptive device by which "the murderer actually says *I*" (113). In *Writing Degree Zero*, he later adds: "The reader looked for [the murderer] behind every 'he' in the plot: he was all the time hidden under the 'I'. Agatha Christie knew perfectly well that, in the [detective] novel, the 'I' is usually a spectator, and that it is the 'he' who is the actor" (34–5).

Interestingly, French archeologist turned detective novelist Fred Vargas, while breaking somewhat from detective narrative convention by not announcing the crime at the beginning of her 1996 novel, *L'Homme aux cercles bleus* [*The Man of the Blue Circles*], nonetheless adheres to tradition through sheer anticipation. When commissioner Jean-Baptiste Adamsberg is transferred from southern France to Paris, his uncanny knack for "feeling" a crime must suffice for several chapters as the man of the blue circles strikes throughout Paris, mysteriously drawing attention to dropped or discarded objects. Thus, despite a narrative in which no proof of a veritable crime has been presented, the prospective crime-story-in-anticipation-of-a-crime continues on as supposedly negligible items such as a hair roller, a metro ticket and a run-over cat are innocuously circled in blue chalk. Of course, as predicted by Adamsberg (and required by the genre), a body eventually appears in one of the circles, Adamsberg's deputies shed their skeptical outlook on the case, and the veritable and thereafter *typologically* legitimate investigation ensues. Despite the novel's ultimate adherence to detective narrative norms, it is thus interesting to note the clever yet seemingly acceptable (or at least critically accepted) overlapping of crime and investigation stories. Given Adamsberg's structurally premature insistence that the investigation begin before the crime story has been evidenced with a body, the two narratives actually share a segment of their trajectory rather than allow the first (crime story) to end before the second (investigation story) begins:

(crime story **[///////) investigation story]**

Such a variation on traditional detective typology is significant in the context of this chapter to the extent that a certain trust linking Vargas's text and its readers is not only manifest but necessary. In other words, not only is the novel generically "bound" as a detective narrative to present a murder and thus to legitimize both the case Adamsberg has begun and, on a greater scale, the novel's adherence to the genre, but in due course the reader is rewarded for this peritextually-crafted promise: a murder is eventually discovered and the case is officially labeled as

[10] Genette explains in *Figures III* (in "Discours du récit" or "Narrative Discourse") that as opposed to ellipsis, which skips over a moment of time, paralipsis "sidesteps a given element" (1980: 52).

such by both Adamsberg's colleagues and the readers of the novel. In this sense, the genre's fundamental structure is tested but ultimately proves reliable.

Before turning to *L'Esclave vieil homme et le molosse*, it is worthwhile to briefly consider two additional detective narratives by prolific Guadeloupean writer Maryse Condé. Rather than win the confidence of the detective-minded reader along the lines of *L'Homme aux cercles bleus*, each novel offers what are arguably misleading typological clues that in due course undermine the very reliability of traditional detective-narrative structures. Condé's 1989 *Traversée de la Mangrove* [*Crossing the Mangrove*] begins much like *Le Meurtre du Samedi-Gloria* when Mlle Léocadie Timothée discovers Francis Sancher's body on a forested path. The question of foul play immediately arises since Francis was only in his thirties and appeared to be in excellent health up until his death. During the subsequent wake, Condé's text becomes a polyvalent narrative as, through alternating first- and third-person narrations, each person present either tells or has told his or her thoughts on the matter.

If at the novel's end no cause of death has been established and the pretension of murder remains largely impossible to ascertain, one might very well challenge *Traversée de la Mangrove*'s categorization in the detective genre—whether it be with respect to traditional detective narratives or in light of more recent *néo-polars*. Contrary to expectation or at least anticipation—after all, the novel has no generic peritextual ties or obligations—an investigator's elucidation of the crime does not effectively bring about the end of the narrative in *Traversée de la Mangrove*; rather, daybreak finds each of the "witnesses" leaving Francis's wake, thus bringing the narrative to a close. While the novel's classification as detective fiction may therefore be questioned, I would argue that the unique context of the Caribbean should also be taken into consideration before the text is prematurely denied such a label. After all, to the extent that Francis's enigmatic death—and indeed life—can be understood as an allegory for Caribbean identity, to suppose a definitive end or solution to the case might be judged presumptuous. In this regard, if one feels duped at the novel's "end," it is clear that a particular structure has been taken for granted and subsequently misread. In the context of the (neo)colonial French Caribbean and France's continued control and oversight of its Overseas Departments, such disillusioned "trust" surely suggests the call for renewed perspectives and methods of interpretation. Consequently, one could assert that the specific context evoked in the novel might warrant modification to detective narrative expectations, all the while adhering to generic conventions such as the opening crime scene and subsequent testimonies of witnesses and/or suspects. Along these (pluralized, rhizomatic) lines, logical, hegemonic processes of deduction and proposed solution are clearly thwarted.[11] In the case

[11] Cf. Édouard Glissant's theory of *racine-unique* (unique root) and *rhizome* as dichotomous identitarian notions in *Introduction à une Poétique du Divers*. Inspired by the distinction first suggested by Gilles Deleuze and Félix Guattari (1980), Glissant likens the *racine-unique* to atavistic cultures that espouse fixed identity and purity while

of *Traversée de la Mangrove*, rather than be sorted and summarily discarded by a single, supposedly superior discerner of truths and lies, each individual's life experiences and discoveries are proven—in light of the very *absence* of a traditional detective—to have equal bearing on the investigation. Reflecting this narratological as well as ideological shift, the novel's detective typology may be formulated as such:

(possible crime story) **[19 proposed investigations]**

A more recent work by Condé provides an altogether different variation on detective narrative typology. *La Belle Créole* (2003), named for the boat inhabited by the novel's protagonist, begins with the latter's release from prison after he has been found innocent of killing Loraine, a rich white woman—or *Békée*—whose garden he tended and with whom he has allegedly had an intimate relationship. Curiously, however, rather than "begin anew," Dieudonné—and the text that recounts his story—continues to return to his life before prison and, more importantly, to the events leading up to the crime for which he has recently been acquitted. In effect, the detective narrative (i.e. the novel itself) does not begin until *after* the initial and supposedly definitive investigation represented by his acquittal at the trial's conclusion. However, when it becomes clear by way of the novel's retracing of past events that Dieudonné may have indeed committed the murder, both the man's innocence and the narrative itself must be reconsidered. After all, given that the narrative begins subsequent to Dieudonné's release from prison, the crime story must effectively be retold—not merely a second time (which was the investigation story that supposedly resulted in the trial), but a *third* time. The slightly veiled detective narrative thereby provides a (re)solution to the initial crime, inviting readers to consider the events of the crime in a significantly different light—and, one could suggest, within the context of postcolonial rewritings and remappings of history. *La Belle Créole* can thus be visualized structurally as a subversive ulterior narrative that proposes a necessarily alternate investigation to a previously definitive crime (story):

(crime story) [trial = investigation story #1 deciding Dieudonné's innocence]
[investigation story #2 suggesting Dieudonné's guilt]

---

the *rhizome* represents composite cultures that allow themselves to spread out and intermingle with others.

The Purloined Crime Scene

As evidenced not only by the traditionally distinguishable (outer) publisher's peritext and (inner) narrative structures of detective novels—not to mention the sections of bookstores reserved specifically for the genre—detective fiction, I would contend, is seldom if ever read *unintentionally*. What would happen, however, if someone were to read the near entirety of a detective novel without knowing it? If, as Uri Eisenzweig suggests, "the narrative structures specific to detective fiction call for a particular method of reading" (78, my translation), what would the implications be when readers realize that the narrative (what they believed to be merely a story) was in fact an investigation—that is, a *search* for the very story they thought themselves to be reading? To what extent can a person be conscious of a crime if the crime scene is not duly accounted for? Once the telling has—after the fact, as it were—been (re)presented as *re*-telling, where does the narration begin and to what end?

Such is the case of Chamoiseau's *L'Esclave vieil homme et le molosse*, in which an old, docile slave of model submission unexpectedly decides to become a maroon, escaping into the hills near the plantation he has long inhabited.[12] To this effect, Lorna Milne remarks:

> The *marronnage* of the old slave in *L'Esclave vieil homme et le molosse* is the first sign of disobedience in a long and exemplary life of servitude, during which he has appeared so docile, discreet and anonymous that no-one notices him or even remembers his name. In this he personifies one of the most important psychological and social effects of slavery according to Chamoiseau, which is to reduce the autonomous individual to a mere component of a single, undifferentiated "magma" or "densité inerte" of degraded humanity. (63)

Soon on the slave's heels are the Maître-béké slave owner and his blood-curdling watchdog. Whereas the novel might therefore present at first glance the trappings of a traditional detective novel—an elusive fugitive, the pursuer hot on his trail, and even the latter's large bloodhound—it is just as soon clear that the slave's actions significantly downplay the necessary mystery to be found in traditional detective fiction. After all, the "criminal" has been identified from the start in the sense that we know *which* of the plantation slaves has fled. Furthermore, as opposed to the conventional criminal who leaves the scene of the crime in the hopes of concealing his identity, fleeing ironically endows the slave with individuality; his act of *marronnage* distinguishes him from the "magma" of which Milne writes. Consequently, from a detective typology standpoint, this early (narratologically

---

[12] *Marronnage* is the term used in French to define slaves' flight to freedom in the Caribbean, primarily from plantations. Maroon settlements and communities were sometimes formed clandestinely in regions where the geography allowed for runaway slaves to remain hidden and live for extended periods of time.

speaking) development and designation of identity proves unconventional and rebukes further investigation. To the extent that the marooned slave has singled himself out, no puzzle remains to be solved in the novel; the ensuing chase aligns itself more readily in the adventure genre, thereby giving the reader no reason to consider the novel in a detective mind-set. If *marronnage* constitutes a serious crime in the context of slavery, it does not after all amount to much in terms of traditional or contemporary detective fiction. As Todorov explains: "The novel must have at most one detective and one criminal, and at least one victim (a corpse)" (49).

It is not until near the novel's end that we learn that a death has in fact occurred, and an unresolved one at that. The final short chapter of the novel begins: "Les os furent retrouvés au fond des bois" (141). ("The bones were found deep in the woods," my translation.) It is interesting to note Chamoiseau's choice of the verb *retrouver*—which can mean both "to find" and "to find again" in the sense of "to recover"—since the reader's discovery of the bones at the end of the novel doubles as a re-discovery of the narrative itself. In other words, in light of the unresolved death, the story can now be reconsidered as a second (investigation) story rather than an initial (crime) story. Not until this moment does the novel reveal itself to be an investigation in *search* of a story rather than the story itself. Chamoiseau intervenes as a narrative agent to recount a conversation he had with a *vieux-nègre-bois*, an old man from the woods.[13] It is in this capacity that Chamoiseau explains how he first came to hear about a Caribbean Rock—*la Pierre*—a volcanic stone hidden in the woods that is covered with the writings of peoples from every era of the island: "A volcanic rock. Imagine it in wonder. Covered with American-Indian signs. Guapoïdes. Saladoïdes. Calviny. Cayo. Suazey. Galibis. All of the eras colliding together there" (143, my translation). The old man then produces a relic that he has found at the base of this monolithic testimony to Martinque's little-known precolumbian past—a tibia that, when touched by Chamoiseau, propels him on an insatiable quest to discover its story:

> I was victim of an obsession, the most trying and the more familiar, from which the only escape was to Write. Write. I therefore knew that one day I would write a story, this story, molded from the great silences of our fused stories, our confused stories. (145, my translation)

Clearly, the investigative nature of *L'Esclave vieil homme et le molosse* is deliberately veiled at the outset. Chamoiseau thereby subverts the detective genre all the while adhering to its structure on a general level—a level to which he makes the reader privy in remarkably belated fashion. After all, it is important to note that to bring the detective novel into clear focus structurally, it suffices merely to place

13 There is no mistaking the author's identification as narrator. Following the passage, "At the time, I was finishing a work on a neighborhood of Fort-de-France, a poor epic that was taking me forever and leaving me at a loss" (my translation), a footnote clarifies: "*Texaco*, roman, Éditions Gallimard, Paris, 1992" (142).

the seventh and final chapter of the novel at the beginning. Doing so effectively recreates the crime scene and identifies the narrative impetus of the chapters to follow. The question of course is why Chamoiseau decides to position the chapter at the end of the novel rather than at the beginning, effectively withholding all mention of what may now be recognized as a crime scene.

In retrospect, *L'Esclave vieil homme et le molosse*'s peritexts provide a preliminary answer to this question. Contrary to a Barthesian world in which the death of the author is often assumed, Chamoiseau's relation to *Esclave* is limited neither to the front cover of the book—his name figures prominently—nor to his explicit authorial intervention at the end (Cf. note 13). In fact, no less than six prefatory statements (an epigraph, a dedication, a table of contents and a chapter heading, followed by two more epigraphs) make up the first nine pages of the novel, seemingly orienting the reader for what will come. The significance of these abundant peritexts are, as Genette indicates in *Paratexts*, not only to *present* the text but "to make present, to ensure the text's presence in the world, its 'reception' and consumption in the form (nowadays, at least) of a book" (1). Consequently, in remaining unanswered, the first epigraph's inquiry—"Does the world have an intention?"[14]—stands as both provocation and warning; although the epigraph is unmistakably addressing the reader and furthermore both influencing and accentuating his or her "reception" of the novel, it remains uncertain as to whether or not the world—and in particular the text itself—indeed has any intended design or purpose and, if so, what it might be.

The irony of Chamoiseau's calling attention to the uncertainty of intentions in the epigraph only to reveal his own late in the novel proves quite significant in the dual contexts of detective fiction and postcolonialism. After all, if the prefix *post* has any true weight with respect to its true connotation, the crimes and struggles of colonialism might well be relegated to the past. Searching for clues in a contemporary context would arguably constitute an unworthy enterprise—an act as unexpected as it is unnecessary. This complacent disposition with regard to inquiry and search is conveyed early on in *L'Esclave vieil homme et le molosse* due to the very *absence* of traditional detective fiction "leads" that evoke irresolution and intrigue, such as a crime scene, the unknown identity of the criminal, clues, and so forth. Whereas *The Murder of Roger Ackroyd* disguised the murderer behind a detective, Chamoiseau disguises an entire investigation in the form of a story. Interestingly, when Chamoiseau's *intention* is eventually elucidated and it is revealed that the text is an attempt to solve what might today be termed a cold case, it becomes clear that the evidence gathered—a single bone—ultimately balks at finite deductions or conclusions. Thus, whereas Chamoiseau's intentions are made apparent to the extent that he belatedly identifies what for all intents and purposes is a mysterious crime scene as the work's central narrative impetus, his first-person narration—contradictorily, it would seem—leaves little doubt that the

[14] "Le monde a-t-il une intention?" The question also figures as the last line of an essay by Chamoiseau entitled *Ecrire en pays dominé* published the same year.

now open investigation *cannot* succeed in telling the crime story. Typologically, the novel can thus be represented as follows:

(crime story) **[fictional, inconclusive investigation]**

In her extensive article on *L'Esclave vieil homme et le molosse*, Doris Garraway suggests that the novel be read as a "Creole myth of origin" despite the evident contradictions the term inevitably evokes in the context of slavery and colonization. Indeed, how can a myth of origin, whose value resides in its "power to justify the presence of a people in its natural environment, and to ground its sense of collective identity," apply to colonial societies "marked by a history of forced deterritorialization, slavery, symbolic loss and cultural heterogeneity" (Garraway 151)? Unpredictable and repeated displacement over time due to what J. Michael Dash has termed "the powerful shaping forces of colonialism" (288), coupled with the resulting loss of collective memory and identity, render it virtually impossible to fathom common beginnings. It is nonetheless from within these inherent pitfalls of cultural and geographical discontinuity that Garraway posits Chamoiseau's project as "a story of symbolic creation that inscribes Caribbean history into a vast temporality reaching back to the precolumbian past and encompassing the origins of the universe" (152). In this sense, a shared suffering becomes the paradoxically privileged historical focal point at which Caribbean cultural generation and creolization may be concentrated. A human tragedy finding commonality in those who have suffered, the destructive forces of slavery are thus re-fashioned as a potentially viable place of collective construct.

Interestingly, the narrative necessary to recount this myth of self-reclamation must therefore claim the Caribbean environment in the name of the people whose story it endeavors to tell: "Through this emotionally charged rewriting of creation from the perspective of a male fugitive, the novel proceeds to debunk the colonial master text of discovery, possession, and exploitation of nature, which was itself arguably a deformation of the Edenic myth" (Garraway 158). Hence, the runaway slave and the precolumbian past merge in Chamoiseau's work when the former comes to the hieroglyphics on the volcanic Rock:

> The maroon, the one who escapes […] and becomes human again in the womb of nature, recreating in the process the world around him, meets the Carib, the primordial ancestor whose knowledge of the "Time Before" ("*l'Avant*") trumps the colonizer's containment of historical memory to the time of discovery. (Garraway 159)

Whereas Garraway goes on to suggest that this meeting of the slave and Carib in *L'Esclave vieil homme et le molosse* cannot function in the one-dimensional time of history and therefore necessitates the atemporal, imaginary space of myth, it is interesting to re-examine the projects that she attributes to Chamoiseau within the context of detective narrative typology. After all, in learning belatedly of the mystery behind the bone that has been found at the base of the Rock, readers are forced to reconsider the properties of the history they have been reading. In other words, they are urged to question the reliability of the "master" text as it devolves into a mere story among imaginably countless possible others. In this regard, it is not so much an atemporal space that readers are subject to as it is an infinite number of would-be solutions to a tragic, enigmatic past. Rather than represent a single story (or myth) freed of temporal constraints, *L'Esclave vieil homme et le molosse* reveals that discovery—as opposed to Westernized ideals and paradigms—can be a necessarily pluralized notion of telling.

It is interesting to note that *L'Esclave vieil homme et le molosse* consequently resists Uri Eisenzweig's criticism of the detective genre in *Le Récit impossible* [*The Impossible Narrative*, 1986]. According to Eisenzweig, the detective novel—because it is essentially a closed narratological system—is a false or impossible narrative. In other words, if the mystery were in fact a mystery, it could never be solved; given that it *can be* implies that the investigation is not truly necessary. Tautologies aside, Eisenzweig insists on these shortcomings of the detective narrative in order to demonstrate at length the necessary process by which a textual absence can logically be transformed into a presence. The mystery at the heart of all detective stories is after all merely a narrative secret rather than a conceptual one (Eisenzweig 53). The investigation's purpose is thus to introduce an acceptable *dis*solution of the enigma rather than propose a veritable solution—in this way, the investigation only modifies the initial evidence that has been present all along in order for the crime to be solved over a given period of time.

In *L'Esclave vieil homme et le molosse*, Chamoiseau effectively reverses this narrative convention. Rather than divulge how a textual absence is transformed into a presence, he announces that what was considered by unsuspecting readers to be a presence should on the contrary be re-interpreted as an irrefutable absence. The slave's story is nothing more than conjecture, as are the elements of the narrative recounting the actions and thoughts of the Maître-béké and his watchdog. The conditional past—the verb tense consistent with such speculation and investigations in general—is thus fittingly present for the first time in the novel when Chamoiseau the narrator announces the unexpected substitution of investigation for (crime) story: "My marooned man *would have crossed* the Great Forest, *would have been injured, would have come to die* directly beneath this rock" (144–5, my translation and emphasis). In identifying—*after* the supposed fact, as it were—the line of inquiry that not only explains the entire narrative but in fact belies its claim to authenticity and singularity, Chamoiseau deconstructs the colonial myth of finite ends and beginnings in the French Caribbean. However, just as a single storyline is deemed grossly insufficient in unraveling the mystery of the bone found in the forest, the inherent opacity and countless crimes of the colonial period render it conversely impossible to discount any particular narrative as false.

Evoking what she terms "the central paradox of Caribbean post-identitarian discourse," Garraway notes: "*L'Esclave vieil homme et le molosse* reminds us of the lure of origins for people whose identity derives precisely from a common loss of origin" (164). In this regard, it is important to recognize the sheer magnitude of the investigation that is announced retrospectively at the end of the novel. As Shlomith Rimmon-Kenan explains in *Narrative Fiction: Contemporary Poetics*, a retrospective gap, as opposed to a prospective gap of which a reader is made immediately aware—whereby "the reading-process becomes (at least partly) an attempt to fill it in"—involves an instance in which "a text can prevent the reader from asking the right question until it is answered. [...] Only after the fact does the reader realize that some significant information has been withheld from him" (129). In this manner, the crime scene's placement at the back of *L'Esclave vieil homme et le molosse* prevents readers from asking the right questions. In fact, they are not prompted to have questions at all, since the narrative—despite its lyrical, poetic tone—is merely presented as a story.

By conceding fact to mere speculation in the final chapter, however, Chamoiseau openly acknowledges the lack of tangible proof linking the tibia to the marooned slave in the narrative: "[The bone] could have been from any one of us. American Indian. Black. Béké. Indian. Chinese. [It recounted] an entire era, but one open to total uncertainty" (144, my translation). The tibia, like the indecipherable Rock, is a crucial yet more importantly *indeterminate* element of a largely unintelligible Caribbean *histoire* —both in the dual French meaning of *story* and *history* and in the detective typology sense of *crime story*. The narrator's limited substantial evidence is thus emblematic of the inherent struggle involved in negotiating identity or Creoleness against the fragmented historical backdrop of slavery, colonization, and Creolization in the French Caribbean.

Rimmon-Kenan's examination of narrative beginnings serves well to accentuate on a narratological level the difficulty associated with adequately accessing the past:

> Narratives are in one way or another expedients for covering over [...] the impossibility of getting started. The beginning must be both inside the story as part of its narrative and at the same time outside it, prior to it as its generative base [...]. Any beginning in narrative cunningly covers a gap, an absence at the origin. This gap is both outside the textual line as its lack of foundation and visible within it as loose threads of incomplete information raveling out toward the unpresented past.[15]

According to Rimmon-Kenan, the past is therefore necessarily problematic in any narrative. However, in stark contrast to detective fiction, in which the entire narrative hinges by definition on this elusive temporal gap, Chamoiseau cleverly refrains from drawing attention to the "unpresented past" until the last possible moment of the narration. Thus it is only at the end of the text that the true *problem* with the story (i.e. the unaccountability of what has just been told) is fully manifest. A seemingly sound generative base suddenly dissolves to expose far more

---

[15] Quoted in J. Hillis Miller's *Reading Narrative* (58–9).

questions than it had originally purported to answer. It is perhaps of no surprise then that in calling attention to detective narrative conventions, *L'Esclave vieil homme et le molosse* nonetheless avoids telling what Robert Champigny refers to as *what will have happened* in his book of the same title. The future perfect that precisely conveys the hermeneutic structure of the detective genre falls short in articulating the often inaccessible or "imperfect" social and historical realities of the French Caribbean—what Chamoiseau terms in *L'Esclave vieil homme et le molosse* as "the not-understandable" or "the unforeseeable to-be-constructed" (145, 146, my translations).

Not unlike Poe's purloined letter that sits in plain view of all yet fails to be judged for its true meaning until appropriately contextualized by Dupin, the crime scene in *L'Esclave vieil homme et le molosse* only becomes apparent once Chamoiseau the narrator reveals the historical and social context from which the old slave's story *originates*. Furthermore, in encouraging the reader to reconsider a story as speculative investigation, the intention that is disclosed at length, as well as its ultimate failure to "unearth" irrefutable answers to the past, might in turn be suggestive or even prescriptive of postcolonial reading and writing practices. After all, Chamoiseau's undeniable *lack* of sufficient evidence is an invitation in itself to question the authenticity of authorial voice—in short, to not judge a book too hastily by its (peritextual) cover.[16] And if the polyvalent, marginalized narrative of *L'Esclave vieil homme et le molosse* appears to challenge hegemonic discourse in this regard, structural conventions are also clearly at stake. Indicative of a new and increasingly accepted typology of historical inquiry, the novel follows in a growing list of French-Caribbean literary works that, in questioning (neo)colonial patterns and practices, propose investigations largely void of crime stories.[17] Of the three protagonists in *L'Esclave vieil homme et le molosse*, it is surprisingly the Maître-béké slave owner who best frames this state of mind when he returns from the forest without the slave he has pursued: "[H]e didn't have the impression of coming back empty-handed […]. He was returning with the weight of something he couldn't name" (137, my translation).[18] In the spirit of Eisenzweig's theory regarding the truly impossible, solution-less detective narrative, it is, curiously, the acknowledgement of the epic proportions of the colonial crime scene that renders such investigations not only possible and justified, but also irreversibly necessary.

---

16 Chamoiseau's first-person intervention is responsible for calling the author's own authority into question on more than one occasion. In evoking the tibia, for instance, he has in effect contradicted himself—the narrator who has until then withheld his identity from the reader and claimed in the first pages of the novel: "At the start of this story, everyone knows that this old slave will soon die. This conviction is not founded on *any* evidence" (18, my translation and emphasis).

17 For a list of such novels, cf. note 1.

18 "[i]l n'avait pas l'impression de revenir bredouille [...]. Il revenait chargé de quelque chose qu'il ne pouvait nommer." In addition to signifying "loaded with" or "weighed down by," the original French *chargé* has the rich (and significant) double meaning of "entrusted with."

Works Cited

Barthes, Roland. "Introduction to the Structural Analysis of Narratives." *Image – Music – Text*. Trans. Stephen Heath. New York: Hill and Wang, 1997. 79–124.

——. *Writing Degree Zero, and Elements of Semiology*. Pref. Susan Sontag. Trans. Annette Lavers and Colin Smith. Boston: Beacon, 1970.

Boileau, Pierre and Thomas Narcejac. *Le Roman policier*. Paris: Payot, 1964.

Chamoiseau, Patrick. *Écrire en pays dominé*. Paris: Éditions Gallimard, 1997.

——. *L'Esclave vieil homme et le molosse*. Paris: Éditions Gallimard, 1997.

——. *Solibo magnifique*. Paris: Éditions Gallimard, 1988.

Champigny, Robert. *What Will Have Happened: A Philosophical and Technical Essay on Mystery Stories*. Bloomington: Indiana UP, 1977.

Chraïbi, Driss. *Une Enquête au pays*. Paris: Éditions du Seuil, 1981.

Christie, Agatha. *The Murder of Roger Ackroyd*. 1926. New York: Berkley, 2000.

Condé, Maryse. *La Belle Créole*. Paris: Gallimard, 2003.

——. *Traversée de la Mangrove*. Paris: Mercure de France, 1989.

Confiant, Raphaël. *La Baignoire de Joséphine*. Paris: Mille et une nuits, 1997.

——. *La Dernière Java de Mama Joséphа*. Paris: Mille et une nuits, 1999.

——. *Le Meurtre du Samedi-Gloria*. Paris: Mercure de France, 1997.

Dash, J. Michael. "Anxious Insularity: Identity Politics and Creolization in the Caribbean." *A Pepper-Pot of Cultures: Aspects of Creolization in the Caribbean*. Ed. Gordon Collier and Ulrich Fleischmann [*Matatu* 27–8; Amsterdam and New York: Editions Rodopi, 2003].

Eisenzweig, Uri. *Le Récit impossible*. Paris: Christian Bourgois Éditeur, 1986.

Frégni, René. *On ne s'endort jamais seul*. Paris: Éditions Denoël, 2001.

Garraway, Doris L. "Toward a Creole Myth of Origin: Narrative, Foundations and Eschatology in Patrick Chamoiseau's *L'Esclave Vieil Homme et le Molosse*." *Callaloo* 29.1 (2006): 151–67.

Genette, Gérard. *Narrative Discourse*. Trans. Jane E. Lewin. Ithaca: Cornell UP, 1980.

——. *Nouveau discours du récit*. Paris: Seuil, 1983.

——. *Paratexts: Thresholds of Interpretation*. Trans. Jane E. Lewin. Cambridge UP, 1997.

Glissant, Édouard. *Introduction à une Poétique du Divers*. Presses de l'Université de Montréal, 1995.

——. *La Lézarde*. Paris: Éditions du Seuil, 1958.

Gorrara, Claire. "Narratives of Protest and the *Roman noir* in Post-1968 France." *French Studies: A Quarterly Review* 54.3 (2000): 313–25.

Herbeck, Jason. "Raphaël Confiant's *Le Meurtre du Samedi-Gloria*: Crime and Testimony." Forthcoming in *The French Review* (Dec 2008).

Hewitt, Leah D. "Inventing Antillean Narrative: Maryse Condé and Literary Tradition." *STCL* 17.1 (Winter, 1993): 79–96.

Leroux, Gaston. *Le Mystère de la chambre jaune*. 1907. Paris: Gallimard, 2003.

Miller, J. Hillis. *Reading Narrative*. U of Oklahoma P: Norman, 1998.

Milne, Lorna. "The *marron* and the *marquer:* Physical Space and Imaginary Displacements in Patrick Chamoiseau's *L'Esclave vieil homme et le molosse*." *Ici-Là: Place and Displacement in Caribbean Writing in French*. Ed. Mary Gallagher. New York, NY: Rodopi, 2003.

Moudileno, Lydie. *Littératures africaines francophones des années 1980 et 1990*. Dakar, Senegal: CODESRIA (Conseil pour le développement de la recherche en sciences sociales en Afrique), 2003.

Pépin, Ernest. *L'Homme-au-baton*. Paris: Gallimard, 1997.

Pineau, Gisèle. *Chair piment*. Paris: Mercure de France, 2002.

Poe, Edgar Allan. *The Murders of the Rue Morgue*. 1841. Oxford UP, 2007.

Rimmon-Kenan, Shlomith. *Narrative Fiction: Contemporary Poetics*. New York: Routledge, 1996.

Roumain, Jacques. *Gouverneurs de la rosée*. Éditions Messidor: Paris, 1946.

Todorov, Tzvetan. "The Typology of Detective Fiction." *The Poetics of Prose*. Trans. Richard Howard. Oxford: Blackwell, 1977. 42–52.

Trouillot, Evelyne. *Rosalie l'Infâme*. Paris: Dapper, 2003.

Van Dine, S.S. "Twenty Rules for Writing Detective Stories." *The Art of the Mystery Story*, 1928.

Vargas, Fred. *L'Homme aux cercles bleus*. Paris: Éditions Viviane Hamy, 1996.

Victor, Gary. *Les Cloches de la Brésilienne*. La Roque d'Anthéron, France: Vents d'ailleurs, 2006.

Chapter 5
Out on *Parole*: Suspending Oral Culture's Death Sentence in Patrick Chamoiseau's *Solibo magnifique*

Greg Wright

The Scene of the Crime

Solibo is dead. From the beginning, the title character is dead, "throat snickt by the word," literally killed by the words he seeks to speak (Chamoiseau 8). During the opening of one of his tales, Solibo the storyteller shouted "*Patat'sa!*" and keeled over dead; the audience, believing his shout and immobility to be part of the story, responded "*Patat'si!*" and waited patiently for the rest of his tale, silently sitting for "eons (exactly three hours, thirty-eight minutes, and twenty-two seconds, says the coroner)" (16). But Patrick Chamoiseau (as both author and metafictional narrator) locates these events in the novel's diegetic past, and though his characters tell many stories of Solibo, the novel never offers any present tense narrative about him; his life and tale-telling are always already in the past. As an oral storyteller, Solibo appears to signal a kind of death of orality through his own demise. This event, however, spawns further storytelling, a struggle between the police's written reports and the tales told by Solibo's audience members. Thus, Solibo's seeming death sentence for oral culture receives an extension (parole) through the untamed storytelling inspired by Solibo's creative embrace of the word (*parole*).

Instead of creating a final, permanent judgment such as the hypercorrected, Frenchified police report that begins the novel, Chamoiseau's *Solibo magnifique* wraps multiple mysteries within its portrayals of the interactions between Creole and colonial culture, of the continual reformulations of the Creole language as a basis of culture, and of the narrative's attempts to Creolize the space between the spoken and written word throughout its own language and structure. The text's ambiguity allows for multiple interpretations of his demise—the doomed fate of oral tradition, a harbinger of Creole culture's extinction, or even what Chamoiseau wrote about with Jean Bernabé and Raphaël Confiant in *Éloge de la Créolité*: the "aesthetic suicide" of old Creole repression due to a lack of Creole self-awareness (106). However one interprets it, the fact remains that Solibo is beyond resuscitation. And yet Solibo's spirit is very much alive in *Solibo magnifique*, as the novel fuses the fictional storyteller's orality with written forms, resulting in a narrative mixture of detective stories, folktales, police reports, memorials, riddles, and jokes. Through this narrative amalgamation, Chamoiseau depicts the plurality of Creole culture, which, while evolved from diverse past cultural and linguistic threads, represents itself as a vibrant part of the present, much as Solibo's audience members keep him symbolically alive after his death by re-narrating memories, rituals, and lies that adapt and thus preserve his stories.

Because *Solibo magnifique* creates uncertainty about the implications of Solibo's death without providing narrative resolution, the text poses the questions inherent in such ambiguity as much to the reader as to the various official and unofficial detectives in the novel. Chamoiseau's open-ended narrative invites interpretation and judgment based on the various "facts" offered up in the novel's glut of eyewitness accounts, police reports, and digressive metanarratives. In this sense, Chamoiseau's text plays with genre as fluidly as it does with language; suggesting the familiar format of a detective story, the novel posits a mystery: "Now that Solibo is dead, what are we going to do about it?" The stakes of this mystery are no less than the interconnected futures of Creole and colonial language, culture, and identity, and so, clearly, *Solibo magnifique* has no simple, unilateral resolution. In this sense, there is no final cultural judgment, nothing to proclaim that oral culture is dead. Instead, the novel's obsessive cultural debates keep the dialogue going, letting what Solibo represents stay alive because his words are still on the lips of his audience.

Although *Solibo magnifique* is first and foremost a detective story, it is also a metaphorical ghost story, haunted by the dual presence of the dead Solibo and the influence of French colonial authority. The specter of France looms throughout Chamoiseau's novel, haunting the Creole culture in the forms both of abstract notions, like language and culture, and of the physical violence sustaining the cultural and linguistic dominance. France never appears in the form of what we might consider official colonial manifestations, but the Martinician institutions of daily life are saturated with French colonial influence to such an extent that local power breaks down along colonial lines. For example, the Martinician police force, the only official, institutional authority to which locals can appeal, derives its power from overseas, as illustrated when Doudou-Ménar—one of Solibo's outspoken audience members who creates her own stories after his death—seeks help for Solibo from a local policeman, calling out "Law! call a doctor [...] you hear me, Law?" (25). He calmly counters her frenzied shouts by deferring his authority to colonial influence: "Madame, I am a guardian of the peace, the law it's another matter, it's made in France, you understand?" (26). Not only does this statement reveal the power of the metropole, it inadvertently confirms the local rift between "peace" and "law," the disparity between the abstract peace written into the police officers' ultra-civilized, Frenchified written reports and the officers' practice of brutally beating innocent bystanders and criminals alike.

Police Reports and the Usual Suspects

Throughout *Solibo magnifique*, Chamoiseau as author weaves the mild-mannered police reports with the more extreme oral accounts (some of which Chamoiseau, as the narrator character of Oiseau de Cham, could not possibly hear), heightening the contradiction between constabulary theory and practice, what Achille Mbembe describes as "banality of power," a term that:

> does not simply refer to the way bureaucratic formalities or arbitrary rules, implicit or explicit, have been multiplied, nor [...] routine—though certainly "banality" implies the predictability of routine, if only because routine is made up of repeated daily actions and gestures. Instead, I refer here to those elements of the obscene and grotesque that [...] are intrinsic to all systems of domination and to the means by which those systems are confirmed or deconstructed. (102)

With this model of legitimation in mind, the police force's official and unofficial actions, the brutal harassment and its benign paper trail, are carefully and deliberately united. The banality of power in Solibo's world kills him as much as it investigates his death. The legal system, in opposition to the heterogeneity of Creole culture, murders to dissect.

The police, of course, do not recognize their own violence. Police power and its application in this case are systemic, so, although there is a cultural and linguistic dissonance between the police reports and "reality," this dissonance does not necessarily imply intention. The officers may at times be conspiratorial in their abuses of power, but the repetitious violence of the law—both on paper and in practice—is simply routine. In this sense, the written word of the reports represents a kind of violence through confinement, a textual limitation of Creole autonomy and oral expression, as when the narrator bemoans how Solibo is remembered: "For him, I would have wished words his size: inscribed in a simple life and yet higher than life. But around his body the police had scribbled 'suspicious death'" (9). The official, legal word maps reality in a way that inhibits the local culture's narrative memory of Solibo; the officers symbolically hurt him in and after his death with scribbled words as much as their billy clubs physically hurt his audience in order to disperse them from the alleged crime scene. The often subtle domination of writing provides only one example of the cultural control and circumscription colonial power exercises throughout the text, and yet, for Chamoiseau (inserted as a self-reflexive character within his own novel), the allure of writing—as a possible future for Creole folktales and collective identity—muddles the categorical binaries of written expression and oral expression, as well as the separate classifications of Creole and colonial culture.

All of the investigation within the novel represents an interaction between colonial and Creole cultures, the two at times blending into one another, as when officers slip into Creole or witnesses translate themselves into stilted French; these complicated interactions form a kind of evolutionary synthesis, a text that includes and adapts these disparate strains of content while also adapting the structural forms of spoken orality and written textuality. To complicate matters further, characters on both sides of the law carry with them a slew of nicknames, aliases, personalities, and roles so that their identities are just as fluid and destabilized as the language they use to express—and even name—themselves. These lines of self, language, and culture are so blurred that Chief Sergeant Philibon Bouafesse (the officer in charge of restoring order and sorting out the mess of Solibo's death through questioning and reporting) and suspect-witness-criminal-troublemaker Doudou-Ménar recognize their old romance during the interrogation and rekindle this passion, a product of ritual celebration, excitement, and softly spoken lies that allows the past to seep into the present through their shared narrative.

When the Chief Sergeant arrives to interrogate Doudou-Ménar, she recognizes him from their passionate affair from years ago, which he then begins again in the police station, letting the seductive woman she used to be excite him in the present. This impromptu union brings together the conflicting cultures (Creole vs. colonial), textualities (oral vs. written), and ideologies (Frenchified law vs. local lawlessness) that these two characters represent, and the narrative similarly shifts between their perspectives and the third person, melding the dialogue into the exposition seamlessly as though the words themselves were part of the sex act, an idea which also enters into the description of the mixed temporality and textuality of their sexual commingling. Chamoiseau—or whichever narrator/character is speaking—illustrates that this sex is part illicit memory and part symbiotic representation, that: "There exists an art of fucking, of fugitive love. You seize the instant to be dazzling" (35). Like most of this ribald, lively novel, the "artful fucking" of Doudou-Ménar and Bouafesse rejoices in the excitement of the present, which Chamoiseau presents as a synergistic fusion of textual forms, temporalities, and textualities. Similar to this illicit sex, the text's ideas mix like DNA, yielding a kind of love between opposing viewpoints that, as the novel demonstrates, parallels Creole history, culture, and literature. After the sergeant and suspect re-consummate their romance, the text recounts the absence of love from most theorizations of Creole identity:

> Our pre-literature is made up of screams, of hatred, of vindication, of prophesies at the inevitable Dawns, of analysts, of lesson givers, guardians of soluble solutions to the miseries of the world, and the blackfolks this, and the blackfolks that, and the Universal, ah yes the Universal! … Conclusion: no song about Love. No song about sex. Negritude was a eunuch. And Antilleanity has no libido. They had lots of children (mostly illegitimate) but without any goddamn love. (37–8)

This quick aside leaves the police station behind to explain how theorizations of Creole identity—presumably excepting Chamoiseau's own *Éloge de la Créolité*—have not been loving enough, not sexy enough to synthesize the disparate ideas which are already in dialogue even if the theorists have not yet uncovered these secret liaisons. Given this textual slipperiness, the mysteries of Solibo's death and the ensuing investigation are directly concerned with representing the "art of fucking" to the extent that different cultures, personalities, and ideas can mix and influence each other through texts. Although characters claim that each other's dialogue is unintelligible, cultural transmission is still taking place, evolving into something more than the sum of its parts.

Interrogation Methods

One example of the dialogic, daily culture-work emerges through the police interrogation, which is as much an interrogation of identity as it is of the homicide in question. The policemen, of course, comprehend and even casually speak Creole, but in front of the witnesses, they refuse to use "black Negro gibberish, just mathematical French" (67). And when an obstinate witness named Congo claims "*Han pa jan halé fwansé*" during interrogation, the officer, though he claims not to speak Creole, understands him well enough to reply "You don't speak French? You never went to school?" (67, italics in original). This deliberate and selective (mis)understanding evokes Édouard Glissant's claim that "the *béké* masters, who know Creole even better than the mulattoes, cannot, however, manage the 'unstructured' use of language" (124, italics in original). The significant distinction from Glissant in Chamoiseau's novel, however, comes from the fact that the *béké* masters have been replaced with black policemen; the French power structure allows the various strata of Martinique to self-colonize through their language use. But linguistic differences are a substitute for violence not far removed from brutality, as an interrogation in French translates effectively to physical punishment for the witnesses. The Chief Sergeant muses that:

> The best way to corner this vicious old blackman was to track him down with French. The French language makes their heads swim, grips their guts, and then they skid like drunks down the pavement. The Chief Sergeant's sixteen years of career policework had roundly shown this technique to be as efficient as blows with a dictionary to the head. (66–7)

In this passage, French becomes another tactic of violent state intervention; the colonial language manifests itself as equally efficient whether in an interrogation spoken in perfect French or in a French dictionary used as both the object and objective for violence. Through these tactics, language and violence act together as a kind of interrogation methodology, with language acting as the "good cop" forever backed up by the brutal force of violence's "bad cop" routine. Together, language and violence have the capacity for devastating power.

Given the police investigation's atmosphere of literal and symbolic brutality, the challenge facing the Creole witnesses is negotiating the double-bind of language and violence in order to tell their versions of the story, even as the police continually reinterpret the witnesses' words as belying their guilty involvement in Solibo's death. Their spectrum of narratives serves as a cultural construction of self-definition in the face of opposition, much like Solibo's tales themselves, performing what Paul Gilroy labels as the function of:

> directing the consciousness of the group back to significant, nodal points in its common history and its social memory. The telling and retelling of these stories plays a special role, organising the consciousness of the [...] group [...] and striking the important balance between inside and outside activity—the different practices, cognitive, habitual, and performative, that are required to invent, maintain, and renew identity. (198)

With Gilroy's framework in mind, Solibo's fatal encounter with the word becomes not the tragic cessation of story-telling, but the impetus for future narratives; his death provides the source of identity formation through orality, not its end. Storytelling is a strategy here, the means by which the survivors survive.

While the allegorical death of a storyteller—written in a novel, no less—might seem like a commentary on the triumph of written forms over oral tradition, Chamoiseau utilizes Solibo's dramatically performed death during a story circle as inspiration for the audience to tell tales of their own. The stories provide a way out, a means of salvation within the grim situation itself. The novel demonstrates that Solibo's death is a cultural loss only in isolation, but no event exists in a vacuum. Although Solibo's audience waits silently for a long time after he dies, as soon as they recognize his death for what it is, they quickly fill the void with words, chattering and screaming narratives to one another.

Getting Out on *Parole*

Although the everyday Creoles prefer oral tales while the police favor written expression, the relationship between orality and writing moves beyond binaries through the novel's complicated form and content. The novel does not imply any absolute transitions between written and oral cultures; instead, these dialogic cycles feed off of each other in all of the citizens' day-to-day wordplay. The text takes an evolutionary stance, as if to say that claims of isolation on the part of oral- or written-focused cultures only do damage to both parties, much like the violent encounters between Solibo's audience and the police. Some scholars, such as Alexie Tcheuyap, on the other hand, claim that Chamoiseau's authorial killing of Solibo represents the strict binary of oral and written culture, signifying the death of oral culture through writing stories instead of telling them. Tcheuyap writes that: "Solibo, however, serves a warning to the narrator: any attempt to immobilize the word through graphemes is vain and even dangerous. For if the word kills him, it is because it is powerful and has magical powers—even mystical powers—that Chamoiseau does not really place in his work" (51). Although there is no literal third space between speaking and writing—a statement is either written or spoken—criticism such as Tcheuyap's overlooks the complexity of Chamoiseau's text. The storytelling word—as parole/*parole*—is a way of getting beyond the confines of colonial power, both linguistic and institutional. There is a survival through storytelling: the survivor is the one who lives to tell the tale, displacing victimhood to others, never oneself. Parole/*parole* delays and defers consequences always into the future.

The two forms of expression—written and oral—inform, transform, and mock each other throughout the course of the novel, suggesting an adaptation of expression that moves away from strict categories toward a fresh understanding of the way that texts can evolve. Although Tcheuyap claims that "orality cannot be reduced to a pragmatic and phonic dimension of textual practice as is done in Chamoiseau's texts; and the somewhat stark and simplistic Creolist opposition between the oral and the written is strictly inadmissible," Chamoiseau's text would itself agree with Tcheuyap's sentiment as *Solibo magnifique* spends much of its time breaking apart such "simplistic Creolist opposition" (45). The novel directly confronts the notion that written or oral culture could exist independently of one another; the text implies many times that those who move toward absolutism—such as Solibo, who rejects the validity of writing and winds up dead, or the policemen, who value only written documents and perpetrate obscene violence—only risk harm to themselves and others. Instead, the narrative calls for a textuality that plays between oral and written, a literary hybrid that pulls together disparate cultural lines into an interwoven whole. But such interaction between and among forms cannot be frivolous or superficial, as the Creole participants hesitate to disclose their stories as novelties.

The locals do not want their treasured texts to be merely written down as anthologized entertainments or exploitative official documents; they are as suspicious of Chamoiseau as a novelist as they are of the police force as an authority. Eventually, Chamoiseau's character admits: "With patience, I got them to accept my notebooks, my pencils, my little tape recorder with batteries that never worked, my unhealthy appetite for tales […] all knew me so well that the talk no longer died out at my approach and eventually no one, instead of hello, would ask me: So Ti-Cham, what's the use of writing?" (21) The transformative mixing of oral and written elements cannot be done casually or quickly. The process takes a level of cultural commitment greater than the police investigators provide, and, as a result, the nature of hybrid resistance is not simplistic but inherently more complex, difficult both to produce and to represent. For example, the Chamoiseau narrator confesses within the story how hard he has struggled to write the story. Such moments focus on the play of diegetic asides, digressions, and metatextual revisions; many of the shifting narrators question their own words, whether written or spoken, like Chamoiseau writing/speaking of the time "when Bouaffesse yelled: *Hey!* … (What the hell is *Hey!?* A vine or a lasso? Glue or a brake?)" (55, italics and ellipsis in original). The implication of such hyperactive, self-referential commentary within the delivery destabilizes the text, illustrating that although the words on the page are by definition finite, their storytelling capabilities are somehow fluid. The tales are under constant revision, just like their tellers' identities, which are narrated and re-created throughout the novel.

As the characters tell stories of their much admired Solibo, they do not create their identities by focusing on the past but through collectively remembering and re-experiencing Solibo's performance. While the audience/witnesses/suspects await the judgment of the police, they tell stories of Solibo, honoring his memory without dwelling in that space of the past; their tales are always in and about the telling. In an interview with Rose-Myriam Réjouis, Chamoiseau describes his novel as adopting "a Creole structure that is very particular. It's a text based on the principle of the Creole wake, with people testifying *in memoriam*" (348). Through this structure, Chamoiseau appeals to a specific type of identity formation, one based on sharing the knowledge of a common history, regaling a prominent community figure. Even though the novel flows from the remembrances of happier days to the present-day interrogation about events surrounding the "crime," the audience of storytellers defiantly hold onto their Creole language and culture even in spite of the police's question-and-answer narratives. Instead of destroying the group's identity by isolating them, the multiplicity of the witnesses' testimonies—often jumbled, digressive, and contradictory—solidifies their pluralistic subject position in that it confounds the detectives' attempts to forge a single, unilateral narrative. Since the witnesses' Creole identity is grounded in their heterogeneity, their stories are polyphonic whether they are cross-examined as a whole group or as individuals isolated from one another. Despite these accounts' differences, the interpretations regarding Solibo's death break down into two basic camps: those who blame the Creole participants for Solibo's death (the official police view) and those who look to more complicated, mystical causes (the opinions of Solibo's audience).

The Death Sentence

Those who create the sentences framing Solibo's death—the interpreting detectives and suspects alike—become empowered as storytellers. The "death sentence" in this way means the power to speak as the survivor. The differences between the interpretive views of Solibo's death initially seem unbridgeable, but the dialogue that develops itself forms a story beyond the simplistic sum of its parts. The "death sentence" becomes dialogic, prolonging the interpretation and thus evading the death of the narrative and the narrative's form itself. Even the novel's beginning alludes to the ideological split inherent in the dialogic form by opening with Evariste Pilon's official police "Incident Report" detailing in staccato shorthand the officers' proceedings in investigating Solibo's death from "The second of February, 06:00 hours" (3) and then following this stilted document with the rollicking Creole-style first-person account of Solibo's final story-gathering which "happened on a day whose date is unimportant since time signs no calendar here" (8). The linguistic, attitudinal, and cultural dissonance between these two narrative methodologies complicates the novel as neither one can form a totalizing narrative as to what happened, leaving the reader to interpret the confusing plot through a synthesis of the pragmatic and the fantastical. Something happened to Solibo, but neither cultural group can entirely envelop the event with an explanation through their narrativization, as some aspect of the incident is always beyond the grasp of one singular, exclusive textual realm.

The allegorical struggle over these interpretations, of labeling the group's identity as guilty or innocent, reveals the competitive, combative narrativizing of Solibo's death. Much like Richard Dawkins's Darwinian framework of meme theory in *The Selfish Gene*, the two sets of narratives attempt to oust each other and thus prove "fittest." In order to detail such a meta-narrative struggle, however, the novel itself takes on a hybrid form. Just like the audience members' various stories, which erupt spontaneously and rely on improvisation and the interjected interactions of audience members of their own—"(Yeah [...] tell it, tell us the tale)"—*Solibo magnifique* tells the story of Solibo while still moving beyond it, rejuvenating Solibo's style (81). Chamoiseau's text aims to capture the rhythmic flows of oral delivery while still retaining the structural and grammatical boundaries of a written text. Within this complicated narrative competition, the police and the witness/suspects race to out-narrate one another, with the ramifications extending beyond identity politics to possible imprisonment or even death. Similarly, Chamoiseau's structure and style pay paradoxical homage to oral storytelling in order to keep such oral forms out of the prison of written limitation as well as out of the cultural boneyard of forgotten practices.

As illustrated above, the oral, Creole versions of Solibo's auto-strangulation cannot exist independently of the official police version, and vice-versa; any such story cannot mean anything on its own. The written and spoken performances are mutually dependent, as Homi Bhabha explains in *The Location of Culture* that:

> The reason a cultural text or system of meaning cannot be sufficient unto itself is that the act of cultural enunciation—the *place of utterance*—is crossed by the *différance* of writing [...] It is this difference in the process of language that is crucial to the production of meaning and ensures, at the same time, that meaning is never simply mimetic and transparent. (36, italics in original)

In order for the versions of Solibo's demise to make sense, the detectives' interpretations violently push the Creole utterances into their written reports. That is to say, the storytellers—whether witnesses or investigators or both—create a synthetic, adaptive narrativization, which may mean "that meaning is never simply mimetic," but which also means that meaning must be memetic. The piecing together of hunks of spoken text into a mutated, evolved, new written whole allows the memes to live on via transformation, leaping out of the threatened extinction of oral culture into the new territory of print culture. The officers understand and even gloat over how dependent the suspects are on the interpretations of the legal system, but the policemen fail to see that they are also bound up in the process of mutual meaning-making.

The police investigators' collective task is to conclude the case file on Solibo's death with some sort of resolution, a feat impossible without the individual, interpretive testimonials of the witnesses, which defy summary. The reader must bear in mind that the witnesses always have some power, that they take part in what Simon Gikandi characterizes as: "the absolute rejection of the popular image of the colonial borderland as a victimized margin, one without a voice in the shaping of the larger imperial event, one without its own strengths and interests, one without agency in the shaping or representation of modern identities" (38). The witnesses are proprietors of a certain type of power through their use of the spoken word; they carry the culture they seemingly mourn whenever they speak and thus replicate the cultural patterns they collectively enjoyed with Solibo. The various speakers are not pushed aside because such an act is impossible; in terms of the investigation the police are trying to conduct, the testifying Creole audience is essential, yet unable to be essentialized.

While the power dynamic cannot be equal, the reader is continually reminded that power involves a constant exchange, with both parties depending on their various means of expression. Thus, when Congo kills himself—"the Chief Inspector was getting his questions in gear, when in a single leap the old man flew right through the window"—the act serves both to release him from the verbal and physical pain of the interrogation and torture, as well as to remove him from the report's equation of meaning (145). The police need Congo's account in order to accuse him; without his narrative agency, their case becomes unsolvable. His awareness of his role in the report's construction makes his suicide a defiance of police authority, not a capitulation to or simple escape from it. Congo's auto-defenestration, like Solibo's auto-strangulation, can be interpreted as a text, but the author himself can no longer contribute to the process; meaning is possible, but it must be assembled without the contributions of its creator speaking or writing in the present tense. These actions-as-texts are typically explained in detective fiction, but, as the narrator notes about Solibo: "if in life he was an enigma, today it is much worse: he exists (as the Chief Inspector will realize after and beyond his inquiry) only in a mosaic of memories, and his tales, his riddles, his jokes on life and death have all dissolved in minds too often sodden" (8–9). By leaving the rest of the community through death, Solibo and Congo actually dissipate more fully into the collective Creole identity, as these deaths—and the lives that preceded them—are left to the re-narration of those Creoles who are still alive and present.

Bearing Witness

The witnesses of Solibo's death also pay witness to his legacy; their testimonies to the police double as testimonials in Solibo's memory. Although the witnesses of Solibo's death, the audience of his final performance, have all developed tactics to distance themselves from official colonial institutions—like refusing formal employment, resisting colonial education, and repelling police involvement—

they cannot completely undermine their subject position within the colonial framework. Because of the police investigation's scrutiny, they cannot physically escape the institutions of power, and they are uncomfortably aware that when police questioning fails in producing the "right" answers from its detainees, the state power's "invented constellations of ideas" will "also resort, if necessary, to the systematic application of pain" (Mbembe 103). To the Creole witnesses, the violent power relationship established by the police is not an unfamiliar one; Creole society, in its attempts to live outside the official institutions, must make constant efforts to avoid even the most basic interactions with institutional establishments invested with colonial power. For example, Doudou-Ménar, after being knocked unconscious by the police, wakes up in the ambulance and finds the restraining medical workers as oppressive as jailers carrying her away in a police van. In response to their monitoring, she "tore off one of the ambulance doors and threw it through the windows of the emergency ward," and her efforts extend to disrupting the order of the hospital even further, in retaliation for detaining her for surveillance (71). From her reaction, the text illustrates that even everyday institutions such as hospitals are inflected with a colonial power that the Creoles refute, directly or indirectly, for holding the authority to place "individuals under 'observation.'" In Michel Foucault's terms, for Doudou-Ménar the hospital creates "a natural extension of a justice imbued with disciplinary methods and examination procedures […] Is it surprising that prisons resemble factories, schools, barracks, hospitals, which all resemble prisons?" (227–8). All of these institutions, along with the prison of the French language itself, emerge as inhibiting factors to Creoles like Doudou-Ménar; they become obstacles even though they are also direct channels of power.

The Creole lifestyle may reject colonial institutions by avoiding them, but when confrontation is unavoidable, as it is following Solibo's death, the Creole citizens openly rebel. Although Martinique is still formally a part of France, Mbembe's characterization of the postcolony accurately addresses Creole insubordination, such as when colonial institutions seek

> to compel submission and force people into dissimulation. The problem is that they do not obey or pretend to obey. Conflict arises from the fact that the postcolony is chaotically pluralistic, and that it is in practice impossible to create a single, permanently stable system out of all the signs, images, and markers current in the postcolony; this is why they are constantly being shaped and reshaped, as much by the rulers as by the rule, in attempts to rewrite the mythologies of power. (108)

The novel's multiple power skirmishes, like the one Doudou-Ménar initiates, undermine the official institutions' efforts to produce a homogenized, unified picture of society. All the social groups vie for dominance, to "rewrite the mythologies of power," but the pluralistic nature of Creole culture enables it to maneuver fluidly around various colonial tactics. The limitations of the Creole subject position, however, also come from this pluralistic approach to culture in that no single member can speak in the plural. In other words, the oral tradition carried on by Solibo cannot be summed up or unified in a statement, and such attempts only wither and die. It is only through a kind of group eulogy, a collective means of bearing witness, that their strategic stories and evasions work.

The absoluteness of orality, as represented by Solibo, cannot exist in isolation, just as Solibo says in his critique of Chamoiseau's attempt at an absolutely removed writing:

> (Solibo Magnificent used to tell me: "Oiseau de Cham, you write. Very nice. I, Solibo, I speak. You see the distance? [...] you want to capture the word in your writing, I see the rhythm you try to put into it, how much you want to grab words so they ring in the mouth. You say to me: Am I doing the right thing, Papa? Me, I say: One writes but words, not the word, you should have spoken. To write is to take the conch out of the sea to shout: here's the conch! The word replies: where's the sea? But that's not the most important thing. I'm going and you're staying. I spoke but to you, you're writing, announcing that you come from the word. You give me your hand over the distance. It's all very nice, but you just touch the distance....") (27–8)

To decontextualize, to remove the written from the spoken, creates a paradox like taking the conch out of the sea. Chamoiseau must find tactics to bridge that distance in order to Creolize his text. Solibo knows that removing himself from the written word will ultimately be his undoing—"I'm going and you're staying"—but if Chamoiseau cannot find a position from which to speak within tradition, yet still manage to embrace newness, his fate will be the same. Instead, as both character and author, Chamoiseau bears witness through his writing, the only way he knows how to capture Solibo's story.

The split of Solibo's final enunciation literally and absolutely separates him from his audience, as the word becomes what stands between the living and the dead. Although his cry evokes the traditional beginning of Creole storytelling, the meaning of his shout signifies nothing clearly; it enters into an ambivalence that cannot be questioned, as its speaker is dead. The stable system of reference is removed, and the linguistic process reverses the mode Jacques-Alain Miller describes in his version of the Lacanian act of signifying: "The real is what it is, but when it is represented, expressed, referred to, connected in some way or another to language, the real begins to be what it is not" (30). Through the act of speaking, Solibo only nullifies himself, not the word he utters; the nullification of reference affects the speaker, not the signified. Solibo's search for the absolute word dissipates his identity completely, since tradition can never be contained through a single act. Although, as Miller observes, "Lacan could say at the beginning of his teaching that '*le mot est le meurtre de la chose*' (the word is the murder of the thing)," Solibo's fantastical death in pursuit of a totalizing oral defiance to the written word leads the word to murder its speaker (30, italics in original). But uniting the oral speech act with death does not limit Creole culture's power to renew tradition through reshaped forms; instead, orality transforms itself through Chamoiseau's characters, through their diverse interpretations, and through Chamoiseau's act of writing itself, which thrives on the contradiction of trying to write orality.

Oral tradition does not end with Solibo, as Tcheuyap implies, but rather changes forms. It evolves. It bears witness. Solibo's audience must take up the part of the speaker in any form they can appropriate, even if the act of enunciation takes the form of mourning or testifying. The many laments over Solibo's death look back to the shared experience of the past, but as cultural formations, they assume what Bhabha calls "the borderline work of culture," a space that:

> demands an encounter with "newness" that is not part of the continuum of past and present […] Such art does not merely recall the past as social cause or aesthetic precedent; it renews the past, refiguring it as a contingent "in-between" space, that innovates and interrupts the performance of the present. The "past-present" becomes part of the necessity, not the nostalgia, of living. (7)

This cultural thinking, outside both past and present, finds a way for the tradition to survive, not as a fixed entity but as a dynamic, constantly reiterated space of living through newness.

Case "Closed"

Even though the police wrap up the investigation, the mystery and violent struggle of language and culture continue. The police reports' closure is impossible. The idea of "case closed" is a fiction, one written as static and homogenous, death-like and incapable of capturing Creole culture. Rather than signifying the death of such a written, conscripted fate, Solibo's case represents an unclassifiable quality that means both his story and his style of storytelling will continue. In a prescient comment to the Chamoiseau narrator, Solibo explains that the transitional phases of tradition signify not death but renewal: "Z'Oiseau, you say: Tradition, tradition, tradition …, you bawl on the floor for the tree that loses its leaves, as if the leaf was the root! … Leave tradition alone, son, and watch the root…" (36, ellipses in original). As Solibo dies entangled with the roots of the tamarind tree, whose leaves scatter on the ground, his metaphor implies that revisions of tradition mirror the transforming tree: simultaneously dead and alive, past and present, continually growing at its base. The mythical and unreal surround Solibo's impossible death—the ants that constantly reappear on the body, the corpse's weight alternating between extreme heaviness and lightness, the strangulation from inside Solibo's throat—since both cultural traditions and "the real" rewrite themselves even while the audience speaks, watches, and participates in these changes. Even in Chamoiseau's final section of the novel, the supposed final words of Solibo Magnificent, the author/character revises even as he writes.

The characters redefine Solibo as they recreate his final words, changing them out of homage as much as out of necessity. This "speech," for lack of a better term, mutates and adapts in their enunciation. The admission "*Oh friends, the word isn't tame!*" produces an instability; although these are written words, they capture the sense of improvisation in that they have morphed in order to arrive on the page (158, italics in original). As Chamoiseau explains:

> Pipi, master jobber, taken with a pronounced desire to save the Magnificent's words, tried to perform for more than three hours at the rate of the wooden horse of our Creole merry-go-round. I taped him and then spent the rest of the season *translating* the whole thing onto a whole bunch of whirling and unreadable pages […] I decided to squeeze out a reduced, organized, *written* version, a kind of ersatz of what the Master had been that night: it was clear now that his words, his true words, all of his words, were lost for all of us—and forever. (158–9, italics in original)

Within this passage, the words themselves are the thing, and, as soon as they are referred to, they evaporate into meaninglessness. But their transmutation, the proof of their revisability, demonstrates the possibility of words to reach across the distance to affect their audience.

In *The Repeating Island*, Antonio Benítez-Rojo links the power of improvisation to a certain time and place, a notion that Chamoiseau reinforces through the impossibility of his translation even as he attempts to translate; Benítez-Rojo explains that:

> improvisation can be taped by a record company, but the product is a recording, not the improvisation, which is linked indissolubly with a space and time that cannot be reproduced […] The deception lies in giving out that "listening" is the only sense touched by improvisation. In fact, improvisation […] has penetrated all of the percipient spaces of those present, and it is precisely this shifting "totality" that leads them to perceive the impossible unity, the absent locus, the center that has taken off and yet is still there, dominating and dominated by the soloist's performance. (19–20)

To the extent that such a locus can ever be even partially represented, Chamoiseau's approach comes asymptotically close; by admitting that the feeling of a live audience cannot be reproduced in written form, yet attempting to capture that rhythm all the same, his writing nearly transcends itself through the immediacy of the rush of words that are falsely attributed (yet openly so) to Solibo. Chamoiseau's project, to Creolize his text between written and oral forms in order to represent a culture chaotically undefinable, provides a sort of elegant failure. In this final gesture of connection between artist and audience that ends Chamoiseau's own barrage of words, the text stops speaking, much like Solibo's own moment of death, and thrusts itself into a type of future. What that future holds is up to each individual reader's interpretation, making the text a synthesis not only of forms but a synthesis between reader and text. The detective work of what happened to Solibo—as well as what his death means—must be sorted out not by the text but by the reader, violating the central premises and promises of most detective stories in favor of creating a new type of narrative. Although *Solibo magnifique* is ultimately a static, bound work (in that it cannot revise or change itself once published), like Solibo's own textual death, which ends his communicative link with the rest of his culture, the novel challenges future storytellers to recreate and refine the tradition the text at once presents and redefines. Rather than closing the case, Chamoiseau's text shows how to reopen the investigation, prolong the mystery, and thus permit the death sentence of Creole culture's oral tradition to be suspended, letting it out on *parole*.

Works Cited

Benítez-Rojo, Antonio. *The Repeating Island: The Caribbean and the Postmodern Perspective, Second Edition*. Trans. James Maranis. Durham, NC: Duke UP, 1996.

Bernabé, Jean, Patrick Chamoiseau, and Raphaël Confiant. *Éloge de la Créolité*. Baltimore: Johns Hopkins UP, 1990.

Bhabha, Homi. *The Location of Culture*. New York: Routledge, 1994.

Chamoiseau, Patrick. *Solibo magnifique*. Trans. Rose-Myriam Réjouis and Val Vinokurov. New York: Pantheon, 1997.

Dawkins, Richard. *The Selfish Gene*. New York: Oxford UP, 1989.

Foucault, Michel. *Discipline and Punish: The Birth of the Prison*. Trans. Alan Sheridan. New York: Vintage, 1995.

Gikandi, Simon. *Maps of Englishness: Writing Identity in the Culture of Colonialism*. New York: Columbia UP, 1996.

Gilroy, Paul. *The Black Atlantic: Modernity and Double Consciousness*. Cambridge, MA: Harvard UP, 1993.

Glissant, Éduoard. *Caribbean Discourse: Selected Essays*. Charlottesville: UP of Virginia, 1989.

Mbembe, Achille. *On the Postcolony*. Trans. A.M. Berrett, Janet Roitman, Murray Last, and Steven Randall. London: U of California P, 2001.

Miller, Jacques-Alain. "Language: Much Ado About What?" *Lacan and the Subject of Language*. Eds. Ellie Ragland-Sullivan and Mark Bracher. New York: Routledge, 1991.

Réjouis, Rose-Myriam. "A Reader in the Room: Rose-Myriam Réjouis Meets Patrick Chamoiseau." *Callalloo* 22.2 (1999) : 346–50.

Tcheuyap, Alexie. "Creolist Mystification: Oral Writing in the Works of Patrick Chamoiseau and Simone Schwarz-Bart." *Research in African Literatures* 32.4 (2001): 44–6.

Chapter 6
A Journey Lost in Mystery: Mario Vargas Llosa's *Death in the Andes*

Haiqing Sun

Ilan Stavans notes that a group of Latin American "mainstream" writers, such as Jorge Luis Borges, Gabriel García Márquez, and Julio Cortázar, have renovated the detective genre, parodically stylizing it as they adapt it to their historical and regional surroundings and bringing it a Latin American personality (42). Peruvian Mario Vargas Llosa, as the author of several criminal mysteries set in his homeland, is one of these writers, yet his detective novels also unveil secrets in the ethical and socio-political landscapes of Peru. In his 40-year career, Vargas Llosa has published a series of novels concerning a variety of crises in Peru, among which *Death in the Andes* (*Lituma en los Andes*, 1993) is unique. It is the first novel written after Vargas Llosa's defeat by Alberto Fujimori in Peru's presidential election in 1990; it marks a new start for the writer; and, unlike all his previous novels, the story is set in the Andes. The writer himself states: "The Andes does not appear in my books or rarely appears, I believe for one reason, because my experience of the Andean world is poor and insufficient."[1] *Death in the Andes*, then, seems to be a break-through for the author, who sets off to solve mysteries in this area by following police sergeant Lituma, a recurrent figure in his fictions.[2] This study examines the detective's crime-solving journey in a world of harsh nature, guilty communities, conflicting ideologies, and desperate struggles for survival; it tries to access the Andes in the text as a literary and ideological space with multivalent meanings of "the postcolonial," and to explore the role the detective plays in a critical and "transhistorical" stage, a stage that does not follow any idealist expectation of progress but rather becomes a site of conflicts among different faiths.

---

[1] "Los Andes no aparecen en mis libros, o aparecen apenas de paso, creo que por una razón, porque mi experiencia del mundo andino es una experiencia muy pobre, muy escasa" (Coloquio 31).

[2] Besides *Who Killed Palomino Molero*, Lituma is also a main character in the story "Los jefes" (1959) and *The Green House* (1966).

Between Crime and Myth

The novel begins with three missing-persons cases in the Naccos area of the Andes, where Lituma has been transferred to protect a highway construction site. The missing people are Pedro Tinoco, a mentally disabled boy who was previously a servant for the police; Casimiro Huarcaya, an albino; and Demetrio Chanca, a highway foreman. Each of the ten chapters contains three sections, following three different narratives. The first section follows Lituma's investigation of the disappearance. The second section narrates incidents happening in the Andes, including attacks by *Senderistas* (members of the "Shining Path," the Peruvian communist guerrillas), and past encounters between this rebellious force and the local people. The third is a love story between Tomás Carreño, Lituma's assistant, and Mercedes, a young prostitute from Lituma's hometown, Piura. Before coming to the Andes, Tomás has killed a drug dealer in order to save Mercedes. The first narrative presents the encounter between Lituma and the Andean society, the second is about the stories in the Andes, and the third is a story outside the Andes, of the policemen's past. The investigation of the missing-persons case provides the connection between the different stories.

From the beginning there are assumptions about the fate of the vanished people. These assumptions are related to two devastating factors in the Andes, one political and the other mythological: that they might have been killed by the guerrillas, or that they might have been taken away by the *pishtacos* (vampires). While Lituma feels helpless with regard to the cases, the second section of each of the first five chapters, which focuses on the *Senderistas*'s activities, reveals more information about the local situation, and forms a background for the cases of the missing persons. Allied to their rigid Marxist doctrines and hostile to government officials, property owners, and foreigners, the *Senderistas* often attack innocent people. Moreover, all three missing people have had previous encounters with the guerrillas. In conjunction with the atrocities that they commit in the mountains, the *Senderistas* are the central source of violence, and they become primary suspects for Lituma. In the second part of the novel, Lituma survives an avalanche, a disaster that terminates the highway project as well as Lituma's duty in Naccos. But he also meets with a Danish professor who informs him about the still-performed indigenous rite that sacrifices human beings to "apus," the Andean spirits, for protection and prosperity. This discovery challenges Lituma's assumptions about the guerrillas as suspects, and he begins to connect the missing cases to the superstitions that reign throughout the local community. Parallel with Lituma's investigation of the mystery, the barkeeper Doña Adriana talks about her and her husband's legendary fighting with the *pishtacos*, and about their history in the Andes. Her stories help Lituma comprehend this couple's role in the criminal cases. By the end of the novel's second part, the missing cases are apparently solved as a tragic result of the superstitions of the indigenous people who try to avoid the recession of the local economy through human sacrifices. But, in the epilogue, while Tomás restores his once-lost love with Mercedes, the road construction site closes, and the two policemen receive orders to abandon their post, Lituma discovers that the human sacrifice is a simulation of not only ancient Indian rituals but also the Christian communion, and some victims are chosen because they seem to have been marked to die by the *Senderistas*. Thus, although the different parties of Andean society—the police, the workers of the highway project, the indigenous people, and the guerrillas—are culturally and ideologically diverse or in contrast, their fate is inexorably intertwined. Throughout the investigation, Lituma is repeatedly struck by nostalgia for Piura, his coastal hometown, which alienates him from the harsh environment of Naccos. The solution of the murder cases does not help him feel adapted to, or accepted in, the Andean region, but rather confirms his status as a stranger.

In their studies of the *Andes* text, critics such as Arnold Penuel, Mary Berg, Hedy Habra, and Raymond Williams have focused on issues other than the investigation of crimes. From their points of view, the rebellion of the Shining Path, the current social crises and the so-called Andean myth are central themes of the novel, and the clouded literary image of Peru is its main stylistic feature. When asked to comment on the novel, Vargas Llosa himself also explicitly connects the guerrillas and the local superstitions, without mentioning the role of crime investigation in the narrative (Rebaza-Soraluz 21).[3] Penuel suggests that the Andes are depicted as a world of different types of violence, and, indeed, the theme of violence functions as a key connection for the stories in the novel (453–4). Berg views the stories as an ambitious "narrative multiplicity" with simultaneously juxtaposing and contrasting representations of the Peruvian life that have "calculated and often very dramatic effects" (25). Williams interprets such "narrative multiplicity" as a way of observing the reality of Peru as a "postmodern country" that escapes rational understanding (150). These critics seem to have examined the phenomena as independent issues, ruling out the criminal mystery as a factor basic to either the representation of different types of violence or the confluence of different stories. However, as the above summary suggests, the criminal mystery is the structural core and uniting feature of the novel. Lituma's detective work serves as a vehicle that moves forward the representations of different problems in the region. The narratives about the Andean life follow the rhythm of Lituma's criminal investigation, unfolding in response to his questions and becoming more mysterious as his uncertainties about the crime itself grow.

Parallel to Lituma and his assistant's attempts to find out possible connections between the missing cases and the guerrillas, the narrative about the past encounters between the three vanished people and the guerrillas reveals more details of the *Senderistas*'s doctrines and atrocities. Such a revelation indicates a site of social

[3] Vargas Llosa comments: "The phenomenon of the Shining Path is present [in the novel] because its members, the Senderistas, appear there [...] there is something more that is not dialogical and not at all political, which is a mythology [...] that is why I have also re-created this in the case of Dionysus, the world of the Pishtacos, and the world of Andean mythology" (Rebaza-Soraluz 21).

conflicts in Peru; meanwhile, it enables the reader to detect and connect pieces of key information of the crime, and puts the reader in a position not inferior to that of the detective character in terms of examining the available clues. These past encounters clear the *Senderistas*, not from Lituma at first, but from the reader's suspicion, as they have spared the lives of the victims.[4] At the end of the narrative, in a panicked moment on the last day of duty, Lituma also learns that the *Senderistas* are more of a red herring than a threat, although they do serve as a link among the various crime-related problems.[5]

Once the *Senderistas*'s image as crime suspects fades out of the picture, they stop being the center of the narrative; Lituma's attention and the narrative focus turn to another dimension of the Andean life—myth and superstition. The protagonists in the middle section of each of the following chapters also shift from the Shining Path to Don Dionisio and Doña Adriana, the barkeepers, whose oral narratives offer another perspective from which to view the Andes and the crimes. Doña Adriana comments that these vanished people all have some defects and are doomed to suffer some casualties.[6] Besides Lituma, the barkeepers are the only people who talk openly about the victims, and they never step out of Lituma's suspicion.

Adriana describes a mythological Andes for Lituma through her own adventure as part of an Andean legend. She has helped her first husband to go inside a labyrinthine cave and kill a *pishtaco* who takes young girls from their village as offerings. In addition to her stories of Andean lore, Lituma also gains some knowledge of the indigenous rituals from the Danish professor Stirmsson, who advises the police from the perspective of a "civilized" outsider:

> Los huancas eran unas bestias, […]. Tú mismo nos contaste las barbaridades que hacían para tener contentos a sus apus. Eso de sacrificar niños, hombres, mujeres, al río que iban a desviar, al camino que iban a abrir, al templo o fortaleza que levantaban, no es muy civilizado que digamos. (177–8)

> The Huancas [indigenous people] are animals […]. You are the one who told us about the barbaric things they did to keep their apus [the mountain spirits] happy. Sacrificing children, men, women to the river they were going to divert, the road

---

4 The guerrillas treated Pedro Tinoco in a friendly manner, and in the albino's case, the executioner chooses to spare his life. See 56–7 and 227.

5 Lituma constantly fears an imminent attack from the guerrillas. In the end of the novel, it is only Mercedes, Tomás's recuperated love, who approaches his post, not the guerrillas. See 285–6.

6 Doña Adriana suggests that one of them deserves to die because he is unclean, and had changed his name to cover a dirty past (41). Don Dionisio suggests another victim has probably been taken by the Andean vampire "pishtaco" (65).

> they were going to open, the temple or fortress they were building—that's not what we call civilized. (152)[7]

Critics have not paid as much attention to Stirmsson's comment regarding the primitive land as they have to Doña Adriana's mythical tales. Based on the matching of the names of Dionisio and Adriana to the original Greek myth of Dionysus and Ariadne and the tales of the killing of the Minotaur, Arnold Penuel suggests: "Of particular interest in *Lituma* are the perspectives issuing from the novel's principal intertexts. The novel displays an impressive interweaving of Greek mythology, Christian iconography, and Peruvian indigenous beliefs" (441–2). Mary Berg suggests that myth "is a central narrative force in Vargas Llosa's novel; references to the Greek Dionysus and Ariadne are conspicuous throughout the book" (30). She concludes:

> Christian communion in which flesh and blood are consumed … Andean belief in cannibalistic pishtacos and expiatory rites involving human sacrifice, Greek accounts of human beings sacrificed to minotaurs … all of these are fused by Vargas Llosa into one powerful meditation on the irrational in human civilization and specifically on the force of the irrational in the Andean areas of Peru. (33)

Such comments reveal a reluctance to comprehend the actual complexities of an ex-colony with hybrid cultures, religions, ideologies, and crises, other than to term them "irrational," or perhaps vaguely label them "postmodern" in their postcoloniality. Even though a parallel is obvious between the Dionisio-Adriana story and the Greek myth of Dionysus and Ariadne, within the context of criminal mystery the myth serves a more complex purpose than just to serve as an archetype or parallel.

Myth is a basic literary form with extensions into different socio-cultural dimensions, as John Vickery explains:

> First, the creating of myths, the mythopoeic faculty, is inherent in the thinking process and answers a basic human need. Second, myth forms the matrix out of which literature emerges both historically and psychologically. […] not only can myth stimulate the creative artist, but it also provides concepts and patterns which the critic may use to interpret specific works of literature. (ix)

The myth represented in *Andes* however, cannot be viewed directly or shared on a single dimension between the artists, the works, and the critics. First, the mythological representation recounted from what is held in the indigenous traditions maintains a certain primitive, symbolic significance that cannot be translated to the modern world. It is a story within a story, told by a witch who

---

[7] The English quotations of the novel are from Edith Grossman's translation. All others are from the original Spanish.

claims to be a heroine, a caring observer of the local area. Although it is arguable that the "myth" told by a character should still be considered a myth, and a story-in-a-story is still the author's creation, one cannot ignore its context of criminal mystery and its possible derivation from political motives. As David Bidney points out, any myth "is said to have its mode of necessity and its own mode of reality [...]. Myth is not something freely invented but a necessary mode of feeling and belief [that] seizes upon human consciousness" (Vickery 5).

In the case of *Andes*, therefore, we must consider the identity and motivations of the myth teller. Doña Adriana is first of all a suspect instead of a "story teller" for the police. Before the account of her *pishtaco*-killing legend in the second part of the text, she has tried to connect the missing people to the Andean monsters (44–5). Her mythical stories—centered on the Andean spirits instead of the victims—start only after the policeman's focus shifts from the *Senderistas* to the local superstition and to her. On examining the story told by Doña Adriana, Madison Smartt Bell praises Vargas Llosa for smoothly braiding together first-person narration and third-person narration (1). But the backdrop of such a narrative mode is that Doña Adriana is under Lituma's inquiry. She is under pressure to answer a policeman's questions and clear his doubts. The Andean myth is apparently the major subject of her talk, which draws the reader's attention to a matter different from the detective's concern, but this does not mean that the myth should be read separately from the mystery.

In his study of myth in modern literature, Michael Bell emphasizes the term "mythopoeia," or mythmaking, instead of "myth," as he believes that the concern is "not with myth as a traditional content or as a means of literary organization. It is rather with the underlying outlook that creates myth; or, [...] sees the world in mythic terms," and therefore, the focus of myth reading should be the question of "what relationship is being suggested between ancient and modern" (1–2). Here one may ask, for instance, what relationship is being suggested between past and present events in the Andes, since, different from a common myth with supernatural factors and symbolic meanings, Adriana's story makes explicit the current economic conditions in the region. After the story of killing a *pishtaco* with her first husband, she comments:

> Así ocurrió cuando [la economía de] Naccos vivía de la mina Santa Rita y así está ocurriendo ahora, que vive de esta carretera. Las desgracias no vendrán de los terruños [...] ni de los pishtacos [...], éstos vienen siempre en los tiempos difíciles [...]. (184)

> That's what happened back when Naccos made its living from the Santa Rita mine, and that's what's happening now, when Naccos makes its living from the highway. Misfortune won't come from the terrucos [...] or from the pishtacos [...] they always come when times are hard [...]. (158)

The region's economy has always been based on a single industry and dependent on the outer world's investment; after the traditional business of the Santa Rita mine diminishes, the local people's only hope rests with the new highway project. However, this project is in fact an attempt at "re-colonization," a symptom of neo-colonial solutions to social problems in a postcolonial era. Doña Adriana, despite her myth-making, reveals a tangible concern with the project:

> Se habló años de años, antes de que se decidieran a construirla. Lástima que cuando empezaron los trabajos [...] fuera tarde. La muerte le había ganado la pelea a la vida. [...] A menos que.... Repito lo de tantas veces: a grandes males, grandes remedios. (269–70)

> They talked about it [the highway project] for years and years before they decided to build it. It's a shame, when they finally started work [...] it was too late. Death had won its battle with life. [...] Unless ... I've said it before: Great troubles need great remedies. (235)

With this premonition of Naccos's fate, Doña Adriana's narration transforms from pure storytelling to a justification of human sacrifice as a means of saving the local economy. In the end, she even insinuates how the victims of the sacrifice are chosen. A differentiation, if not a gap, is notable between the beginning of her narration—a detailed mythical story with specific characters from long ago, and its ending, which comments in general and abstract terms on the current socio-economic situation. Nevertheless, two basic ideas remain unchanged throughout her story: that of the superstitious belief in the Andean spirits, and of herself as a heroine who tries to save her village. Since the development of her story corresponds to the pace of the narrative of the criminal mystery, and to the moves of the detective, her narration should be examined not only in the scope of myth, but also under the specific circumstance of an effort to investigate actual crimes in the region. Standing in the detective's shadow, Adriana's narration provides a broad overview of the local life, while leaping over the crimes that currently threaten the area, and her possible involvement in the murders. At this point, the reader can play the role of a detective and doubt whether her legends are borrowed from the Greek myth by the author to depict Andean life, or by the character Adriana for her own escape from Lituma's inquiry. Then, it is observable that her mythical story avoids a direct answer to the police's question on the one hand; and on the other, voices up the problem of local people's suffering and her proposal of solution—"Great troubles need great remedies" (235).

The reader can see that under the specific social conditions presented by Adriana, the criminals that perform human sacrifice and the detective who tries to solve the crime actually have the same mission in mind—to protect the highway project that may bring hope to the local economy. Doña Adriana's decrying of social miseries and her attempts to justify human sacrifice, then, form a response as well as a challenge to the police who apparently fail to guard the region's well-being. Although related to different parties involved in the mystery, the economic depression is explicitly presented only by Adriana. Her story can be considered truth-telling that affords the reader access to the solution of the crimes, because, under the disguise of "Andean myth," it strongly implies the nature and motive of the human sacrifice. William Righter notes that "to represent something is to become the mark of a truth, either occult or abstract" (8). In this sense, the more supernatural or irrational the barkeeper's story seems, the closer it gets toward an answer of the criminal mystery. Therefore, it is arguable that the "myth" is not born from a culture in general terms, but rather from a guilty community, and it serves the purposes of an increasingly realistic and suspect character before serving the construction of an Andean cultural image.

Some critics like John Updike lament that the author does not develop thoroughly the variety of topics touched upon in the narrative: "there are arresting, plausible evocations in *Death in the Andes* … they exist as adumbrations of some larger, more relaxed, less manipulative work, with the same title, which has not been written" (86). But the different themes of the Andean life—from the *Senderistas* to the mountainous vampires, are not independent of each other in the textual scope. They are presented within the detective's tracing of a crime, and as representations for key actors in Peruvian socio-politics. Both are revealed first as suspects of the crime, then as factors that strongly motivate the guilty party. Arguably, it is the persistence of the generic form, detective fiction, that supports the representation of details of the social, religious, economic, and political complexities that obtain to postcolonial experience. Through the genre's ability to expose different kinds of crises, the crime investigation itself expands to represent a more complicated experience, and the detective begins to observe the entire Andean world as a mystery.

It is not unusual for detective stories to present a criminal case as related to pressing contemporary social issues, but *Andes* does so to develop a sense of mystery not only around, but also well beyond, what is typically the primary tension of a mystery—that between the detective and the criminal. The narrative mystifies the Andean world and puts under examination not only a concrete crime but also the malaise of a whole region. At this novel's end, it is not the missing-persons case but the Andes that remains inaccessible for the detective; and it is not the crime nor the guerrillas, but a natural disaster, an Andean avalanche, that decisively interrupts the highway construction in Naccos, and therefore terminates a local people's hope as well as Lituma's duty in the mountains. Facing the Andes, the police sergeant has no privilege over the local people, as his fate is actually also decided by vast and mysterious forces out of human control. The detective journeys through the secrets of a crime only to encounter a greater mystery. By the time Lituma abandons the Naccos post, things remain chaotic, justice cannot be recuperated for the victims, the guerrillas are still to come, and the local community is hopeless. The unpredictable natural disasters also leave no solution for the afflicted people.

The Detective of Loss

Vargas Llosa presents the mystery of the Andes as a case of loss. First, it is a loss of social resources. The impact of economic depression and poverty is a common link among different parties in the crime: both the soil for the growth of the communist rebellion and a threat that local people try to avoid by committing human sacrifice. This differentiates the mountainous region from the outside world, branding modern Peru with a primitive mark.

The mystery comes in part from the loss of a sense of time. In other words, the Andean mystery significantly bears "untimely" factors of harm. The uncontrollable superstition of the Andean monsters has persisted through pre-colonial and colonial eras to become a major force in present social life. As the Danish professor observes:

> Cada elevación de los Andes, [...] tiene su diosecillo protector. Cuando llegaron los españoles y destruyeron los ídolos y las huacas y bautizaron a los indios y prohibieron los cultos paganos, creyeron que esa idolatrías se acabarían. Lo cierto es que, [...] siguen vigentes. Los apus deciden la vida y la muerte en estas tierras. (174)

> Every peak in the Andes, [...] has its own protective god. When the Spanish came and destroyed the idols [...] and prohibited pagan cults, they thought they had put an end to idolatry. But in fact it still lives. [...] The apus decide life and death in these regions. (149)

The modern construction of highways with support from Europe is, in the beliefs of the local people, at the mercy of some mystic ancient force. The communist movement of the *Senderistas* represents another aspect of the persistence of idolatry. It has its life in the novel, as in reality, with an anti-historic sense, as is indicated by the fact that their powerful presence in the Andes is contemporaneous with communism's global recession. As Armas Marcelo points out, Marxist forces remained agressive in Peru even as communist regimes fell like dominoes across Eastern Europe (222). The *Senderistas*'s anti-historic presence and the local community's "historic" fear of the *Pishtacos* both contribute to the chaos in the region; they blur the sense of time and logic necessary to a westernized view of history. Ulf Hannerz has observed the transnational status of the postcolonial land, where "the actors may now be individuals, groups, movements, business enterprises" under the economical and political trends of globalization (6). Similarly, the crises Lituma encounters in the Andes are "transhistorical" in the sense that the different actors in the Andes carry burdens from past historical periods; the mountainous region seems to have marshaled forces from both ancient and modern times against the "progress" pursued or imposed by western society. In other words, besides displaying the presence of different nations, the Andes see conflicts among different histories. The Andes can therefore be observed as one space with multiple, transhistorical times, and with diverse perceptions of "progress."

The multiple conflicts at various social levels also incur a loss of power for the powerful—the ruling machine of the country, as Gareth Williams has argued in his essay. Although they are the official representatives of surveillance and disciplinary force in Naccos, Lituma and his assistant are isolated from the community, estranged from the natural environment, and threatened by the *Senderistas*. Local people have no belief in them to either restore the social order or impose justice. Even before the government's decision to close the police post at Naccos, the social order in this area has already degenerated into disorder, and the policemen helplessly expect an attack from the guerrillas. So, it is also the loss of social confidence that results in the loss of lives.

The detective's loss of power brings up another aspect of the mystery. If the *Senderistas* movement and the "myth" of local superstition color the criminal mystery as problems *for* the detective, a third one, the problem *of* the detective himself, clearly marks the "expanded" mystery of the Andes. Traditionally the "troubled detective" comes with the development of sub-genres such as the hard-boiled thriller.[8] As Cawelti observes, this type of detective story "embodied significant shifts in both archetype and cultural mythology" within a context of social chaos and breakdown; and the detective "had his own code of behavior that did not correspond to that of society" (61). Such seems to be Lituma's situation in the Andes, but Lituma is obviously an isolated figure, unlike the detective in a thriller who, according to Todorov, "constantly risks his life [...] he is integrated into the universe of the other characters, instead of being an independent observer as the reader is" (51). Lituma's role seems to combine elements of the classical and hard-boiled detectives, using both as lenses through which the reader can investigate the postcolonial experience of the Andes.

Throughout the investigation of the crime Lituma personally faces homesickness and a hostile environment in the community and in nature. But these problems are partially due to Lituma's own multiple identity in the mountains: he is not merely a coastal native, stranger to the mountains, but also a representative of the ruling force, apparent rival and potential victim of the *Senderistas*, an outsider for the Andean community. Lituma considers the local people ignorant, the *Senderistas* monstrous, and his view of the natural environment of the region is that of a cautious stranger:

[8] John Cawelti notes that this sub-genre appeared in the United States during the 1920s and 1930s, typified in works by Dashiell Hammett and Raymond Chandler. In their novels, the detective often finds himself in fatal encounters with the criminal. He can no longer remain a calm and meticulous analyst, but must become a vulnerable anti-hero, facing not only challenges from the criminals but also the indifference of society (61).

> —No tengo más remedio, entiéndeme—[…]. Esas tormentas andinas, con rayos y truenos, no lo hacían feliz; nunca se había acostumbrado a ellas. Siempre le parecía que iban a aumentar, aumentar, hasta el cataclismo. (135)

> You understand, there is nothing else I can do […] these Andean storms, with their thunder and lightning; he had never gotten used to them. It always seemed to him that they would become more and more violent until they exploded in a cataclysm. (114)

Such a view does not demonstrate how the natural environment forms a significant challenge for Lituma as much as how he subjectively perceives the Andes as a tremendous mystery—"this mysterious, violent sierra" (121). Different from some classical detective figures who are sharp-eyed and guide the reader through a tale's riddles, Lituma sees the truth of the criminal mystery actually handed to him through the narration of Doña Adriana and the comments from Professor Stirmsson, while he feels confused: "Nunca entendré una puta mierda de lo que pasa aquí" ("I'll never figure out what […] is going on here," 35). Moreover, many of his immediate concerns are apart from his duty as police: "Por más que lleve uniforme, yo no existo" ("I may wear a uniform, but I'm a nobody," 105). Only his homesickness keeps him conscious of who he is—or who he was. Therefore, while a reader of conventional detective fiction usually expects to find out the truth about a crime through a detective's moves, the reader of *Andes* can also expect to see the extent the detective gets lost in the mystery of the Andes through the different roles Lituma plays beyond the investigation.

Lituma's strong sense of being a coastal native, a counterpart to the *serruchos* (people from the mountains), frames the image of the Andes throughout the narrative.[9] While the foreign tourists—those killed by *Senderistas*—see the culturally heterogeneous nation as a whole, Lituma possesses an insider's view of his country, not necessarily as "rational," but with a sensibility of the differences and contrasts in both its natural environment and social values. The world outside the Andes, represented by Piura, as Lituma constantly recalls, is "de la civilización y el calorcito" ("of civilization and warmth," 288), an image which reflects Lituma's feeling of strangeness in the mountains:

> Como otras veces, sintió la presencia aplastante y opresiva de las montañas macizas, del cielo profundo de la sierra. Todo iba hacia lo alto, aquí. Con todas las células de su cuerpo añoró los desiertos, las llanuras sin término de Piura, alborotadas de algarrobos, de rebaños de cabras y de médanos blancos. ¿Qué hacía aquí, Lituma? (103)

---

[9] Lituma views his life in the harsh Andean environment as a coastal person's adventure, and his sensation of being a Piuran native is often noted. See pages 71, 73, 177, and 208.

> Again he felt the oppressive, crushing presence of the immense mountains, the deep sky of the sierra. Everything here moved upward. With every cell of his body he longed for the deserts, the endless Piura flatlands studded with carob trees, flocks of goats, white sand dunes. What are you doing here, Lituma? (86)

Nostalgia for the outside world also represents a rational life for Lituma, which he perceives in opposition to the superstitious mountainous region: "Allá en el norte, en Piura y Talara, Lituma nunca creyó en brujas ni brujerías, pero aquí, en la sierra, ya no estaba tan seguro" ("Over in the North, in Piura and Talara, Lituma never believed in witches or magic, but here, in the sierra, he is no longer sure about that," 40). In such a situation, Tomás becomes important to Lituma's investigation and survival, not only because he is familiar with the mountainous area, but also because his narration of a love adventure with a girl from Lituma's hometown becomes a spiritual shelter for his homesick officer. Part of Lituma's life in Naccos is spent detecting a "hometown" mystery from an apparently simple romance: the identity of Tomás's girlfriend Mercedes. The mystery of Mercedes connects to Vargas Llosa's previous novels, such as *The Green House* (1966) and *Who Killed Palomino Molero* (1986), which implies that Lituma's journey is not only through the Andean mysteries, but also through an intertextual space.[10]

At the beginning of the text, Tomás's love adventure seems to be an independent episode, but, gradually, Lituma, as a curious and nostalgic story listener, actually participates in its narration. Tomás's story often intertwines with Lituma's requests for more information and clues, and is often interrupted by Lituma's memory of Piura.[11] When the policemen see their life in the Andes as a prison, Tomás's story provides a temporary escape and allows Lituma to recall his hometown as a lost paradise ("paraíso perdido," 177). Some critics show little interest in Tomás's love story. Smartt Bell calls it "absurdly naïve" (1). Mary Berg considers it a "soap-opera-like love interest" (27). But this episode's value may be perceived as not for the reader outside the text, but for Lituma, whose active participation in the narration of this story interferes with his mystery-solving journey and eventually digs a new mystery out of the "absurdly naïve" love that the tale recounts.

In the second half of the text it is in Lituma's interest to connect Mercedes's image with a "Meche" that he has supposedly met in Piura in the time of "the Green House."[12] For the two policemen, the mystery of Mercedes in the past and the missing-persons/murder case in the present are equally challenging. Tomás's story provides a mystery that Lituma can investigate with the kind of rationality

---

[10] Both novels, in which Lituma appears as a main character, are set in the coastal area (Piura and Talara).

[11] See examples in pages 63, 87, 89, 91, 131–2, 164, 166.

[12] The brothel "the Green House" is a major site in the novel by the same title, but "Meche" is not an original figure from that novel; she is created in *Andes* as a possible trace of Mercedes's identity, and a connection between the two novels. See pages 196–7, 289, 296, 304.

that does not serve him well in the Andean case. Ironically, Mercedes's mystery from outside the Andes is the only "case" for which Lituma reaches a firm solution during his duty in the Andes.[13] This story helps expose the detective's own status as a figure situated between different textual and ideological dimensions. If in his investigation of the crimes Lituma is tormented by the irreconcilable conflicts between different ideologies (from Marxist doctrines to indigenous superstitions and degrading Western views) and regional cultures (Piura and Naccos), then his examination of Tomás's story provides an extra space—an intertextual space immune to any present crisis—for him to survive. With his multiple roles in the text, Lituma can be a connector between two different worlds, between the world he comes from—represented by homesickness and Mercedes's mystery, a world pre-existing in the author's other novels, with the values of the coastal people—and the Andean world in which he is now lost. Although Lituma feels that his status in Andean society is unstable and marginalized, as a central figure in the narrative, he possesses an important space of "in-betweenness," a space where the modern meets the indigenous, the familiar meets the strange, nostalgia meets indifference, and the current text meets the author's previous ones. Lituma's "space" cannot be located in a specific territory, but he maintains it even as he is drawn back into his investigation in the Andes.

Lituma does not much resemble the classical or hard-boiled detective of Western tradition, but he in some senses invokes Ed Christian's proposal of the "post-colonial detective." Christian points out that just like the postcolonial elites who function as mediators between Western influence and their homeland, in the case of the postcolonial detective—the detective in the postcolonial land—there is the condition of "being within a space made by the meeting of two borders, a space which serves as a threshold between the two [...]. Often, the detective is this space, this area of overlap, this space of meeting" (13). Christian also suggests that such detectives "are themselves sites of hybridity," comparable to "other post-colonial elites, such as academics" (12–13). Considering that the mystery in the Andes expands to include cultural and regional sensibilities, one may tend to interpret Vargas Llosa's text with overly utopian postcolonial rubrics, celebrating Lituma as the "site of hybridity" and "space of meeting." Christian may take for granted that an "elite" with experience from both the Western world and his homeland would automatically carry values from both sides. However, Lituma's situation in the Andes does not resemble Christian's formulation, and even contradicts it; Lituma is a passer-by, not because he is transferred to Naccos and then transferred away by the police department, but because his life in the mountains is comparable to those foreign visitors who are considered strangers by the Andean people. The local Andeans do not consider Lituma as one of their own, even if they are all Peruvians.

---

13 When Mercedes comes to reunite with Tomás, Lituma is able to confirm that she is the Meche that Josefino rented to la Chunga for one night, the one who later disappeared (289). Both Josefino and Chunga are main characters in *The Green House*.

Lituma's contact with the mountainous culture is cautious, and is dominated by the view that barbarism is a factor in all primitive civilizations.[14] Similar to a visitor who already holds his own cultural mindset, he needs help from "tour guides" to decipher what to him seems mysterious events. Vargas Llosa illustrates such a relationship through Lituma's meeting with the Danish professor Stirmsson, whose Western-centered view enlightens the detective with information about the human sacrifices. Lituma sees the indigenous culture as a negative influence in local society, which also results in his feeling of being lost in the Andes. But his journey is already colored by nostalgia for the outside, the modern world, and by his sense of the conflict between his values and those of the Andes. Therefore, he hardly makes any rapprochement with the primitive land.

The representation of Lituma's view of the Andes sets the mountains and the outside world in opposition. For Lituma, the Andes symbolize a mystery that he could not handle but has to leave alone. The Andean people appear as parts of a community that holds its own view of life and mystery, one rooted in the social and natural conditions, which Lituma feels no obligation to understand, and which he detests as barbaric and unacceptable to a modern *modus operandi*: "Le juro que hubiera preferido no averiguarlo [el crimen]. Porque eso que les pasó es lo más estúpido y lo más perverso de todas las cosas estúpidas y perversas que pasan aquí" ("I swear that I'd rather not investigate it. Because what happened to the victims are the most stupid and perverse thing," 261). He cannot observe the indigenous world from a position of "in-betweenness," nor can he measure the differentiation between his world and the Andes from an objective perspective. The conclusion of his journey in the mountains is pessimistic: "Ya no me importa .... ya bajé la cortina, [...] Me iré ... y me olvidaré de la sierra" ("I do not care any more ... the curtain is down [...] I am leaving ... and I'll forget about the sierra," 304). Lituma sees that his identity dwells in a "civilized" world, and under the cover of nostalgia for his hometown, he displays skepticism and hostility toward the Andes as a land of terrorism, barbaric rituals, and unpredictable natural disasters. Thus, it is arguable that, along with his mystery-solving experience, Lituma may not carry the "space" where the borders of two worlds meet as Ed Christian sees, but rather serves as the border of his own region, against which the primitive land is defined and deemed inferior.

Another trait that delineates the "primitivism" of the Andean people, the superstition of the *pishtacos* or *apus*, forms part of a serious critique, if not accusation, against the local community's ignorance and cruelty within the frame of crime and mystery. Therefore, the author's motive for such rewriting of myth is questionable. Vargas Llosa himself explains

---

[14] Lituma seeks explanations of the human sacrifice, and is advised by the Danish professor that the indigenous people are "beasts," that none of the ancient tribes could pass the test of civilization, and that they are all deemed as "cruel and intolerant" from today's (Western) standard (178).

> [t]he actual characteristics of the novel were born of the impression that the news of the invasion of Pishtacos in Ayacucho left upon me. [...] It provoked a huge commotion in the shantytowns, [...] a phenomenon of mass hysteria and even lynching. Evidently, this was coming from the sediment that had been stirred about and brought up to date, due, of course, to the very particular political and economic circumstances that the region was experiencing. This struck a vein with me. (Rebaza-Soraluz 21)

Vargas Llosa claims that his motivation here is to show "how certain myths are perennial, are always there because evidently the types of questions that brought them about have not been completely resolved (they are questions that reappear under certain circumstances)." He also points out that "the idea of modernity and progress is such a precarious idea; and [...] beneath all this lies an atavistic force belonging to a certain tradition that is not easily uprooted" (Rebaza-Soraluz 21). Arguably, like the story of the *Senderistas*, the mythical story has as its background what the author perceives as social vulnerability and the loss of order, and contributes to an allegorical representation of the writer's loss of confidence in this society.

Vargas Llosa has previously seen himself as a stranger to the mountainous region, thus, for some readers, *Andes* may be considered a breakthrough into what was for him once a forbidden land. However, the novel's examination of the Andean mysteries from a stranger's perspective, one marked by nostalgia and confusion that recognizes only chaos in Andean society, puts up yet another "mystery": should this novel be read as an entry into the Andes or as an alienation, mystification, or demonization of this site? Besides a case of loss, in which the *Senderistas*, the *pishtacos*, and even nature are depicted as similarly untraceable and life threatening, Vargas Llosa does not provide further observation of the Andes. Moreover, Lituma, who is more familiar with the outside world, does not provide any insights into this primitive land, but must himself depend on a European professor to uncover its secrets. From the beginning and throughout the narrative, Lituma's feeling of being lost in the mysteries and his shock at the natural and human atrocities leave little space for further understanding of this land, and thus remind the reader of the potential biases, sometimes hidden, in postcolonial studies.

Conclusion

Death in the Andes confronts its detective with crimes, myths, and challenges that emerge from different social and textual scopes to project a critical view of a community under the control of unimaginable forces. To deal with any of these issues is eventually to deal with a hostile Andean world, which perplexes and finally halts Lituma's mission. The detective's journey through a criminal case diverts into a wider, intertextual dimension that interweaves the author's previous works to instigate the reader's participation in uncovering the text's riddles; meanwhile, the Andes, ruled by complex natural and social forces, makes any specific solution insignificant, and the detective's effort to reason and justify meaningless. With his mission ended, the mystery persists, positing the Andes as a postcolonial site and a meta-mystery, in which there co-exist irrational factors from primitive times that remain inaccessible to the "neo-colonizers," and from modern times that shadow the future of human progress.

Through the representation of the criminal investigation, Vargas Llosa may seem to mount an effort to unveil the Andean secrets from different distances. But while Lituma might appear to be an insider, either as a detective or as a Peruvian in a Peruvian site, his investigation reveals he can only observe the Andean community, and Vargas Llosa can only represent him, as an outsider. "Lituma in the Andes" is actually Lituma in exile. At least the key issue in Lituma's investigation—the criticism of the local region based on Western standards—cannot escape this externality. This detective novel is no longer merely an addition of Latin American surroundings to the original genre. The mystery of the Andes, rooted in rich representations of historical, ideological, and social conflicts, is supported by, yet well beyond, the generic tradition. It overpowers the self-sufficient criminal case, and questions the textual stability of the detective as well as the fate of the land and time that he serves.

Works Cited

Armas Marcelo, J.J. *Vargas Llosa: El vicio de escribir*. Madrid: Alfaguara, 2002.

Bell, Michael. *Literature, Modernism and Myth: Belief and Responsibility in the Twentieth Century*. Cambridge: Cambridge UP, 1997.

Bell, Madison Smartt. "Mountains of the Mind." 18 Feb. 1996. *New York Times on the Web*. 28 Jun. 1998. <http://www.nytimes.com/books/98/06/28/specials/llosa-andes.html>.

Berg, Mary G. "Narrative Multiplicity in Vargas Llosa's *Lituma en los Andes*." Claire Paolini ed. *La Chispa '95*. New Orleans: Luisiana Conf. of Hispanic Lang. and Lit, 1995. 25–38.

Bidney, David. "Myth, Symbolism, and Truth." Ed. Vickery. *Myth and Literature: Contemporary Theory and Practice*. 3–13.

Cawelti, John. *Adventure, Mystery and Romance*. Chicago: U of Chicago P, 1976.

Christian, Ed, ed. *The Postcolonial Detective*. New York: Palgrave, 2001.

Habra, Hedy. "El detective entre el inconsciente personal y el inconsciente colectivo en *Lituma en los Andes*." *Alba de América: Revista Literaria*. (2001 July): 315–36.

Hannerz, Ulf. *Transnational Connections: Culture, People, Places*. New York: Routledge, 1996.

Huggan, Graham. "Postcolonialism, Globalization, and the Rise of (Trans)cultural Studies." *Towards a Transcultural Future: Literature and Society in a 'Post'-Colonial World.* Geoffrey V. Davis et al. eds. New York: Rodopi, 2004. 27–36.

Penuel, Arnold M. "Intertextuality and the Theme of Violence in Vargas Llosa's *Lituma en los Andes.*" *Revista de Estudios Hispánicos.* 3 (1995): 441–60.

Rebaza-Soraluz, Luis. "Demons and Lies: Motivation and Form in Mario Vargas Llosa." *The Review of Contemporary Fiction.* 1(1997): 15–24.

Righter, William. *Myth and Literature.* Boston: Routledge & Paul, 1975.

Stavans, Ilan. "Parody and the Police." *Antiheroes: Mexico and Its Detective Novel.* London: Associated UP, 1997. 31–42.

Todorov, Tzvetan. "The Typology of Detective Fiction." *The Poetics of Prose.* Ithaca: Cornell UP, 1997. 42–53.

Updike, John. "Mountain Miseries: Mario Vargas Llosa Returns to the Novel." *The New Yorker* (April 15, 1996): 84–6.

Vargas Llosa, Mario. *Lituma en los Andes.* Barcelona: Planeta, 1993.

——. *Death in the Andes.* Trans. Edith Grossman. New York: Penguin, 1996.

——. "Coloquio/Respuestas." *Semana de autor: Mario Vargas Llosa.* Madrid: Instituto de Cooperación Iberoamericana, Ediciones Cultura Hispánica, 1985. 30–35.

——. "El Perú en llamas." *Desafío a la libertad.* Madrid: Aquilar, 1994. 37–41.

——. *A Fish in the Water.* Trans. Helen Lane. New York: Farrar Straus Giroux, 1994. 218–19.

Vickery, John, ed. *Myth and Literature: Contemporary Theory and Practice.* Lincoln: U of Nebraska P, 1973.

Williams, Gareth. "*Death in the Andes*: Ungovernability and the Birth of Tragedy in Peru." Ileana Rodríguez ed. *The Latin American Subaltern Studies Reader.* Durham: Duke UP, 2001.

Williams, Raymond. "Los niveles de la realidad, la función de lo racional y los demonios: *El hablador* y *Lituma en los Andes.*" *Explicación de textos literarios.* 25 (1996–97): 141–54.

Chapter 7

The Hunt for the World's Greatest Outlaw: Imperialist Policing, the Journalistic Novel, and the "War on Terror" in Colombia*

Robin Truth Goodman

> It is true, ascendancy of the secret police over the military apparatus is the hallmark of many tyrannies, and not only the totalitarian; however, in the case of totalitarian government the preponderance of the police not merely answers the need for suppressing the population at home but fits the ideological claim to global rule. For it is evident that those who regard the whole earth as their future territory will stress the organ of domestic violence and will rule conquered territory with police methods and personnel rather than with the army.
>
> —Hannah Arendt, *The Origins of Totalitarianism*

The Police and Future Territory

After much controversy in the mainstream news media, in June of 2000 the Clinton administration finally passed a $1.3 billion aid package to Colombia called Plan Colombia—including military training, helicopters, and intelligence—despite various confirmed reports of widespread human rights abuses on the part of the Colombian government as well as growing evidence of its escalating support for paramilitary death squads.[1] The Colombian government at the time made a show

---

* Reprinted by permission from *Policing Narratives and the State of Terror* by Robin Truth Goodman, the State University of New York Press © 2010 State University of New York. All Rights Reserved.

1 "Both international and Colombian human rights organizations now attribute the large majority of atrocities to paramilitaries, who are so closely, and so visibly, allied to the military that Human Rights Watch calls them the 'Sixth Division,' alongside the five official divisions. There's overwhelming evidence of intimate connections and cooperation, both from ample personal testimony and published reports of the major human rights organizations, which are detailed and informative [...] The transfer of atrocities to paramilitaries is a form of privatization that fits well into the 'neoliberal model,' of which Colombia is a stellar example generally. U.S. participation in state terror is proceeding along a similar track. Increasingly, it is privatized. The tasks are handed over to companies like MPRI and Dyncorps that hire U.S. military personnel and operate on government contracts, but aren't subject to the congressional surveillance that somewhat constrains direct participation in state terror" (Chomsky).

of assuring the out-going Clinton administration that the money and equipment would not be used in counter-insurgency but instead would be strictly confined to use in the "War on Drugs," even as these two projects were becoming increasingly difficult to distinguish.

With barely a whimper in the mainstream news media, in July of 2001 the Bush administration pushed through an additional $676 million package called the Andean Counterdrug Initiative,[2] having defeated Democrats Nancy Pelosi and David Obey's House Foreign Appropriations Committee amendment that would have directed some of the funds towards domestic drug treatment.[3] Secretary of State Colin Powell, speaking before the Senate Appropriations Committee, said, "These funds begin to apply the President's decision to shift from a strictly counterdrug effort to a more broadly based effort targeted at helping Colombia fight the terrorists in its midst as well as the drugs" (Dudley, "War"). As Mark Bowden observes in his book *Killing Pablo*, "The drug lords would eventually become not just law enforcement targets but military ones" (42). From the perspective of Colombia—and Nicaragua, El Salvador, Guatemala, Panama, Chile, and most of the rest of Latin America—it would be difficult to argue that the U.S. "War on Terror" began on September 11, 2001 or focuses solely on routing out al-Qaeda and related operatives for reasons of internal security.

The Bush bill not only escalated, through U.S. involvement, Colombia's bloody civil war, but it also allowed U.S. money to support private military contractors. It uncapped the number of U.S. advisors and the amount of money private contractors could use in purchasing weapons and provided assistance to Colombian eradication efforts with additional spray aircraft, the benefits going again to U.S. private military contractors.[4] Additionally, in March of 2003, the

---

[2] Even when, as Steven Dudley has pointed out, "the multi-billion-dollar *Plan Colombia* had brought the country little relief. Although a massive aerial eradication campaign had destroyed thousands of acres of coca fields, these fields had been replaced by new ones in other, more ecologically fragile areas" (*Walking Ghosts* 211).

[3] According to a report by the Rand Corporation, out-of-country operations like the Colombia initiative are the least cost-effective way to combat drugs. The most cost-effective way is through public assistance in the form of publicly-funded drug treatment programs; police protection (including longer sentencing) is seven times more expensive, border patrols are 11 times more expensive, and out-of-country operations are 23 times more expensive and, with the evidence of Colombia and now Afghanistan, the least effective (Caulkins et al.).

[4] "Opponents say 'outsourcing'—from consultancies to flying eradication missions over guerrilla-infested coca fields—has reduced public accountability just as U.S. involvement grows," reports Jared Kotler of Common Dreams. Meanwhile, in a country with 1.2 billion people living on less than $1 a day, fumigation efforts have only led to rising drug prices as supply diminishes and demand in consuming countries stays steady, in the end creating an encouragement for *campesinos* to produce larger crops and to extend areas of cultivation. As crop diversity is limited by the lack of access to markets, infrastructure, roads, transportation, and programs for developing sustainable alternatives, suppression

U.S. Congress passed the Iraqi war bill, which budgeted $105 million in aid to Colombia,[5] and on 21 January 2004, with Colin Powell's nod of assent, the U.S. State Department authorized an additional $34 million in military aid, certified under conditions that Colombia's army "break ties to illegal paramilitary groups, arrest their leaders and suspend officers implicated in rights abuses" (Weinberg). Ten days later, the paramilitaries continued their extrajudicial assassinations in the Cimitarra Valley and elsewhere. Under such U.S. assistance in 2004 over and above the hundreds of millions of dollars pouring in annually,[6] 23,000 people were killed in the Colombian war—hundreds being trade unionists, human rights activists, teachers, and civilian peasants—with both the FARC guerrillas[7] and the paramilitary (Autodefensas Unidas de Colombia, or the AUC, included on the Bush administration's terrorist blacklist) building standing armies of 15,000 soldiers (Barnett). At the time, Colombia was the third largest recipient of U.S. military aid in the world after Israel and Egypt.

This paper compares two journalistic novels about the past fifteen years of the "War on Terror" in Colombia—U.S. reporter Mark Bowden's 2001 *Killing Pablo: The Hunt for the World's Greatest Outlaw* and Colombian novelist Gabriel García Márquez's 1996 *Noticia de un secuestro (News of a Kidnapping)*. Literary texts participate in a broader public culture of media, entertainment, education, and political rhetoric that together lay out the possibilities for what can and cannot be done within a social, democratic sphere of political action. In contrast to Hardt and Negri's claim that policing is called upon as a mode of Empire because

---

has only led to a doubling in levels of coca harvesting in the Andes over the last 15 years, according to Alfred McCoy, author of *The Politics of Heroin* and professor of Southeast Asian History at the University of Wisconsin, Madison (Ungerman and Brohy).

5 U.S. State Department, as cited in "Harper's Index," *Harper's Magazine* (June 2003): 13.

6 These rates continue through 2008 and are projected into 2009, with 80 percent of such aid going to military and police assistance ("U.S. Aid to Colombia, All Programs, 2004–2009").

7 The FARC started out as the militant wing of Colombia's Communist Party, founded on an interpretation of Lenin's strategy of mass struggle in progress, where all the means at disposal were to be employed, military and political, what they called *la combinacion de todas las formas de lucha.* In the eighties under the presidential administration of Belisario Betancur, the FARC formed its own political party because it was hindered by some of the Communist Party's policies, particularly the expansion of its army and its organization of the peasantry. For a compelling report on this history and its eventual demise, see Steven Dudley's *Walking Ghosts: Murder and Guerrilla Politics in Colombia.* Though FARC originated as an association of peasant self-defense organizations with part of its agenda being agricultural reform, after 3000 political assassinations and their failure to control the demilitarized zone, it has become impossible for them to continue public projects (Podur and Shalom).

policing carries with it a moral structure,[8] I view policing as an obsessive focus of political storytelling and cultural production now predominantly because of a crisis in democracy, a weakening of the public sphere of democratic practice and agency caused by a reconfiguration of the nation-state and its institutions on a global scale—that is, a turn from a welfare state to a state of war. Narratives of policing bring to the fore the changing politics of national sovereignty at this time when domestic law is increasingly shaped by international interventions dressed up as transcendent universal norms.[9] "Bush had always pledged that military action would depend on the approval of the host country," writes Mark Bowden in *Killing Pablo*, "but even that caveat had begun to erode [...] the U.S. Justice Department was working on an opinion that would approve unilateral U.S. military action against *narcos* and terrorists in other countries, *with or without* the approval of host governments" (65). The current conflict in Colombia is playing out as a battle between the national public and the forces of imperialism, that is, the private economic sectors representing themselves as the borderless popular will to freedom. Not only has the nation lost its exclusive hold on the liberal democratic principle of acting in the public's name, but the global corporate order has also envisioned a new post-national phase of public participation, reconstructing the universalized rational actor model of economic agency—the ideal consumer—as no longer bound by the borders, morals, and laws of national instigation. The struggle over what policing means reflects a conflict over whether sovereignty as practiced counts as an empirical fact or as an always anticipated transformation, whether as a liberal principle of broadening the sphere of citizen agency on the one hand, or, on the other, as a widespread belief that the institutions of the democratic nation operate only in the interests of powerful economic forces.

This comparison between *Killing Pablo* and *Noticia de un secuestro* shows this conflict is constructed within discursive calls to citizenship and literary formations of the national and the "post-national." García Márquez foregrounds literature itself as standing in for a much broader political ideal of sovereign national institutions. Appropriating the hard-boiled detective's demeanor for his characterization of U.S. and allied forces, Bowden's work, on the other hand, has

[8] "Empire is formed not on the basis of force itself but on the basis of the capacity to present force as being in the service of right and peace" (Hardt and Negri 15). "Moral intervention often serves as the first act that prepares the stage for military intervention. In such cases, military deployment is presented as an internationally sanctioned police action" (Hardt and Negri 37).

[9] This is not a call for protectionism. Clearly, history has shown instances where a moral basis for interventions can be argued, and the histories of nationalisms and regionalisms also indicate that national sovereignty cannot be romanticized as a political solvent applicable in all cases for everybody's benefit. Rather, I show that the private concerns that profit from neo-imperialism in the Colombian case and others have usurped claims to morality and used them against the politics of national sovereignty, particularly in the Third World.

elevated "the popular" to a form that counters the national and its civic institutions in favor of corporate-produced virtuoso expressions of physical and emotional violence. Part of this difference is played out in opposing views of the police. García Márquez can project a police force that would ideally be held "responsible for acting without prudence or orders" (190) and would stand to defend the public against extralegal acts of violence or face state punishment for dereliction (189). Bowden, meanwhile, envisions the future of a police force capable of "cooperating with ugly people to get a good job done" (170) even if this means making alliances with "vigilante murderers" (170), that is, fighters who appeal to a higher, more universal point of justice than the corrupted national law. The conflicting sense of what counts as the work of the police demonstrated in this comparison indicates that the practices of public institutions like the police are constantly reconstituting the private, self-interested power of the universalized economic actor under liberal capitalism even as they define and defend a sphere of deliberative action outside of particularized interest, promising expanding access to citizenship protections: the public good. I do not use "literature" and "the popular" here solely to represent different classes of projected readership, even though my analysis will show that García Márquez is targeting a Third World or cosmopolitan, middle-to-upper class of educated and professional literati while Bowden addresses a U.S. masculinized working class with a military ethic. Rather, I use the terms to distinguish a category of writing that defines itself through appeals to the national from a type of writing or experience that, like consumption, formulates itself as antithetical to borders of all sorts, and particularly to national ones.

Bowden's other works also elevate "the popular" to a possible alternative to national agency. His 2002 book *Finders Keepers* tells the story of a pot-head from South Philadelphia who, jonesing for cash on his way to a fix, happens upon a yellow tub containing $1.2 million in unmarked bills mistakenly dropped off the back of a Federal Reserve armored truck. Temporarily invoking an alternative to nationalized forms of capital, the situation calls out a bunch of popular characters, from the Italian mob ("a long-standing, hierarchical, *neighborhood* crime organization" [33; emphasis Bowden's]) to local drug pushers, small-time contractors, and working-class families. This idea of a social disruption through which a national interest gives way to a popular one—"the ultimate triumph of the little guy" (149)—repeats itself in Bowden's journalistic forays onto the international stage. The most famous example is *Black Hawk Down*, made into a film in 2001 by Ridley Scott, focusing on the U.S. Special Forces' 1993 attempted ambush in Mogadishu: "It had been easy to believe, prior to this day, that the Somali warlord Aidid lacked broad popular support. But this fight had turned into something akin to a popular uprising" (230). Similarly, in a 2004 *Atlantic Monthly* article where he interviews those students who had been involved in the 1979 take-over of the U.S. Embassy in Tehran, Bowden sees the possibility of reading in this episode "an epic story of a small group of devout young *gerogan-girha* (hostage takers) who, armed with only prayer and purity of heart, stormed the gates of the most evil, potent empire on the planet" (82). This "popular" sovereignty that wants to transcend the nation-in-crisis is mostly, in Bowden's view, either corrupted through its nationalized institutionalization and religious fanaticism, as in the case of the Iranian Revolution, or misled by its own exuberance and finally quelled by the federal police, as happens in *Finders Keepers*. In *Killing Pablo*, however, "the popular" that has been taken over by nationalistic fanaticism is quite literally demolished by a combination of criminal rogues privately organized into death squads and the raw emotional energy and intelligence of the international police in the form of U.S. Special Forces and other specialized units. This leaves the popular sovereignty of the democratic promise residing in the "muscular modernity" (70) of the de-nationalized detective-hero.

I substitute the oxymoronic term "journalistic novels" for the Spanish term *reportaje* that has no English equivalent. Often allying the popular classes with an expert or academically-trained researcher, the genre in Spanish is linked to the contemporary tradition of *testimonio* that focuses on eye-witness reports of political atrocities and popular oppositional movements, often written as ethnographic dialogues. It is also connected to the much older, historical, and indeed foundational Spanish genre of *crónicas* which were the texts of conquest, telling the tale of violent national foundation through cross-cultural encounters.[10] *Reportaje* is a recounting of a current event—often a cataclysmic historical event—in a realist style, in the dynamic present, and often (as in these two cases) by a trained journalist, where conversations and character development re-envision the story according to the narrative conventions of the novel. This is not to imply that Bowden and García Márquez equally fall under the conventions of Spanish-American histories of violence and conquest, but rather that the label *reportaje* brings into play the differences drawn through the similarity in form. García Márquez consciously and ironically reimagines such histories in an attempt to reclaim a national experience of sovereignty, linking literary production to national justice. Bowden, meanwhile, funnels journalistic-style story-telling through the conventions of a fictional form—the detective novel—in order to impress the current war with the excitement and adventure of a suspenseful popular story, an investigation appealing to all, suggesting a strong agency outside the national form.

Impressing a popular detective model of investigation onto a story of war and conquest, *Killing Pablo* participates in a broader ideological project where imperialist policy is often sold as policing to demonstrate the benevolent translatability of moral and democratic practices, while the popularity of global popular consumption is used as a synecdoche for the end of the nation.[11]

---

[10] García Márquez's renowned novel *Cien Años de Soledad* (*100 Years of Solitude*) purposefully reappropriates the conventions of the *crónica*.

[11] An example of this can be found most compellingly in the work of one of the most foremost popular apologists for corporate globalization, *New York Times* foreign correspondent Thomas Friedman. For example, in *The Lexus and the Olive Tree,* Friedman writes, "And they may want strip malls along every street and Taco Bells on every corner—even though in the short run that will steamroll their local and national cultures" (241).

This mainstream distrust of public institutions—which labels weakened states as cause to many social ills including, in this case, Third World anarchy—attests to an anxiety over the future of public institutions while global capitalism is overriding many of the political roles and democratic assurances formerly residing in the nation-state, in the U.S. as in Colombia and elsewhere. As Zygmunt Bauman has eloquently shown:

> The extant political institutions, meant to assist them [the citizens] in the fight against insecurity, offer little help. In a fast globalizing world, where a large part of power, and the most seminal part, is taken out of politics, these institutions cannot do much to offer security or certainty. What they can do and what they more often than not are doing is to shift the scattered and diffuse anxiety to one ingredient of *Unsicherheit* alone—that of safety, the only field in which something can be done and seen to be done. The snag is, though, that while doing something effectively to cure or at least to mitigate insecurity and uncertainty calls for united action, most measures undertaken under the banner of safety are divisive; they sow mutual suspicion, set people apart, prompt them to sniff enemies and conspirators behind every contention or dissent, and in the end make the loners yet more lonely than before. (5–6)

The contention that public institutions are failing in their public responsibilities has led to a translation of public need into justification for building up private power. "In Colombia," writes Bowden, "one could waste a lifetime waiting for state-administered justice [...]—that's what lay behind the long and bloody tradition of *autodefensas,* or private armies" (30). As military functions are increasingly privatized, military acts have moved increasingly outside of public oversight and democratic judgment, while attacks against private contractors as in Iraq and Afghanistan become a foreign relations nightmare with no procedures in place about how the public sector or the national government should react if private companies are attacked.

From 1989, when, during the death throes of the Soviet Communist regime, the U.S. started investing heavily in the militarization of Colombia, the war has taken shape as an uneven match between the warriors of privatization and civil society, or, as an informant told Marc Cooper of *The Nation*, "a war of the armed actors against civil society." The Colombia example demonstrates that the "War on Terror" did not originate as a "clash of civilizations" or as a battle pitting the forces of freedom against fundamentalist conspirators or as a rather hyped-up concern about who might develop and trade weapons of mass destruction. On the back of continually recurring political conflicts going back one hundred years, the economic crisis of the 1970s hit Colombia hard, with the closing of textile mills in Medellín spurring vast unemployment alongside growing urbanization and a simultaneous intensification of commercialism in the form of shopping malls. In Medellín as elsewhere in Latin America, Eduardo Galeano has pointed out, the shutting down of public schools and other supports has encouraged criminal training for teenagers and the escalation of their participation in the drug mafia, in the guerrilla, and in police-commanded death squads. As, for example, kids smoking pot on doorsteps who were interviewed by reporter Alma Guillermoprieto in 1991 testified that there was nowhere in the neighborhood to feel safe and no point in making plans for the future, they were also being offered the highest in commercial fashion when they got "more than four thousand dollars for every cop killed" (231): "the traffickers said 'You, too, can have a swimming pool, and you don't even have to work for it'" (237). Lured by the "prospect of earning some fast money," Pablo's "army of teens" was recruited as *suizos*, a term, says Steven Dudley, "derived from *suicidio*" and meaning suicide bomber as "These kids were [...] cheap, bountiful, and best of all, disposable" (*Walking Ghosts* 154). Augmented by the desperation and joblessness caused by the breakdown in public order, the promise of corporate-commercial paradise spurred the street-level narco-economy. As one of Michael Taussig's Colombian informants tells him, "the principal arm of the culture of terror is unemployment" (130).

The comparison between these two novels indicates how the "War on Terror" picks up on a broader conflict between the "post-national" goals and strategies of private corporate power, on the one hand, and, on the other, the public sector as a stronghold of democratic action. Bowden's *Killing Pablo* tells the story of a degenerate nation personified in the character of a barbaric and atavistic Pablo Escobar, the cocaine kingpin who was once the head of the Medellín drug cartel, the largest in the world. Caught in a culture of spiraling violence, Bowden's Colombian nation can only be rescued and set right by the sophisticated surveillance technology of the Special Forces, the Seals, the CIA, and the DEA, assisted by "extralegal muscle, some hands-on players who didn't mind crossing the lines of legality and morality" (176). As members of Colombia's popular classes join the U.S.-sponsored death squad *Los Pepes* to take over where the police had failed, the denationalization or privation of the police's monopoly on legitimate violence undergirds the extension of the U.S. police beyond the borders of its own national law in the name of a universalized moral right. Bowden concludes, "The issue of whether the United States should target foreign citizens for assassination merits scrutiny and discussion, but I think this story makes it clear that on occasion it still does so" ("Acknowledgments"). Through military technologization, surveillance, and policies of national security, the police provide the entry-way for moral interventions and infringements on national sovereignty by private and other extra-national interests, contesting a liberal version that would represent the police—as in *Noticia*—as embodying the idea of autonomous controls, self-imposed by the nation-state, over methods of coercion.[12] Gabriel García Márquez's

[12] Private defense firms in the U.S. have profited greatly from the U.S. initiatives in Colombia that have only served to escalate coca leaf production and enrich global criminal transportation, trade, and financial networks. Adam Isaacson of the Center for International Policy has indicated that Sikorsky United Technologies—which makes the Blackhawk helicopter—has received $250 million from Plan Colombia, Bell Helicopter of Texas—

rendition sees Escobar's dominance as arising in the power vacuum left open by weakened public institutions. What Bowden sees as a militarized police action on a violence-infested city incapable of self-government, García Márquez translates as a political negotiation for a developing nation to build public institutions through constitutional reform, a nation whose sovereignty has been undermined through U.S. incursions. As Pablo holds Colombia's elite hostage, he negotiates with the ruling classes and the state to change the terms of his surrender, extend the dates for his capitulation, and, most importantly, end extradition, situating the criminal as a tool for stopping U.S. interventions in Colombia's practices of justice and securing national sovereignty. In other words, what causes the terror in García Márquez' depiction is what ends the terror for Bowden.

Killing Pablo

Linking crime to national character, *Killing Pablo* describes Pablo Escobar as "an ugly caricature of his country, unthinkably rich in natural resources but violent, stoned, defiant, and proud" (47), evoking nineteenth-century racial tropes in order to naturalize national chaos and national degeneracy, making unquestionable the need for intervention (the reference to "the Hunt" in the title also underscores Pablo's primitive animality). Bowden fashions Pablo's criminality into a showcase of police ineptitude: "Police raids were [...] disruptive, and occasionally scary," Bowden explains.

> Pablo was usually tipped off well in advance of any effort to arrest him [...] but now and then the police achieved enough surprise to catch him, literally, with his pants down. In March [...], about one thousand national police officers raided one of his mansions in the mountains outside Medellín. They arrived

which makes Huey upgrades—has received $100 million, and Lockheed—which makes the B3 and P37 aircrafts—$70 million, as well as several million going for the purchase of spray aircraft (Ungerman and Brohy). Private policing companies like Dyncorp, with 300–600 contracted employees on the ground (Singer 207), and formerly MPRI (Military Professional Resources Inc.)—both now active in Iraq as well—were awarded multi-million dollar contracts to pilot fumigation planes and to supervise combat and training. According to P.W. Singer, "Congressional investigators estimate the figure being spent on these [privatized military] firms [in Colombia] at between $770 million and $1.3 billion" (207). As Sanho Tree of the Institute for Policy Study has pointed out, subcontracting bypasses the need for public support: with no more than 800 U.S. military personnel on the ground in Colombia, contractors can be outsourced, getting around restrictions like those on involvement in combat and counterinsurgency as well as quantity ceilings on troop deployment and direct participation. Further, selling military functions and responsibilities to private companies does not require clear articulations of endgames and exit strategies while generating a confusion about what the U.S. government's role should be when military contractors and private citizens are killed on the battlefield (Ungerman and Brohy).

> in helicopters and in tanks and encircled the area. Pablo fled in his underwear, avoiding the police cordon on foot. (57)

Equaled by a similar quasi-slapstick framing of the municipal police, this absurdist parody of the national police extends into a sense that Colombia's national institutions, particularly its institutions of discipline and justice, are chronically depraved and ineffectual to the point of being funny, like the helmsman in *Heart of Darkness* who appears to Marlow like a dog in britches.

Throughout Bowden's report, Colombia's public institutional infrastructure continues to be reduced to the comic exploits of a degenerate policing interchangeable with the malfunctioning of justice. "Pablo practically owned Medellín," Bowden pronounces, "including [...] its police force" (67). Pablo's containment in La Catedral, a maximum-security prison of his own design—with "stereo equipment, big-screen TV, giant bed" (130), imported furniture and tapestries, and wired with computers and all switch-board activity monitored by Pablo himself—was the result of elaborate negotiations with national and local authorities.[13] When President Gaviria decided to transport Pablo to another jail, he could not depend on the municipal prison guards who had been chosen by Pablo, but instead sent in Eduardo Mendoza, national Vice-Minister of Justice. Mendoza went into La Catedral accompanied by Hernando Navas, director of the Bureau of Prisons, and fifteen armed prison guards "representing," Bowden interjects into Mendoza's thinking, "the power of the nation" (124). Later, however, when Pablo easily manages to overpower the police in a bloody shoot-out, Mendoza is forced to renege: "What a fool he had been to believe in the power of the state" (129), he confesses in interior monologue, and the text justifies this condemnation of Colombia's civil institutions by showing Mendoza crouching behind Pablo's toilet bowl to hide from the gunfire (132). The belittlement of justice underlines Bowden's prevalent and reiterated conviction that U.S. police action benefited

---

[13] This kind of absurdist humor in reporting on Pablo Escobar's imprisonment repeats the tone in the mainstream media at the time. Wrote James Brooke in a 1992 article in *The New York Times:* "The image of Pablo Escobar lounging on his prison water bed while coordinating shipments of tons of cocaine to the United States on his cellular telephone is not quite accurate, say lawyers who visited the trafficker in his hillside jail here. First of all, Colombia's wealthiest citizen had to make do with a foam mattress until his water bed was installed last year. Second, until he received his cellular phone he had only the rustic services of the 50 carrier pigeons in his personal prison aviary. Finally, the lawyers say, the 42-year-old Mr Escobar was not one to work in bed, and presided over his business meetings at the head of a proper boardroom table. He also enjoyed the use of an office equipped with a computer linked by a modem to a national computer network" (A1). The humor found in such situations by the Western media has to do with the breaking of modernist stereotypes of primitivism by the advent of technology (further enhanced by the reference to animalism in the article's title) as much as by the collapsing of technological miracles into primitivist magical rituals. As well, it works to ridicule the very idea of Third World sovereignty by collapsing Third World governance into comedies of crime.

Colombia even as he chronicles an ascension of terrorism and assassinations: "It implied that the nation was too weak to administer justice itself (which was true) but that the United States represented some higher moral authority" (51).

Composed of body-builders and football heroes, the bored U.S. agents waiting in a school house to advise the Colombian police from the sidelines were themselves inept in following orders and would often make forays into town and get young women pregnant to escape from the drudgery of endless video games.

> Embassy officials received undeniable evidence of this when a young woman arrived at their door from Medellín with a baby and the name of the red-haired Delta sergeant she said was its father. The baby's red hair lent credence to her story. The operator was sent home and kicked out of the unit. That these men were straying outside the fence should not have come as a surprise. Delta operators were handpicked for their independence and war-fighting skills. They were daring, highly trained men used to accomplishing what they set out to do. There was little chance they would happily sit around playing games for weeks on end while there was action just a few miles away. (170)

The disorder in the ranks of U.S. operatives resulted not from clownishness as with the Colombians, but rather from a vital desire to get into battle: "*Damn, this is going to be fun*" (71), announced one U.S. army officer when he realized that he had an excessive number of explosives. The characteristic exuberance and spontaneity explain why the command could suspend state legality, even hiring killers and terrorists, transforming the law into a privately-decided spectacle of independent force justified through scoring rather than legitimated through law. Admits General William F. Garrison, head of the Joint Special Operations Command and Delta Force authority, "The death squads were horrible, but nothing equaled them for striking fear into the hearts and minds of would-be Marxists," while U.S. Ambassador Bugsby agreed that "virtuous goals sometimes demanded hard methods" (178).

What distinguishes the U.S. "players" (176) from the Colombian police is technological knowledge, in part attributable to the translation of video game leisure time into military support—even when the military support they practiced was often illegal—in part attributable to their disregard for the rules of the game if technology offered ways around them for greater efficiency. The remarkable U.S. surveillance equipment and expertise catalyze the Colombian police force's pursuit of Pablo: "The airborne equipment substituted the three separate ground locations by taking readings from different points along the plane's flight path. As soon as a target signal was received, the pilot would begin flying an arc around it. Using computers to do precise, instantaneous calculations, they were able to begin triangulating off points in the arc within seconds" (73). This new surveillance technology, called Centra Spike, was so precise that it would make the difference between finding a needle in a haystack and walking in somebody's front door, informs a U.S. Embassy official in the video that accompanies *Killing Pablo.* At the end of the documentary, the voice-over proudly lists the other "great successes" of Centra Spike (and I mean this with irony though Bowden does not): pinning down warlords in Somalia, providing support in Bosnia, and, finally, locating Osama bin Laden in Afghanistan after the bombing of the U.S. embassy in Tanzania in 1998. Nevertheless, both the book and the movie allege that the feeble Colombian police apparatus needed bolstering by a private mercenary army supplied with these supposedly superior contracted U.S. weapons and strategies, and that this alliance was what built competence in the Colombian police. Rather than constituting the police as the extension of national law and order, the focus on technology reshapes policing as an engineering challenge or a mechanical feat, measurable by its capabilities, its range, or its success rate.

Affirming material *and* political salvation in following the terms of U.S. development, the promise of technology in producing public security increases as the Colombian police acquire and learn to use U.S. equipment. "The only way we will ever find Pablo is with your equipment," the police chief interjects. "The technology! It is our advantage over him. Technology!" (226). The gradual acquisition and training in the uses of technology allow the Colombian police to replicate U.S. bravura, going undercover in the best tradition of the popular hard-boiled detective or police procedural, and building an aura of heroism and suspense through courting danger: "The more dangerous his job was, the more he seemed to enjoy it" (152). Here, technology, like the dramatic expertise of the Seals, has universal application, constituting power as instrumental and not regulatory. Pablo is apprehended when he is talking on a cell phone with his son Juan Pablo; the son Hugo of the federal police chief Colonel Martinez tracks him, by learning to apply Centra Spike's devices through trial and error. The successful use of technology exhibited by the police culminates a series of experiments, rehearsals, observations, and evolving methodologies that show Hugo—as the prodigal son—gradually acquiring the scientific mastery of the father nation, the U.S. imperialist power that grants him the machinery, a curiosity about it, and a faith in its ultimate triumph. The scene leading up to the shoot-out is cross-cut between the succession of electronic conversations—expressions of love, trust, strategy, sometimes boastfulness, and often impatience—between a fleeing Pablo and Juan Pablo, his son, held in police custody and, in pursuit, a series of call-ins and technical reports from Hugo's mobile operator to his father Colonel Martinez at central control. In a sense, the Centra Spike surveillance technology secures the family and the nation in the father-son bond, while Pablo's failing use of technological communications sets the stage for his son's betrayal (which leads to Pablo's bloody death). Centra Spike as policing power proves its moral superiority when the competition loses out to its own Oedipal crisis.

Reducing the imperialist mission to technological training of the Colombian national police, policing carries moral force without needing to legitimize the type of morality. This means, for example, that morality gets translated into an instrumentalist, presentist fascination: if it works, the logic dictates, then it must be good. As the different U.S. agencies in Colombia competed to demonstrate the superiority of their own equipment, each apparatus had to prove its speed and efficiency, a proof which would promise future federal funding, surviving the budget cuts. Once Centra Spike proves it is more successfully applied to Colombian security, criminal baiting, intelligence gathering, and terrorist apprehension than the CIA's surveillance machines, then the U.S. efforts with Centra Spike are sanctified and justified, no matter what such applications entail, even if they include wire-tapping, kidnapping and intimidating Pablo's wife and kids, assassination, and similar suspensions of Colombian sovereignty.

Nor with hindsight would Bowden pass judgment on such operational "success" even when he could easily see, after nearly a decade, that the break-up of the Colombian drug cartels only led to a decentralization of the drug economy, making any stop-gap measures nearly impossible, if not completely futile to conceive or to implement (even though, as Plan Colombia shows, that has not deterred U.S. efforts)—as Sanho Tree of the Institute for Policy Study has described it, "the only thing we've succeeded in democratizing in Latin America is the drug trade" (Ungerman and Brohy). Contingently, Bowden justifies other methods of disciplining Colombia's civil infrastructures on the assumption that U.S. policing methods are themselves unquestionably in the service of right because they could "win" the competition in catching the most bandits and rogues the fastest, "prov[ing] that its men, equipment, and methods were most useful" (171). Therefore, "the U.S. embassy was silent on the appearance of *Los Pepes*" (176) [Perseguidos por Pablo Escobar, or People Persecuted by Pablo Escobar], the paramilitary group that assisted U.S. efforts by staging acts of violence and intimidation against suspected Pablo supporters: "What was needed," the embassy men understand, "was some extralegal muscle, some hands-on players who didn't mind crossing the lines of legality and morality that Pablo so blithely ignored" (176). Though it is not indelibly clear who funded or organized *Los Pepes*—whether, for instance, it was the CIA, a rival cartel, a powerful family, or an indigenous guerrilla group—the U.S. command agreed with former kingpin Carlos Lehder that Pablo's apprehension would only come about with the establishment—in the U.S. tradition of the Green Berets—of "a freedom fighters brigade, controlled by the DEA, and independent of the Colombian politicians, police or army" (184). *Los Pepes* were commanded by Fidel and Carlos Castano, who would expand the private army into the AUC paramilitary organization which, with 70 percent of its financing coming from contributions from drug lords (Dudley, *Walking Ghosts* 205),[14] protected international companies like Dole, Chiquita, British Petroleum, and Coca-Cola. The AUC's targeting of the Marxist-Leninist guerrilla group, FARC, and the political party—*Union Patriotica*, or UP—which sought to build peace by bringing the militants into the process of political and institutional reform has led to its appearance on the Bush administration's terrorist blacklist, not unlike a U.S.-funded Cold War ally that transformed into a terrorist cell. Nevertheless, the private militia for Bowden replicates the ethical neutrality promised in both technology and independence from national law: outside of public

---

[14] *Los Pepes* was established by the same commanders, the Castano brothers, who founded and controlled the AUC until May of 2004, when Carlos Castano was found strangled.

oversight and national debate, *Los Pepes* are evaluated on whether or not they catch the prey, on winning the competition.

The Delta Force commander's justification for militarization on the grounds that it silences Marxists repeats the book's own gestures in ridiculing and ruling out politics and, particularly, the politics of need. In other words, the farce of the national public sector in the police represents a further insufficiency of public institutions in general, and therefore an absence of democratic mechanisms for citizen agency, the rebalance of equality, the scrutiny of moral values, and the pursuit of justice, with a contingent deficiency of a language of redress and critique. Pablo's character bubbles over with the desire for pure, brute power. This idea that power is simply about the acquisition of power nullifies the possibility of thinking about power as a social relation or as an instrument of material distribution. Any of Pablo's statements about human rights or national sovereignty, therefore, Bowden translates into comedic but strategic moves to poke fun at authority, neither substantive nor serious but dripping with public relations motivations. For example, at one point Pablo reasons that "terrorism […] 'was the atomic bomb for poor people. It is the only way for the poor to strike back'" (111). Bowden immediately disqualifies this analysis by indicating that Pablo's identification with the poor—when he is really one of the richest men in the world—absurdly positions him as the victim of unjust governmental violence.

In contrast, Gabriel García Márquez centralizes the class politics and issues of national sovereignty invoked in what Bowden underscores as Pablo's joke. Instead of foregrounding the strategies of capturing Pablo, García Márquez frames the story through a series of kidnappings of journalists, members of Colombia's elite, and their long-term captivity in the charge of Medellín's renegade teenagers and other of Pablo's supporters. This means that Pablo himself does not play a dominant role in the narrative, but rather operates invisibly as a distant but marginal commander while the managers of the kidnappings always appear hooded or masked. The story unravels through encounters between Colombia's ransomed ruling classes and their ghetto guards, set against the backdrop of Colombia's elections for their *asemblea constituyente*, the extradition debates furnishing the national project of rewriting the constitution with an anti-imperialist thrust. In debates between differently located actors in the national drama—mostly about what constitutes the criminal and what kinds of police procedures and oversight should be instituted—García Márquez develops his plot by creating a sense of a national forum with its various parts contesting implications of the law:

> The guards talked a good deal among themselves, taking no precaution except to speak in whispers. They exchanged blood-soaked news about how much they had earned hunting down the police at night in Medellín, about their sexual prowess and their melodramatic love affairs. Maruja had succeeded in convincing them that in the case of an armed rescue attempt, it would be more realistic to protect the captives so that they at least would be sure of receiving decent treatment and

> a compassionate trial [...] Little by little, their mutual dependence and shared suffering brought a thin veneer of humanity to their relations. (98–9)

Here the conversations turn around shared life histories, and the telling of these histories foregrounds the narrative conventions underlying public debate and the formation of a public forum. Certainly, García Márquez's sympathy towards the captives might be mitigated by the fact, as he admits in the Acknowledgments, that they are his friends. Certainly, as well, the impetus towards social change, their compassion for their guards, and pressure on their friends and relatives in government to acknowledge the demands for equality made by their captors—certainly, these conditions of the ruling class's role in the national conversation are, to say the least, idealized, along with the novel's hopeful suggestion that class antagonism can be resolved in simple dialogue and storytelling leading to sympathetic agreement and understanding. However, rather than concurring with Cabanas that Pablo is too much favored and redeemed—"Pablo Escobar se habia convertido en 'empresario benefactor', capaz de crear puestos de trabajos y mejora social" (11)[15]—I argue that Pablo is made by the text to mark the absence of social institutions, particularly institutions offering safety and care, and to call for a political articulation around the possibilities formed through that absence; in other words, Pablo's character draws attention to a central emptiness inviting a national speculation on the need for socialism.

Additionally, the exertion, on the part of the powerful families of the captives, to change national law and extend the dates of surrender for the benefit of the kidnappers of their children depicts the ruling Colombian elites as taking personal and political risks for the public good and for national sovereignty (meaning, erroneously, that the elites are not allied with foreign interests) and reveals the government as autonomous from elite interest in ways that let the upper classes off the hook too easily in *Noticia*. Dona Nydia Quintero, for example, mother of the captive Diana Turbay—famous news reporter and daughter to a former president—angrily argues with president Gaviria against police raids on the houses where the prisoners were being detained, suggesting that the police were out of government control (bringing the idea of the paramilitaries into the debate only as an insinuation): "She [Nydia] had to control her rage as the president explained that law enforcement was not a negotiable subject, that the police did not have to ask permission to act, that he could not order them not to act within the limits of the law" (90). Nydia manages partly to persuade the president of her conviction by talking about a guard who had been informing to the police and had subsequently been killed in a raid, but President Gaviria denies Nydia her request by insisting that the *asemblea constituyente*—which, he believes, would be indefinitely delayed if the terms of extradition had to found the basis for the new law—could not be held hostage to criminals. García Márquez certainly glosses

[15] "Pablo Escobar had turned into a 'benefactor entrepreneur,' capable of creating jobs and social betterment."

over the obvious problems of representing class antagonisms from the perspective of the upper class. Yet he still narrates how the problem of Third World national sovereignty is the same as the foreign control of criminality which allows foreign control of their public institutions, particularly in questions of justice: "[A]lthough conclusive evidence against the drug dealers lay outside the country, the entire question of cooperation with the United States had reached a critical state, and the time limits for obtaining evidence were too short. The solution […] was to extend the time limits and transfer to the presidency the responsibility for negotiating the return of evidence to Colombia" (96).

Nor does García Márquez critique harshly enough the ruling class's control of the media. Many of the captives worked as journalists and had families who managed television stations and so were able to set the tone and framework of political discussion—without resorting to the violence perpetuated in Medellín—to get the message of desperation out to audiences. In fact, the book starts with a description of Maruja Pachon and her cousin Beatriz as they leave the sanctuary of "FOCINE, the state-run enterprise for the promotion of the film industry" (6), where they worked as executives and managed the press, only to fall into the hands of the delinquents. Unlike in Bowden, surveillance and communications technologies in *Noticia* do not function to prove morality in the winning of a competition or to instrumentalize politics. Contrasted with the lambasted sentimental family bond that betrays Pablo through his cell phone in Bowden's account, *Noticia* favors media production as securing a sentimental familial connection which has been threatened by the national crisis: "And almost all of Maruja's children worked in the media. Some had regularly scheduled television programs and used them to maintain communication that they assumed was unilateral, and perhaps useless, but they persisted [… Their] primary consideration was to select topics that Maruja and Beatriz would find interesting and to conceal personal messages that only they would understand" (50–51). This personalized and intimate relation with the television, of course, can only extend to those who own and control the means of symbolic production (the guards' families were *not* on television) but, in *Noticia*, it serves rather as a figure for national bonding that makes birthdays and Christmas bearable even in separation, isolation, and loss, reflecting a broader family of nation promised in the idea of state-run television. The moments when the television gets removed are the most heart-wrenching and desperate as they re-enforce the sense of emptiness and human suffering in state abandonment. In the end, the television—as a Colombian owned and operated public utility, which differentiates it from the global media consolidation and the resulting narrowness of programming worldwide, amounting to censorship—is primary in forming a national resolution as the television evangelical preacher sends messages out to Pablo, calling him into the national debate and thus articulating the initial outline of a social institution built through the sovereign actions of citizens.

Meanwhile, the United States hovers backstage, referenced as the power of empire that validates Pablo's resolve to defend a non-extradition platform to the point of bloodshed. "[A]s long as Colombia did not have an effective judicial system," the narrative concludes, "it was almost impossible to articulate a policy for peace that would position the state on the side of good, and criminals of any stripe on the side of evil" (132). Instead of translating Pablo's degenerate violence into a call for the morality of imperialism, García Márquez shows Pablo's confrontation as resulting in a viable political discussion about the shaping of public law in defense of citizens' rights and in opposition to the production of poverty, terror, and war for imperialist advantage and exploitation. As García Márquez puts it, the country was preoccupied with the question of "how to create a judicial alternative to the war against terrorism" (69).

Most telling, the police in García Márquez's account do not work as a foil to Pablo's power, as a proof of Pablo's ultimate control, or as evidence of national degeneracy and incompetence underscoring the need for intervention. For García Márquez, the police function most efficiently and rationally for the capitalist state to terrorize the poor. "He would wake with a start in the middle of the night," García Márquez says of one of the guards. "'Listen!' he whispered in terror. 'It's the cops!'" (62). In fact, García Márquez attributes Pablo's ascent to the social discontent caused by police night raids and the summary executions of teenage boys in the ghettos of Medellín: "Escobar had denounced in all the media the fact that the police would go into the Medellín slums at any hour of the day or night, pick up ten boys at random, ask no questions, and shoot them in basements or empty lots" (129). Later, García Márquez writes, "Pablo Excobar threaten[ed] to set off fifty tons of dynamite in the historic district of Cartagena de Indias if there were no sanctions against the police who were devastating the slums of Medellín: 100 kils for each boy killed outside of combat" (201). The collapse of the police's public role is mirrored in the crumbling of other public functions. One of the guards, a 24-year-old called Ant, for example, joined Pablo's crew when his parents died and he had to quit his university studies because he had no other recourse (207). Pablo's explicit motive was to allow for national institutional intervention, "not asking for criminal prosecution but for disciplinary action against the police wreaking havoc in the slums" (243).

García Márquez's tale ends immediately before Pablo's surrender and apprehension in La Catedral, when the U.S. policing forces, as shown in *Killing Pablo*, wreak havoc to the process and the new constitution altogether. What appears as justice in Bowden's work is non-conditional, disciplinary, lawless, and repressive imperialist control in the face of a culture that cannot help its regression to violence, rather than a nationalist legal reform, the disciplining of privatized police gangs, and the fortification of institutions for justice, educational accessibility, and democracy in defense of the public. In Bowden, the use of the police shows U.S. power treating foreign territory as though it were domestic territory, deploying in Colombian cities the same as it would deploy in Detroit. Public institutions of oversight here shrink down and are replaced by the brute desire for force that Bowden identifies as a product of popular consumption. Meanwhile, the series of conversations about the future of the legal system in *Noticia* links the production of literature—the telling of the story—to the building of a public sphere, its own institutions not merging with foreign power of the police and of imperialist force but rather contesting it, imagining its difference as new institutions are articulated through the public interrogation of justice.

For García Márquez, struggles for justice arise from a basic incompatibility between the egalitarian discourse of politics on the one hand and, on the other, the population and territorial control grounded in the logic of the police. Another way of stating this would be that the basic ambiguities over the social meaning of the police point toward the historical tension between the liberal welfare state's promise of equality on the one hand and, on the other, its mechanisms for social control through the containment, maintenance, and constant reinstitutionalization of inequalities. At this time when the compassionate social institutions which historically underlay the promise of political equality in the democratic state have been severely crippled under the forces of global capital, militarism, and privatization, talking about the police needs to provide a way for rethinking the public sphere. As anthropologist Michael Taussig remarked during his fieldwork in a small town outside of Cali, "People who support the paras [paramilitaries] do so in part because the Colombian state can not protect them from anything, not just from the guerrilla […] the very authority you might want to turn to for protection is likely to make things worse […] the law, meaning in the first instance the police, is likely to make you into a suspect" (30). Here, the absence of the police has sparked a desire for state interventions in the form of institutional democratic protections and the promise of equality, even when the police also represent authoritarian power, severe repression, assassination of oppositional political leaders, the weakening of state institutions for justice, daily violence, and the illegal expansion of military force over civilian populations. Turning the nation into a mechanism of repression or the law into an obstacle to be transcended, the imperialistic, realpolitic alternative of disregarding the politics of national sovereignty has empirically sideswiped the liberal ideology separating the political sphere from strangulation by economic imbalances. Still, even in the wake of its history on the side of capital, the nation-state remains as a ghostly script that democratic sovereignty still needs to reference in order to alter.

Works Cited

Barnett, Antony. "Price of Cocaine Paid With Blood." *Guardian* (13 Feb. 2005). <http://observer.guardian.co.uk/-international/story/0,1411812,00.html>.

Bauman, Zygmunt. *In Search of Politics*. Stanford, CA: Stanford UP, 1999.

Bowden, Mark. "Among the Hostage-Takers." *Atlantic Monthly* (December 2004): 76–96.

——. *Black Hawk Down: A Story of Modern War*. New York: Penguin, 1999, 2000.

——. *Finders Keepers: The Story of a Man Who Found $1 Million*. New York: Atlantic Monthly P, 2002.

——. *Killing Pablo: The Hunt for the World's Greatest Outlaw.* New York: Penguin, 2002.

Brooke, James. "How Escobar, a Rare Jailbird, Lined His Nest." *The New York Times* (5 August 1992): A1.

Cabanas, Miguel. "El sicario en su algoria: La ficcionalizactión de la violencia en la novela colombiana de finales del siglo XX." *Taller de letras* 31 (2002): 7–20.

Caulkins, Jonathan et al. "The Benefits and Costs of Drug Use Prevention: Clarifying a Cloudy Issue." In *An Ounce of Prevention, a Pound of Uncertainty: The Cost-Effectiveness of School-Based Drug Prevention Programs.* Drug Policy Research Center DPRC, 1999. <http://www.rand.org/publications/RB/RB6007/>.

Chomsky, Noam. "Cauca: Their Fate Lies in Our Hands." Interview with Justin Podur. *Z-Net* (12 July 2002). <http://www.zmag.org/znet/viewArticle/11898>.

Cooper, Marc. "Plan Colombia." *The Nation* (19 March 2001): 11–18. <http://www.thenation.com/archive/-detail/4213727>.

Dudley, Steven. *Walking Ghosts: Murder and Guerrilla Politics in Colombia.* New York and London: Routledge, 2004.

——. "War in Colombia's Oilfields." *The Nation* (5–12 August 2002): 28–31. <http://www.thenation.com/archive/-detail/7014355>.

Freeman, Laurie. "Colombia's 'Drug War.'" *Washington Post* (26 January 1999): A18.

Friedman, Thomas L. *The Lexus and the Olive Tree: Understanding Globalization.* New York: Farrar, Straus & Giroux, 1999.

Galeano, Eduardo. *Upside Down: A Primer For the Looking-Glass World.* Trans. Mark Fried. New York: Picador, 2000.

García Márquez, Gabriel. *News of a Kidnapping.* Trans. Edith Grossman. New York: Penguin, 1998.

Guillermoprieto, Alma. "Medellín, 1991." *Reconstructing Criminality in Latin America.* Eds. Carlos A. Aguirre and Robert Buffington. Wilmington, DE: Scholarly Resources, 2000.

Hardt, Michael and Antonio Negri. *Empire.* Cambridge, MA and London: Harvard UP, 2000.

"Harper's Index." *Harper's Magazine* (June 2003): 13.

Kotler, Jared. "Outsourcing War: $43M Report to Colombia Questioned." *Commondreams News Center.* 21 May 2001. <http://www.commondreams.org/headlines01/0521-04.htm>.

Lazarus, Edward. "The Upcoming Supreme Court Cases Involving the Guantanamo Detainees: Why They Will Be Transcendently Important." 13 Nov. 2003. *FindLaw's Legal Commentary.* <http://writ.news.findlaw.com/lazarus/-20031113.html>.

Leech, Garry. "Plan Petroleum in Putumayo." *NACLA Report on the Americas* (May/June 2004). <http://www.nacla.org/art_display.php?art=2404#>.

Lenin, V.I. *Imperialism: The Highest Stage of Capitalism, A Popular Outline.* New York: International Publishers, 1939.

Podur, Justin and Stephen Shalom. "Colombia Interview." *Z-Net* (22 March 2002). <http://www.zmag.org/znet/-viewArticle/12328>.

Renda, Mary A. *Taking Haiti: Military Occupation and the Culture of U.S. Imperialism 1915–1940.* Chapel Hill and London: U of North Carolina P, 2001.

Singer, P.W. *Corporate Warriors: The Rise of the Privatized Military Industry.* Ithaca and London: Cornell UP, 2003.

Taussig, Michael. *Law In a Lawless Land: Diary of a* Limpieza *in Colombia.* New York and London: The New Press, 2003.

Ungerman, Gerard and Audrey Brohy. *Plan Colombia: Cashing-In on the Drug War Failure,* with accompanying video interviews. Free-Will Productions, 2003.

"U.S. Aid to Colombia, All Programs, 2004–2009." *Just the Facts.* <http://justf.org/Country?country=Colombia>.

Weinberg, Bill. "Terror in Colombia." *The Nation* [online]. 23 March 2004. <http://www.thenation.com/doc/-20040405/weinberg>.

Chapter 8
"Sympathetic Traveling": Horizontal Ethics and Aesthetics in Paco Ignacio Taibo's Belascoarán Shayne Novels

Jennifer Lewis

Despite a nineteenth-century war of independence waged in the name of republican values, and a twentieth-century revolution fought in the name of democracy—its "verbal banner" was "Valid Voting, No Reelection" (Krauze 239)—Mexico has remained locked within a pyramidal structure that has consistently and aggressively denied political, cultural, and economic freedoms, centralizing and concentrating power in the hands of an authoritarian few. According to historian and activist Enrique Krauze, the repeated failure of democratic ideals in Mexico has in large part been due to the fact that "across the centuries," it has submitted to the "concentration of power into a single person (*tlatoani*, monarch, viceroy, emperor, President, caudillo, *jéfé*, *estadista*)" (244). In *Mexico: Biography of Power*, Krauze describes the failure of decolonization and the Mexican Revolution to achieve emancipation and democratization as the result of a peculiarly Mexican inability to shake off an "historic" habit of elevating "personages" over ideals; the result, then, of a mass capitulation to "emblematic" all-powerful individuals (243). Such a habit, which Krauze interprets as a remnant of both Indian and Spanish traditions of absolute power, "one emanating from the gods and one emanating from God" (xiv), institutionalized a "social pyramid" (220) in which a virtually untouchable paternalist leader and state presided over a mass of Mexicans who were positioned as "submissive children" (Braun 513). In Mexico, then, power and authority have historically been mapped onto a vertical axis, with the President a personification of power at its apex, the Mexican *pueblo* on a horizontal plane at the pyramid's base.

Towards the end of the 1950s, however, this pyramid appeared to be on the point of being dismantled. Divergent groups of the population began to take to the streets in order to protest against different manifestations of state oppression, and relations with the government began rapidly to deteriorate. The integrity of the paternalism upholding this "vertical" system began to be questioned and a new kind of connection began to be forged in which Mexicans found their political identity, not through a relationship with the "paternal and authoritarian Mexican state," but through a shared "uncompromising opposition to it" (Hugo Hiriart, cited in Braun 512).

This crisis in confidence reached its zenith in 1968 when an unprecedented number of students and activists took to the streets, demanding that President Díaz Ordaz should listen and respond to their grievances. The students were themselves responding to the government's increasingly brutal suppression of minor acts of rebellion. In Morelia in October 1966, a student from Guerrero had been shot to death by police during a demonstration against an increase in bus fares. Having ominously decreed earlier that year, that "No one ha[d] rights against Mexico," Díaz Ordaz had sent in paratroopers to break up the crowds and ordered the army to enter and search student residences and to carry out a series of evictions, "at bayonet point" (Krauze 689–90). A few months later he sent Mexico City's "tear gas brigades," the *granaderos,* to "pacify" skirmishing gangs of high-school students, and used them again violently to disrupt a routine pro-Castro march, killing three students and injuring and imprisoning hundreds (Braun 519). In late August 1968 the students staged walkouts, closing every school and university in Mexico City. During the next few weeks well over 140,000 students and left wing sympathizers marched on their city, their protests culminating in a mass assembly in the Plaza de las Tres Culturas in the Tlatelolco neighborhood. This time, Díaz Ortaz's propensity to act violently spiraled out of control. The army, the police, the *granaderos*, and a specialist security force trained to police the imminent Mexico Olympics encircled the protestors and opened fire, creating "a closed circle of hell" (Krauze 719). Thousands were injured and thousands arrested. "Agitators" were rounded up, accused of robbery, assault, incitement of rebellion, and even homicide. An unknown number were killed; their bodies disappeared.

For some, what was lost at Tlatelolco was a sense of Mexican modernity. Abandoning history, as history seemed to have abandoned them, these survivors interpreted the massacre as part of a death-driven cycle, in which a peculiarly Mexican "relationship" with murder (Paz 52) manifested itself—the slaughter a kind of return of the repressed that re-enacted the blood-letting of the Aztec human sacrifices and conquistador slaughters, signifying the "stubborn return of the blood" in a place that seemed to "attract death" (Krauze 722). Others, though, interpreted it as another kind of return; a reprisal of brutal colonial ideology in which slaughter was used as "a mode of terror and control" (Krauze 722). For all, though, Tlatelolco symbolized the final collapse of the liberal ideals that the Revolution begun in 1910 had briefly seemed to hold out as a possibility, and the final demise of any hope of a society freed from the authoritarianism inherited from the colonial past and governed instead by the principles of liberal democracy.

Though, "for a time," immediately after Tlatelolco, "it seemed that nothing had happened," the student protests had "opened a crack in the Mexican political system" (Krauze 733) and the government's pyramidal structure began to disintegrate. Having failed to respond "paternally" to the students' demands, the state "had lost its most praised resource: the ability to negotiate and conciliate" (Monsiváis 27) and as a consequence it had lost its power to claim paternal authority. However, although this system started to give way it did so only in order to make way for a new, aggressively anti-egalitarian structure, an intricate, all-pervasive, inherently antisocial vertical system founded on state-sanctioned corruption. Ordinary citizens consequently found themselves newly ensnared in the same old state of "isolat[ion] […] intimidat[ion] and divi[sion]" that Benito Juarez had diagnosed as Mexico's colonial legacy over a hundred years before (cited in Krauze 242). Thus, although they had freed themselves of deference to a "tyrannical and omnipresent father" (Monsiváis, cited in Braun 511), Mexicans found themselves maintained in a state of powerlessness by a new kind of tyranny, symbolized by the omnipresent kickback.

It is this corrupt world that Paco Ignacio Taibo II unmasks in a series of detective novels that are centered upon the adventures of Héctor Belascoarán Shayne, a one-eyed, part-Irish, part-Basque naturalized Mexican "private detective in a country where such a thing was unheard of" (*An Easy Thing* 65). These novels, with their unlikely (anti)hero, fantastic plots, and playfully ironic style, respond in different ways to an array of questions triggered by this violent history: how to represent a city that is both "magical" and monstrous (*An Easy Thing* 50); how to respond both to the burden of history and a kind of cultural amnesia; how to imagine a kind of "Mexicanidad, Mexican-ness" that does not simply reproduce "exotic delusions" (*An Easy Thing* 67). At the heart of each novel, though, lies a fascination with the way in which "the masses of men" (*An Easy Thing* 56) are caught within this system that institutionalizes corruption and inculcates social, cultural, and political alienation. *Some Clouds*, the third of Taibo's detective novels, for example, is a novel that describes the detective's attempts to track down the murderer of a childhood friend's family. Like most of the novels of this series the plot moves quickly from a description of personal tragedy to an uncovering of political and corporate corruption. The family is found to be caught up in a web of illegal dealings that implicate police chiefs, politicians, and big business and is therefore ultimately unfathomable. Like most of these novels, the detective's quest in *Some Clouds* ultimately ends in a kind of failure; the system proves unstoppable. Yet what is won is a glimpse of this system and its workings and a gradual understanding of its affect. Though *Some Clouds* ends with death and with exile, it also ends with a "consciousness-raising session" (141) through which Taibo articulates a corrupt vertical structure that ensures not only the enrichment of those in authority, but also the alienation of those at the bottom of the pile:

> You know what happens to the lowly motorcycle cop who puts the bite on you for three hundred pesos because you ran a stoplight? At the end of the day he has to kick back fifteen hundred or two grand to his sergeant for letting him work the intersections, and if he doesn't, he'll be sweeping streets or directing traffic, left to eat shit. The guy has to pay for the maintenance on his own bike, because if he takes it to the shop at the station they'll steal everything down to the spark plugs and, boom, the guy's back on the streets again, on foot. And he starts every day with eight litres of gas instead of the twelve he's allotted, because

> his major and his chief skimmed off the other four. He pays into a pension plan that doesn't exist either. His sergeant kicks back twenty-five grand to the district chief, who runs hot plates on the side and takes a bite out of the phoney pension fund. You know how the commanders call roll at the start of each day at district headquarters? With an envelope in their hand. Officer so-and-so reporting for duty, and there goes the money into the envelope. The district commander must take in half a million pesos every day. He's got two officers and all they do is collect money… *That's* the system. (*SC* 140–41)

Taibo uses his novels to describe this new, or perhaps newly exposed, system and to suggest this vertical system of fraudulent economics is even more oppressive, more alienating, and more powerful than the one that had preceded it. For the traditional pyramidal structure of the pre-Tlatelolco Mexico at least had at bottom a horizontal plane within which the mass of Mexicans could connect through some kind of shared consciousness (even if it was the "false consciousnesses of blind obedience" [Krauze 242]). This new system, described by Taibo in all of his Belascoarán Shayne novels, though, has no base, no end. The "motorcycle cop" in the passage above is "lowly" but not the lowest. He is part of a structure that not only towers above him but also tunnels beneath him, eroding even "the earth beneath [his] feet" (*No Happy Ending* 204). It is a chain of exploitation that extends well beyond what Jason Demers calls the "structured sites of institutions" (5) that had, previously, to some extent contained authority, while also plumbing new, apparently infinite depths. Even the sewers, which seem implied here as a kind of absolute—being "left to eat shit" signifying a kind of end point—are nothing of the kind. A truly "fluctuating network" (Demers 4), they appear in the novels as a diabolical extension of the system, forever on the brink of filling up the relatively few cities which possess them "with shit" (*An Easy Thing* 28).

As there is no base to this power structure, as it is no longer a pyramid but rather a vertical sewer—an endless "Drainage Network" (*An Easy Thing* 28)—there is little potential for a political base either. Little chance then, for solidarity, communication, or anything other than scattered, atomized, ineffectual resistance. Though the demonstrations of 1968 suggested a society on the cusp of real revolutionary action, the system that survived the aftermath was one that rendered popular resistance almost unthinkable. Reluctant acceptance "of being the forced vassals of a corrupt autocracy" seemed to become the new national reality (Monsiváis 29). Perhaps inevitably, in the post-Tlatelolco era, Mexican resistance continued to find expression, not in revolutionary ideals, but rather in the cult of revolutionary heroes which simply replaced one paternal leader for another.

Detective Fiction in a Mexican Context: "Thou Shalt Not Trust American [Genres]"

In light of this it is perhaps easy to see why, despite the fact that it "bears the imprint of other cultural and historical realities" (Simpson 10), detective fiction has proven enormously popular in Mexico in the years since the uprisings. This genre, after all, presents its readers with a fantasy of an heroic individual pursuing "natural" justice, plunging into chaos and ultimately bringing it to order. The detective exposes corruption, gives voice to grievances, and offers redemption. In this sense detective fiction offers the perfect escape from Mexican political realities, satiating that desire to believe in "heroic personalities" (Monsiváis 15), and enabling a vicarious experience of liberation from disorder.

While detective fiction has enjoyed a boom in the post-Tlatelolco era, however, some Mexicans have been unwilling to acquiesce either to this form of literature, or to the form of hero worship it seemed to feed. The journalist, critic, and activist Carlos Monsiváis, for example, has repeatedly criticized this genre, arguing that it is entirely anachronistic within a Mexican political landscape, requiring a kind of belief in the possibility of justice that he sees as untenable in Latin America: "The exception, the out-of-the-ordinary, isn't that a Latin American is a victim, but rather that he or she isn't one" (Monsiváis cited in Simpson 21).

Monsiváis's attack on detective fiction goes beyond critiquing the extent to which its form could be said realistically to reflect Mexican society. He also has a more serious ideological objection to the writing and reading of detective fiction. He suggests that both activities are, in fact, politically irresponsible. To create fictional mysteries while surrounded by real ones, he implies, is decadent: "Who cares who killed Roger Ackroyd [...] if no one knows (officially) who was responsible for the killings at Tlatelolco" (Monsiváis in Braham 5).

As his reference to Agatha Christie's Roger Ackroyd makes clear, Monsiváis is implicitly responding here to only one form of the genre: classical, predominantly English detective fiction. This form, which developed mainly in England and France alongside industrial revolutions, burgeoning middle classes, and the development of relatively stable bourgeois legal systems and modern police forces, certainly does depend on an ideal of an ordered society in which a sense of what is naturally just is ultimately reflected in the actions of the police. Though these stories articulated, or fed upon anxiety about social order—their plots flirting with anarchic forces and legal transgressions—each story more or less began with an ordered universe and culminated with the reassertion of order and the enactment of what was generally presented as natural and social justice.

The form that has achieved enormous success in Mexico, though, is predominantly the American hard-boiled variety which comes via Dashiell Hammett and Raymond Chandler rather than Arthur Conan Doyle and Agatha Christie, a form in which society is represented as falling apart: hierarchies inverting, institutions of order breaking down, government shown to be crooked. It conjures up a world of corruption and disillusionment and it creates detectives whose task is not to "restore lost order" but rather to "reveal its fissures" (Colmeiro 52). It is a form that generally culminates, then, not with narrative or ideological closure, but rather with unresolved breaches of morality, legality, and—in the case of Chandler—even logic. While this dystopian vision of society resonates with Mexican experience, the Chandleresque detective also seems a perfect fit for the culture of submission that Krauze identifies as inherently Mexican. For the Marlowe figure offers the fantasy of a return to a stable, vertical world, in which power is held by a benign authority; a benevolent father. Even though his investigations seldom accomplish a complete return to order, his own integrity, separateness, and fidelity to a more ancient authority means that he simultaneously personifies its loss and symbolizes its potential. Thus, a Mexicanized Marlowe has the potential to become another magical name in the pantheon of heroes.

Furthermore, while hard-boiled American detective fiction's focus on institutional corruption creates a point of contact with Mexican experiences and goes some way toward answering Monsiváis's claim that the genre is fundamentally incompatible with Latin American realities, it still leaves unanswered his accusation that to care about fictional crimes when surrounded by all too real and all too irresolvable ones is itself a kind of intellectual crime. And it raises another problem. For though there are correspondences between the social world conjured up by Hammett, Chandler, and the rest and that experienced by Mexicans, this is an American form, reflecting American ideologies. And throughout Mexican history, North American ideologies have regularly denied, and consistently conflicted with Mexican rights. This has literally been the case, with the United States of America invading Mexican territory, meddling in Mexican political affairs, and exercising catastrophic influence over the Mexican economy,[1] leading many Mexicans to consider "Thou Shalt Not Trust Americans" to be "the eleventh commandment" of their "official [...] mythology" (Krauze 773). But there are more subtle reasons for this deep distrust too, reasons that call into doubt hard-boiled detective fiction's adaptability, or its potential as a form to create a narrative space within which experiences and subjectivities other than those of the white Americans who are inevitably its heroes can be inscribed. For while the hard-boiled stories of the thirties, forties, and fifties imagined a society in which there was no institutional order, they continued to be organized around another kind of regulatory principle—another kind of order—repeatedly using race as a still-legible sign, even in the chaotic noir universe.

Time and again in these stories American hard-boiled detectives were delineated through their distance from and antagonism to ethnic others. These others, often indistinguishable, tended either to symbolize the depths of the depravity that the detective had to plumb, or to function as stooges who enabled the white hero to shine. Mike Shayne is a case in point. The creation of "Brett Halliday" (one of

[1] One of the most Machiavellian instances of this is, perhaps, U.S. Ambassador Henry Lane Wilson's involvement in the plot to overthrow Francisco I. Madero, one of Mexico's few "scrupulously" liberal Presidents. See Krauze, pp 265–7.

the pseudonyms of Davis Dresser), Shayne was the protagonist of a long line of novels beginning with *Dividend on Death* (1939) and ending with *Murder and the Wanton Bride* (1958) (though the series continued, ghosted until the 1980s). What follows is an excerpt from an essay published in Otto Penzler's *The Great Detectives* in which Halliday described the inspiration for Shayne:

> I first saw the man I have named Mike Shayne in Tampico, Mexico, many, many years ago. I was a mere lad working on a coast-wise oil tanker as a deckhand when we tied up at Tampico to take on a load of crude oil. After supper, a small group of sailors went ashore to see the lights of a foreign port. I was among the group.
>
> We didn't get very far from the ship, turning in at the first cantina we came to. We were all lined up at the bar sampling their tequila when I noticed a redheaded American seated alone at a small table overlooking the crowded room, with a bottle of cognac, a small shot glass, and a larger glass of ice water on the table in front of him. He was tall and rangy and had craggy features with bleak grey eyes which surveyed the scene with a sort of quizzical amusement [...] there was a certain quality of aloneness about him in that crowded cantina. He was part of the scene, but apart from it. There was a Mexican playing an accordion in the middle of the room and several couples dancing. There were other gaily dressed senoritas seated about on the sidelines and some of the sailors went to them to request a dance.
>
> I don't know what started the fracas. Possibly one of the sailors asked the wrong girl for a dance. Suddenly there was a melee which quickly spread to encompass the small room. There were curses and shouts and the glitter of exposed knives. We were badly outnumbered and getting much the worst out of the fight when suddenly, out of the corner of my eye, I saw the redheaded American shove the table away from him and get into the fight with big fists swinging.
>
> Each time he struck, a Mexican went down—and generally stayed down. I was struck over the head by a beer bottle and was trampled by the fighting men [...]. Then I was dragged out of the tangle and set on my feet by the American redhead. He gave me a shove through the swinging doors and I stumbled and went down, to be picked up by my comrades who were streaming out the door behind me.
>
> We got out of there fast, back to the ship where we patched up broken heads and minor knife cuts.
>
> We went to sea the next morning and none of us knew what had happened to the redhead after we left the cantina. (146)

It's all here—the critical signs of the hard-boiled detective. He's alone but not lonely. He's independent but not indifferent. He's at ease anywhere, but he's not *of* anywhere. He's skeptical but not scornful. He's silent but his presence speaks volumes.

The signs of the Other are here too, of course, in the stock characters: accordion-player, colorful (provocative?) dancing women, and dirty-fighting, unindividuated, previously scarcely acknowledged Mexican men whose obscene "exposed" knives suddenly threaten American innocence abroad. When the two come together there's only one possible outcome; the American soon-to-be detective will swat the others like flies. The crowding, chaotic Mexicans in this passage create the sense of menace, cause the confrontation—those polite sailors, with their "sampling" of the local liquor and decorous "requests" to dance are not to be held responsible for what happens. But they also provide the occasion for the detective to show his honor, his integrity, his moral and physical impregnability.[2] They are then interesting only to the extent to which they illuminate our detective, rendering him more clearly and completely our hero.

"All right, enough already": Colonizing the Genre

There seems little potential here for any Mexican writer, let alone a left-leaning, politically engaged writer like Taibo, who has protested American interference in Mexican economic, political, and cultural life, who claims to want to create literature that acts as "subversive subversion," rather than a sop designed to "satisfy" reactionary "desires and whims" (Taibo in Stavans 1994, 36, 34), and who is iconoclastic to the extent that he uses his novels to question the relevance of even Mexico's untouchable hero, Zapata—"the legend of Zapata had never managed to break free from the hollowness of the towering monuments or the frozen metal of the statues" (*An Easy Thing* 4). Like Carlos Monsiváis, Taibo is suspicious of literature that aims only to provide an escape from the vertical "immoral reality" of Mexican life (Stavans 1994, 36). Like Enrique Krauze he is also conscious of Mexico's historic habit of fetishising authoritarians, and is equally unwilling to submit to it. However, while Monsiváis bewails Mexicans' submission to foreign fantasies and calls for literary models that engage more directly with Mexican political realities, and while Krauze diagnoses the Mexican cult of heroes and prescribes a psychoanalyst, Taibo holds to the radical potential of the colonized *novella negra* and offers instead a "democratic detective" (*Some Clouds* 98).

Taibo's Héctor Belascoarán Shayne series colonizes hard-boiled American detective fiction, mixing its formulae with other, more indigenous forms to create fiction that displaces the white American at the center of the genre's origins, clearing a space within which another subjectivity can emerge (presenting Mexico as a country that exists outside of the American experience of it; imagining, in a sense, the Tampico bar *before* the Americans get there). With this series Taibo answers Monsiváis's persistent question, creating a literary form that uses fictional mysteries

[2] Detectives in this genre are not always so physically impressive, of course. Chandler's Marlowe, for example, spends a considerable amount of time being knocked unconscious.

to address factual ones—inculcating not an escape from political realities but instead a reengagement with them—and, most importantly, assembles iconoclastic narratives that dismantle the culture of dead heroes, replacing "vertical," politically ineffectual hero-worship with an ethics and aesthetics of horizontality.

So far there are six novels in the Belascoarán Shayne series (five of which have been translated into English), all of which in many ways self-consciously imitate their American precursors, replicating the central elements of the hard-boiled style. For a start there is the city—Mexico City—that looms large over the proceedings, a sign both of ruin and redemption; "a holy mess" (*An Easy Thing* 151). Then there are the stock characters: pornographers, crooked cops, corrupt old patriarchs, beautiful and duplicitous women. There are the conventional sub-plots too: women being blackmailed over comprising pictures; captains of industry using the detective to cover up corruption. There is the underlying acknowledgment of deception and duplicity, the detective at once knowing that he is being deceived and yet going along for the ride, biding his time until the truth, or perhaps small fragments of truths, start to shine. There is the detective too, of course. His very name sounding echoes of an earlier incarnation, he presents himself, like Mike Shayne, like Spade and Marlowe, as a lone hero, a "solitary hunter" (*An Easy Thing* 216) whose destiny it is to feel forever "like an outsider, strangely alien to the whole environment" (*An Easy Thing* 75); a man whose "dry, cold, detached" style is the only protection he has from the corruption he immerses himself in, the only thing that stands between him and a city "filled up with shit" (*An Easy Thing* 75, 57, 28).

However, Taibo's novels pull in two directions, and thus, while these points of contact are palpable, they are also constantly undermined, or perhaps, brought to the surface in such a way that they are simultaneously celebrated and critiqued, creating a reading experience in which the reader alternately wallows in the familiarity of the genre's clichés and revels in the revelation of them *as* clichés. Though all of the familiar motifs of the genre are there in Taibo's work, then, the hackneyed nature of their presence is fully acknowledged by a narrative that draws attention to their tiredness and frames their appearance with self-conscious flourishes of metatextual irony. When Héctor first meets the blackmailer and pornographer Burgos in *An Easy Thing*, for example, he responds as Marlowe might have, with a judgment that manages to be both jaded and lyrical, and that is, of course, prophetic (as he does turn out to be a real snake): "Burgos, thought Héctor. Another name on the list. He had cold, teary eyes. Snake's eyes" (*An Easy Thing* 86). With its pared down language, its spare syntax and its emphatic simile, this is Hector thinking like Marlowe, and Taibo writing like Chandler. This statement is immediately followed, however, with a sentence that draws back from such stylistic symbiosis and calls it into question (Taibo's detective collapsing into Chandler's collapsing into Greene's): "All right, enough already," the narrative continues, "it was starting to sound like a Graham Greene novel" (*An Easy Thing* 86).

This is also the case in Taibo's representation of the detective Belascoarán Shayne. Almost all of the books begin with gestures towards the conventions of noir: the detective a personification of alienation and existential ennui, standing at a bar, draining drinks, while "letting the time slip by" (*An Easy Thing* 1); sitting in his battered old leather swivel chair, "whil[ing] away what was left of the afternoon" (*No Happy Ending* 3); or standing at the window, smoking Delicados in the dark, silently "watch[ing] the green lights that the streetlights threw on the trees" and thinking about death (*Return to the Same City* 3). He has all the conventional props too: a "wrinkled trenchcoat" (*An Easy Thing* 104); a gun; a constant supply of cigarettes; a body that aches with the memory of old injuries when it rains; a dusty, paper-strewn desk in the corner of a "grimy office" (*An Easy Thing* 103) situated on the third floor of an anonymous building in a dubious part of town. Yet for each cliché of noir iconography, there is a qualifying deviation, a parodic extension of the ideal, or an equally satiric retreat from it. In addition to the limp and the scars and the ubiquitous "craggy features" (Halliday 147), Belascoarán Shayne has a glass eye, which he doesn't always bother to wear, though he sometimes covers the "scarred socket" (*Some Clouds* 6) with an eye patch which, he imagines, makes him more Count of Monte Cristo than Marlowe (*An Easy Thing* 228).[3] Likewise, as well as constantly being knocked out, tied up, or shot at in the way that the genre demands, Belascoarán Shayne is actually killed. At the end of *No Happy Ending* a "shotgun blast" catches him "mid-torso and lift[s] his torn, broken body into the air" (171). When, due to public demand, he is resurrected, reappearing in *Return to the Same City*, his deliberation on the meaning of death on the first page is therefore as much an ironic acknowledgment of authorial (or perhaps readerly) power as it is conventional expression of world-weariness.

Perhaps more interesting though, are the ways in which Taibo draws back from the hard-boiled ideal, for it is at these points that Taibo begins to develop a kind of metatextual antiauthoritarianism that "deliberately incit[es]" readers "to be suspicious and aware of those established codes, discourses and patterns" that "exud[e] power, control and authority" (Vieira 584).[4] One example of this retreat is at the beginning of *An Easy Thing* when the detective is presented as standing at the bar, drinking steadily, apparently an embodiment of noir cool: "'One more, boss,' said Héctor Belascoarán Shayne." As soon as this tableau is established it is undermined, though. Héctor has, "[f]rom the beginning," it transpires, been "emptying the rum on the sawdust-covered floor and pouring Coke into the glass," "spiking it" with nothing other than lime (1). This subterfuge "save[s] him the embarrassment of not drinking liquor in a cantina," but it hardly adds to his image. Though in this case the "virgin" drinks are explained as a tactic, allowing the detective to do his job more effectively, as this novel develops it becomes clear that he is, essentially, a virgin drinker and a man of basically adolescent tastes. His favorite tipple is orange soda pop and all he ever seems to eat is ice cream. In fact he loves ice cream so much he even has a theory about it that he explains, apropos of

3 This eye patch is possibly a parodic reference to Brett Halliday, the creator of Mike Shayne, who lost an eye as a child and wore an eye patch for the rest of his life.

4 Vieira is referring specifically here to Brazilian postmodern writers. There are correspondences though, between these writers' project, and Taibo's own.

nothing: "His personal theory was that the more complicated the dish of ice cream, the more calories it contained." Whereas his namesake, Mike Shayne, uses cognac to focus his thoughts, Belascoarán Shayne uses complicated sundaes "made with six different flavors of ice cream, nuts, whipped cream, fresh strawberries, melon, and cherry syrup" (*An Easy Thing* 215). The (perhaps unsurprising) effect of this ice cream is not clarity at all, or at least not the kind we might expect. For when Belascoarán Shayne has finished his ice cream the narrative states that "[n]ow it seemed to him that even if things had become a whole lot clearer than they were before, it was with a particularly dense and impenetrable brand of clarity" (215). The detective's thoughts have achieved a kind of lucidity, but it is a lucidity that only serves to illuminate the confusion, not end it.

It is clear from the excessive detail included here, in what is essentially an episode in which Belascoarán Shayne takes stock, that Taibo is deliberately creating a distance between his Shayne and Halliday's, between his detective and the iconic detectives who cast shadows over these books. But this stylistic distance is only part of the point. The real gulf that Taibo opens up in this passage is that between the kind of genre writing that allows readers to indulge in the fantasy of a superhuman individual who can read the chaotic world they inhabit with clarity and confidence, and this kind of writing, that expresses an anxiety about knowledge and power, an understanding of the embeddedness of the one within the other, and a desire to posit uncertainty and provisionality as dignified, intelligent and empowering responses to the chaos of Mexican life. So while Belascoarán Shayne's revelation is a dispiriting one—he is always measuring himself against "fictional" detectives and finding himself wanting—it is not disabling. In fact, Taibo implies, the "myth" of the hero, the "super-detective" (*Frontera Dreams* 67) is by far the most dangerous force described in these books. Far more perilous even than drug runners, crooked police or government conspirators, this myth threatens to "eat" anyone who falls for it "alive" (*Frontera Dreams* 67).

Horizontal Ethics and Aesthetics

Taibo does not only counter this myth by creating a detective willing to admit both to ontological and epistemological uncertainty. He also takes the "solitary traveler" (*No Happy Ending* 87) cliché that is central to the iconic detective's heroic status, and, demonstrating its complete inadequacy, creates plots in which the detective only survives, let alone solves anything, by virtue of his being embedded within a series of familial and social networks that stretch across the city and beyond.[5]

---

[5] Braham cites an unpublished essay by Glen Close that seems to be arguing a similar point. Close also seems to interpret Taibo's detective as one whose "effectiveness depends almost entirely on the collaboration of (...) friends, acquaintances and strangers" (84). Close also draws attention to Belascoarán Shayne's horizontal "interaction with the city." Rather than interpreting it as a way of resisting Mexican corruption and authoritarianism,

While he repeatedly and self-consciously plays the role of the lone hero, therefore, Belascoarán Shayne is almost never alone, and almost never unprotected. For a start he has a brother, Carlos, and a sister, Elisa, who drive him around, cook for him, even educate him when necessary, whether he likes it or not—"Enough, Carlos. The last thing I need right now is a consciousness-raising session" (*Some Clouds* 141). He has a lover—an enigmatic woman with a ponytail—who appears and disappears with a freedom usually reserved for men. He has a landlord whose own antiauthoritarianism makes him a willing accomplice, union officials whose connections with Carlos give him access to the last vestiges of organized political resistance in Mexico, and an old school friend turned radio DJ, "skinny little Valdivia" (*An Easy Thing* 88), who, in *An Easy Thing*, becomes the detective's own "helping hand on the airwaves" (90). He even has "assistants," three "very efficient secretaries" who keep him in soda pops, follow up on clues for him, cash in favors to get invaluable information, take or convey "messages without complaint" (*An Easy Thing* 68), and even participate in gun fights when necessary.

What is interesting abut these relationships, apart from the fact that they provide Taibo with another way to unravel the hard-boiled genre—in Jorge Hernández Martín's words, "neatly defus[ing] the cosmopolitan and exotic connotations of the detective myth"(165)—is the fact that they are all, in a sense, horizontal. His familial relationships are almost completely intra-generational and although the siblings repeatedly jostle for position, each is presented with their own area of expertise so that no enduring ascendancy is ever established.[6] His relationship with the woman with the ponytail is characterized by mutual vulnerabilities and toughness. They are both equally capable of sentimentality and physical violence, the woman often intervening in order to save her lover's life: "a gloved hand smashed El Chato's head with a wrench. The big man collapsed over the steering wheel, and Hector had a laughing attack. 'What are you laughing about, asshole?' She said, taking off her helmet and swinging her ponytail in the rain" (*No Happy Ending* 144). His relationships with his landlord and old school friend are also marked by mutual respect.

Which just leaves Belascoarán Shayne's "assistants," who might seem to contradict this horizontal network. Yet of course these aren't "assistants" in the conventional sense. Rather they are a plumber, a sewer and drainage specialist, and an upholsterer who sublet a part of their office to the detective. They aren't employed by him and are his equals in (almost) every way. Nor are they assistants in the sense usually implied in this genre, wherein the relationship is almost always one-way, the (female) assistant demanding nothing in return for her services

---

however, he seems to read it as a device that "complements" Taibo's use of the "vertical" mass media (91).

6 Though *An Easy Thing* begins with Belascoarán Shayne's mother's funeral and the revelation of a letter written by his father that to some extent casts a shadow across the narrative, these remain rather digressive facts within the novel and Belascoarán Shayne's emergence as a "democratic detective" coincides with his final acceptance of his orphaned state.

(sometimes, when times are hard, not even a pay check). Belascoarán Shayne's relationship with his assistants is much more mutual, much less one-sided. It depends less on the assistant's slavish admiration of the man she understands to be her superior and more on a system of reciprocity in which all men take turns to occupy this "feminine" role: "In return, Héctor was obliged to take job orders for the upholsterer and the plumber, quote prices on the repair of Naugahyde love seats or broken taps, and every now and then, take a message from the engineer's girlfriend" (*An Easy Thing* 68).

The one exception to this pattern of egalitarian relationships is the uneasy relation he has with the unionists in *An Easy Thing*. In this novel Taibo creates a back-story for Belascoarán Shayne which implicates him in the system he now opposes. Giving him a history of complicity within that vertical structure that is shown to create mass poverty, Taibo creates space within the narrative for a clear critique of both the system and the role of the middle-classes in the perpetuation of that system. Called to the "industrial suburb of Xalastoc" (57) in order to investigate the murder of a company executive, Belascoarán Shayne recounts a degraded past during which he was a white-collar engineer:

> Twice a day for four long years he'd driven that same stretch of highway [….] He'd tried to ignore it all, driving home in the evening toward the comfortable security of his nauseatingly middle-class neighbourhood […] trying to separate himself from that industrial wasteland raised up amid the dust and the misery of one hundred thousand new immigrants from the countryside, the sulphurous puddles, the air thick with dust, the drunken cops, the rampant land fraud, the illegal slaughter of infected cattle, the sub-minimum wages, the cold that rides in on the east wind, the unemployment [….]
>
> At the end of every day his car waited for him at the factory gate, and he drove the next three miles without ever leaving the main road, with his windows rolled up and the stereo on.
>
> His eyes and ears had been closed. (58)

It is this willfully blind, willfully silent complicity that the detective is atoning for in this novel. He wants to "escape, forget his past" (62), to change sides. He wants to move from the atomized stratified world he inhabited as a "foreman-accomplice to The Bossman" (62), into the harsh, vulnerable, but communal world of the "workers." However, these workers will not allow it. The union men with whom Carlos associates with such ease resist Belascoarán Shayne's attempts at comradeship. When they meet, their refusal to recognize either his name or his right to ask them questions are clear signs of their moral authority, while the detective's unusual, demeaning, and unsuccessful attempt to ingratiate himself with them marks him as obviously subordinate: "He paid for the juice, and ventured a weak smile in the direction of the workers. They ignored him" (*An Easy Thing* 59). Taibo burdens his protagonist with a truly antiheroic past, one in which he has passively accepted a position of privilege. Consequently he owes a debt to the working men that is only cleared through the loss, at the very end of the novel, of one of those formerly "closed" unseeing eyes. It is, then, only when he is physically marked by his active opposition to the state, that he achieves a kind of correspondence with these workers, the gunning down of the detective correlating with the running down of the striking workers, allowing their fates briefly and symbolically to intertwine:

> They broke the strike about three days after you went into the hospital—with the cops charging in on horses, the whole shooting match. They brought the scabs in, but our men refused to go back to work for fear of reprisals [....] Of course, the struggle goes on inside. It ebbs and flows. (232)

Inevitably, it is a connection forged through suffering violence at the hands of "the system". (232)

After this, Belascoarán Shayne's penance is complete, as is his transformation. The detective is, from this point, represented as a man who has fully extracted himself from the vertical system of exploitation and has the scars to prove it. Henceforth he is recognized everywhere and by everyone as a fully "democratic" man:

> He got off the bus, balancing carefully on his cane, and walked toward the three-storey building. Three men were pitching pennies in the street in front of an autoparts shop.
>
> "Got room for one more?"
>
> They looked him over from head to toe, and smiled among themselves.
>
> "Sure. Why not." (*An Easy Thing* 233)

What interests me here, though, is the way this antagonism between two different ways of being—complicity, acquiescence, and financial reward versus resistance, solidarity, and extreme hardship—is represented. For it is predominantly described in spatial terms, symbolized through the ways Belascoarán Shayne moves across a landscape that is, perhaps because of its obviously makeshift nature and apparent fragility, a "real Mexico" (67).

Taibo chooses to symbolize Belascoarán Shayne's political shame as a car ride. In order to describe the calculated blindness that the middle classes inculcate in order to insulate themselves from a recognition of the fact that hundreds of thousands of Mexicans, trapped in urban "wastelands," are paying the price for the middle class's "nauseating [...] neighborhoods" (*An Easy Thing* 57), Taibo puts his not-yet-detective in a private car that seems magically to appear "at the end of every day" at the factory gate, and has him drive in shameful solitude through a devastated landscape that encapsulates a history of political, geographical, and environmental exploitation. The car, with its wound-up windows and its expensive stereo, enables class stratification and atomization, and prohibits meaningful, horizontal exchange. The very fact that the car is described in a narrative focalized through Belascoarán Shayne as "waiting for him at the factory gate" every night shows just how complete this insulation is; he does not for a moment pause to wonder how this car materializes so magically every evening. Taibo subtly suggests that such a man is more likely to anthropomorphize the car (it "waited" for him), than to acknowledge the invisible workers whose role it is to uphold a form of privilege they will never themselves experience.

What Taibo pits against this, especially in *An Easy Thing*, is a different kind of spatial engagement with the city and its inhabitants, one that physically and culturally reintegrates the detective. Retracing his steps, re-enacting the journey he used to take as a fully fledged collaborator, Belascoarán Shayne distances himself from his previous self by taking the bus. Traveling this time with the workers, whose presence he previously refused to register, he reclaims a kind of horizontal relationship with the land and its people. No longer "trying to separate himself" (*An Easy Thing* 57), he steps out of the temporal, spatial, and political limbo of the car and enters a public space in which physically, intellectually, and even spiritually he experiences a kind of connection the vertical sewer is designed to militate against:

> [O]ne's city creates its own sympathies, tepid dams made of toothpicks that occasionally resist the spate of the flood. The smile of the clerk in the paint shop; the wink of casual complicity on the bus with the guy who's reading the same novel [...]; the hostile look shared by the passersby before the corner cop who is chewing out a motorcyclist. And inside one's own city, other cities are made [...] that connect every once in a while with other people's cities. (*Return to the Same City* 21)

The self-styled "solitary traveler" therefore takes instead to "sympathetic" traveling, and the horizontal network reaches out across the city. Henceforth, bus rides, metro rides, and even walks through the city "reaffirm" Belascoarán Shayne; they convince him that he belongs, that he is "just another mexicano trying to make it in the Mexican jungle" (*An Easy Thing* 67).

What being a mexicano actually constitutes, however, is not straightforward. Taibo's books are full of casual references to Belascoarán Shayne's "Mexican-ness," yet what this might actually signify is more difficult to ascertain. Belascoarán Shayne, with his unpronounceable name—"You cannot—you never—I cannot pronounce it" (Taibo cited in Goodman 2005)—is, of course, part Basque, part Irish; a migrant to Mexico, rather than a native. According to his genealogy he should be as incongruous within the Mexican landscape as his namesake was drinking Cognac in that Tampico bar. Yet the detective has little trouble fitting in; little trouble persuading other, indigenous Mexicans of his "Hispanic" (Martín 161) characteristics, his credentials as a "sympathetic" fellow traveler.

He has little trouble convincing his readers either. In episodes such as that in which Belascoarán Shayne and his siblings gather to pay their respects to their dead mother, Hispanic motifs dominate. The description of the aunts "dressed in black, s[itting] in the corner opposite the door, whispering among themselves," to say nothing of the appearance of the dead woman whose grey haired head is covered by a "Spanish mantilla," seem to produce a convincingly, if rather hackneyed,

Latin-American scene. Similarly, when the siblings, Héctor, Carlos, and Elisa, gather to eat and talk and energetically discuss the minutiae of Mexican politics and life, it is generally their localism—their embeddedness in what Héctor calls "the real Mexico" (67)—rather than their genealogical distance and difference that is emphasized. Thus even critics have been lulled into repressing through their readings the extraordinary, to use Salman Rushdie's word, "impurity" of these texts and their characters (Rushdie 394), falling instead for the rather romantic ideal of a distinctive Mexican "spirit" (Martín 161) that they often seem to privilege.

In, for example, an essay that stresses the "particularly Mexican" aspects of these novels by reading them as books that are interesting primarily because they help to "create a national literature, forged with national rules that make it verisimilar to the particular context of origin," Jorge Hernández Martín suppresses full acknowledgment of the hybridity of the Belascoarán Shayne siblings in favor of a claim of an overarching and apparently homogenous "Hispanic nature" (Martín 161). Despite the fact that he fully acknowledges the detective's immigrant status, outlines the father's history, and briefly references the nationality of his mother, Martín's argument seems to protect Héctor, Carlos, and Elisa from the complexity of this cultural inheritance, presenting them not as multiculturalists who have brought with them segments of other cultures, nor even as creolists, who, out of the cultural mix have created something new, but rather as indigenists; migrants who have no remnants of cultural otherness but who have instead found themselves in their adopted home, found a "common destiny," a way of "sort[ing] out [their] life," a "spirit" (163–5) in Mexico. Consequently, though they are half Irish and half Basque, Martín's logic insists that they are model Mexicans, siblings whose relationship, with its "spirit of camaraderie and mutual support" is a "notable characteristic" of their and the novels' "Hispanic nature" (161).

Of course, in a sense, Taibo's narratives invite us to respond in this way. The three siblings are characters who deliberately and often quite self-consciously participate in what I am calling indigenization. Taibo presents them as immersing themselves in local cultural forms, perpetually authenticating themselves and, in turn, re-authenticating this local culture in two ways: through the self-conscious consuming of Mexican goods that function as symbols of resistance to the kinds of global homogenization that threaten to flatten out cultural difference and diminish the meaning of the kind of nationalism Martín celebrates, and through participation in established rites and rituals that maintain a sense of cultural particularism. In this way, both Héctor's devotion to sickly "soda pop" and his concomitant dedication to "recurrent discussions of the rise in [its] price" explicitly function as "daily dose[s]" of local culture that maintain and "reaffirm" his "mexicanidad, Mexicanness" (*An Easy Thing* 67–8).

On the surface, then, it can seem that Belascoarán Shayne's hybrid genealogy is a rather empty gesture on Taibo's part—a device used simply to add a non-elitist, postcolonial exoticism to his character (his pedigree ensuring that his ethnic difference symbolizes persecution and perpetual struggle rather than privilege). For it is localism that seems repeatedly to be reasserted; a localism that seems determined to tie these texts and the cultural life they describe to a specific Mexican national history and to issues that, in Schulze-Engler's words, can be "defined in self-enclosed cultural [and] political terms" (59); failed revolution, the "social pyramid," Tlatelolco. I want to suggest, though, that Taibo's representation of "Mexican-ness" might be more complex than this, or at least more tangled. For though Hispanic motifs certainly dominate, the detective's ethnic inheritance ensures that the novels are peppered with signs that hint at creolization, ensures that the horizontal ethic, which explicitly creates a lateral intra-national network enabling interconnectivity and solidarity, also implicitly extends beyond the boundaries of the nation, reaching out to a multitude of other states, each with their own individual experience of colonization and "vertical" power structures: Ireland, Basque, Morocco, Tunisia, even Canada are drawn into this network through the experiences and inheritances of the Belascoarán Shaynes.

For example, the aforementioned image of the mother lying serenely in her coffin, which seems one of uncomplicated Mexican conformity, is, as the book continues, thoroughly challenged by details that depict her not simply as a suffering but resigned traditionalist, but rather as an internationalist; a woman who, through a spirit of transnational solidarity, left a home in Ireland to join the socialists in Spain, who took her Irish folk songs to New York City, who cherished her very un-Hispanic "beautiful, bright red hair" (*An Easy Thing* 8). The sister Elisa is similarly unconventional. Though hints of the clichés of Mexicanness are inevitably there—she plays the guitar and secretly writes poetry—she also deviates from the norm. She is different physically, with her freckles and red hair, and culturally. She has recently returned from Canada when the first novel begins, a place which, though it often "bored [her] to death" (*An Easy Thing* 78), has left its mark on her. For as a consequence of this traveling, it seems she has developed cosmopolitan tastes in sharp distinction to her determinedly parochial, sweet-toothed brother:

> Elisa dedicated herself to the plate of spaghetti in front of her [...].
> "Do they eat a lot of Italian food in Canada?"
> "Plenty," she said with her mouth full. (*An Easy Thing* 136–7)

It is, however, the dead father's letter that most powerfully extends the boundaries of this and the other novels' physical and imaginative geographies. This letter, inserted into the main narrative as *An Easy Thing* comes to some kind of conclusion, creates lines of continuity that stretch from Basque country to Spain, to the northern tip of Africa, and finally to Mexico. It articulates a form of sympathetic traveling that extends beyond the nation-state, stretching across a Western colonized world and hinting at, to borrow Jürgen Habermas's phrase, a kind of "world citizen's solidarity" (Habermas in Schulze-Engler 56):

> The revolution broke out in October 1934 [...] I was compelled to spend more than a year working out of the south of Spain as a sailor on ships bound for Morocco [...] After a while I renewed my contacts with the [socialist] party, and

> collaborated in writing and distributing *The Southern Seaman*. We organized the cadre of the longshore union, and helped comrades escaping to Africa. During this time I came to know the Moroccan and Tunisian coastline like the back of my hand, or perhaps better, if that's possible, as well as the untamed coast around Spanish Sahara, Guinea, and Sidi Ifni. I made good friends, and I found out that the white man's world isn't the only one there is. It was an amazing revelation for a twenty-five-year old Basque. (*An Easy Thing* 170–71)

"Mexican-ness" in these novels must therefore be understood as, to some extent, creolist—not merely because of the country's colonial past, with its enforced mixing of Amerindians and Europeans, but also because of its postcolonial present, through its inevitable participation in an increasingly transnational world. Though Taibo's novels are in some ways thoroughly attached to the romance of beleaguered indigeneity—to Mexican-ness as something homogenous and bounded—the internationalism of the central character's inheritances and experiences demand that we question this indigeneity. They demand that we understand the culture that Belascoarán Shayne participates in so enthusiastically, not as a pure expression of bounded place, nor as a unique response to an enclosed national history, but rather, to use Ulf Hannerz's words, as "a combination of diversity, interconnectedness, and innovation" that can only be understood in "the context of global center-periphery relationships" (Hannerz 1996, 67). Seen in this light Belascoarán Shaynes's apparent localism is revealed to be part of something much wider. The mother's wearing of a Spanish mantilla is a gesture that reminds us of international struggles against oppression. Brother Carlos's commitment to the unions and their struggle against corporations is not simply a local affair—a response to the verticality of the Mexican economic and political system—but rather both an echo of his father's internationalism and a response to "transnational dynamics" which exaggerate this verticality, "widening [the] gap between the political sphere of democratic participation and control" (Schulze-Engler 56). Even Héctor's commitment to Mexican soda pop is a reflection on global economics and a deliberate example of innovative cultural "counterflow" (Hannerz 1996, 6); a self-conscious participation in the so-called soft-drinks war in which Mexican brands attempt to resist the hegemony of the American giants, Coca-Cola and Pepsi.

The spatial horizontality that I am suggesting develops this understanding of Mexican culture as "diversity, interconnectedness, and innovation" is not just present in the content of these novels, though. It is apparent too in their aesthetics, in the kind of textual landscape they sketch. For, though these novels more or less follow the requirements of the genre, beginning with a mystery and ending, if not in resolution, then certainly with a discourse on the desire for resolution, the path these novels take between these two points is digressive and often ostensibly arbitrary—"horizontal" in its placing of apparently contiguous, disparate literary forms alongside one another.

An Easy Thing, for example, mixes conventional chapters with ones given titles that echo the so-called "Red News" crime pages popular in Mexico for nearly a century (Monsiváis 148). Disrupting things still further these chapters are themselves interrupted with the voice of "El Cuervo" (the skinny Valdivia), whose enigmatic late night broadcasts offer to be "a guide and companion [...] ready to lend a hand where help is needed" (129). In *No Happy Ending*, things become even more tangled as Taibo throws *testimonios* into the mix as well as chapters that forgo narratorial consistency in favor of a kind of reportage.[7] Added to this are a plethora of iconoclastic acts of irreverent name-dropping (Octavio Paz, for example, is the name given to a duck in *Return to the Same City*), quotations and intertextual references that embed Taibo's texts within a cultural network that, again, stretches beyond Mexico's borders, encompassing Chandler novels, Paul Newman films, Vietnamese protest poetry, African music, even the philosophical writings of Jean Paul Sartre. Through this placing of different indigenous and imported traditions, genres, styles, and formats alongside each other, Mexico becomes a "magical" space (*An Easy Thing* 50) of connectivity and creativity, while Mexican-ness becomes creolist, perhaps even, to borrow from Édouard Glissant, rhizomatic.[8]

One of the effects of this unremittingly digressive prose, which is forever shooting off in different directions, is a repeated refusal to provide answers to virtually any of the questions the narratives raise, from what becomes of Octavio Paz, to whether Zapata is really alive, to what happened to the bodies of those students killed in Tlatelolco in 1968, to who the Halcones were and why were they never brought to justice. The answers to these questions, ultimately, prove as impossible to pin down as the question of "Mexican-ness," and in their refusal to give answers—in their determination to return again and again to the central question of culpability—Taibo's novels keep the questions, and the spirit of questioning, alive. Rather than offering resolution then, his texts, in their playful, ironic way, model a kind of perpetual "struggle" (232) through which a kind of liberation from the tyranny of blind obedience is effected, and an on-going process of political, cultural, intellectual, and spatial "reappropriation" (Hardt 363) is established:

> "Well ... the people have to learn from the struggle. That's the only way to do it. [The strike] wasn't a victory, that's for sure, but in this town, it takes a lot of work ... I don't know what to say, exactly. It wasn't a victory or a defeat..." explained Carlos [...]
>
> "Not one or the other ..." said Héctor. (*AET* 232)

---

[7] For a comprehensive account of *testimonios* and their place in Latin American literature see Gugelberger's *The Real Thing*.

[8] Glissant describes the rhizome as "une racine demultipliee, etendue en reseaux dans la terre ou dans l'air, sans qu'aucune souche y intervienne en predateur irremediable. La notion du rhizome maintiendrait donc le fait de l'enracinement, mais recuse l'idee d'une racine totalitaire" (23). It is suggestive here, I think, not only because of its spatial implications, which echo those I've been outlining in this essay, but also because of the idea it articulates of culture as interconnective and always in process.

Works Cited

Braham, Persephone. *Crimes Against the State, Crimes Against Persons: Detective Fiction in Cuba and Mexico.* Minneapolis: U of Minnesota P, 2001.

Braun, Herbert. "Protests of Engagement: Dignity, False Love, and Self-Love in Mexico during 1968." *Comparative Studies in Society and History,* 39.3 (July 1997): 511–49.

Colmeiro, Jose F. "The Hispanic (dis)connection: Some leads and a few missing links." *Journal of Hispanic Culture* 34.4 (Spring 2001): 49–66.

Demers, Jason. "Fingering the Fringes of the Global Façade: Towards a Mobilization of Latin American Hybridity." <www.culturalstudies.ca/proceedings04>.

Glissant, Édouard, *Poetique de la Relation.* Paris: Gallimard, 1990.

Goodman, Amy. "An Hour With Mexican Writers Elena Poniatowska and Paco Ignacio Taibo." <http://www.democracynow.org/article.pl?sid=05/04/18/1411203>.

Gugelberger, Georg M. Ed. *The Real Thing: Testimonial Discourse and Latin America.* Durham: Duke UP, 1996.

Halliday, Brett. "Michael Shayne", *Great Detectives.* Ed. Otto Penzler. Boston: Little Brown & Co, 1978. 146–52.

Hannerz, Ulf. *Transnational Connections.* London: Routledge, 1996.

——. "Flows, Boundaries and Hybrids: Keywords in Transnational Anthropology." 2000. <http://www.transcomm.-ox.ac.uk/working%20papers/hannerz.pdf>.

Hardt, Michael and Antonio Negri. *Empire.* Cambridge: Harvard UP, 2000.

Krauze, Enrique. *Mexico: Biography of Power.* Trans. Hank Heifetz. New York: HarperPerennial, 1997.

Martín, Jorge Hernández. "Paco Ignacio Taibo II: Post-Colonialism and the Detective Story in Mexico." *The Post-Colonial Detective.* Ed. Ed Christian. New York: Palgrave, 2001. 159–75.

Monsiváis, Carlos. *Mexican Postcards.* Ed and trans. John Kraniauskas. New York: Verso, 1997.

Paz, Octavio. *The Labyrinth of Solitude.* 1961. Trans. Lysander Kemp. London: Penguin, 1967.

Rushdie, Salman. *Imaginary Homelands.* London: Granta, 1991.

Schulze-Engler, Frank. "From Postcolonial to Preglobal: Transnational Culture and the Resurgent Project of Modernity." *Towards a Transcultural Future: Literature and Society in a 'Post'-Colonial World.* ASNEL Paper 9.1. Eds. Geoffrey V. Davis, Peter H. Marsden, Bénédicte Ledent, and Marc Delrez. New York: Rodopi, 2004.

Simpson, Amelia S., *Detective Fiction from Latin America.* London: Associated UP, 1990.

Stavans, Ilan. "A Brief talk with Paco Ignacio Taibo II." Trans. Carrie Van Doren. *The Literary Review* 38.1 (Fall 1994): 52–5.

——. *Antiheroes: Mexico and its Detective Novel.* Trans. Jesse H. Lytle. London: Associated UP, 1997.

Taibo II, Paco Ignacio. *An Easy Thing (Cosa Facil).* 1977. Trans. William I. Neuman. London: Friction Books, 2005.

——. *Some Clouds (Algunas Nubes).* 1985. Trans. William I. Neuman. Scottsdale: Poisoned Pen Press, 2002.

——. *No Happy Endings (No Habra Final Feliz).* 1981. Trans William I. Neuman. Scottsdale: Poisoned Pen Press, 2003.

——. *Return to the Same City (Regreso a la Misma Cuidad).* 1989. Trans. Laura Dail. Scottsdale: Poisoned Pen Press, 2005.

——. *Frontera Dreams (Suenos de Frontera).* 1990. Trans. Bill Verner. El Paso: Cinco Puntos Press, 2002.

Vieira, Nelson H. "Metafiction and the Question of Authority in the Postmodern Novel from Brazil." *Hispania* 74.3. (Sep. 1991): 584–93.

Chapter 9
Hot on the Heels of Transnational America: The Case of the Latina Detective

Wendy Knepper

In P.D. James's *The Murder Room*, one of the characters suggests that "Murder, the unique crime, is a paradigm of its age" (9). Crime fiction plays an integral role in highlighting and interpreting the representative potential of a crime (whether murder or another act of wrongdoing). Generic features, such as the figure of the detective, the accounts of witnesses, and investigative processes, focus attention on the elucidation of a crime in relation to its contexts. Potentially, crime fiction introduces a far-ranging reclamation and analysis of formative events and histories that shape an understanding of a crime as a paradigmatic event. The detective as an interpretive, mediating figure plays a central role in the disclosure of hidden relations and contexts. Indeed, every age demands a detective who is uniquely equipped to interpret the representative dimensions of crime: an individual whose character, intelligence, identity, and methods of detection enter into a truly dynamic relationship with the horizons of a given world order. In this context, the relatively recent emergence of the Latina detective in crime novels, television, and film warrants particular attention. Her presence attests to changes in the demographics of America, shifts in feminist perspectives from the 1980s onwards, and the increasingly transnational dimensions of the contemporary world. Just as the Latina in the United States represents a hybrid figure, someone who negotiates aspects of her American and Latina selves, the Latina detective novel represents a hybrid discourse, a blend of the feminist detective novel and ethnic detective novel. Responsive to the insights of the detective herself, the Latina detective novel introduces transnational, cross-cultural feminist perspectives, incorporates aspects of the Latino/a experience, and draws on Latino genres of investigative and testimonial narration.[1]

Crime series, which trace the history of a particular detective over several cases, are particularly intriguing because they allow for a sustained exploration of the detective's character and life history. In this chapter, I focus on three authors and their representations of a particular Latina detective over the course

[1] The term "Latino/a" (as I use it in this chapter) encompasses all citizens of the United States whose heritage is Mexican, Puerto Rican, Cuban, Central American, and South American, as well as descendents of those who became U.S. citizens when Mexico ceded territories under the Treaty of Guadalupe Hidalgo in 1848.

of several works: Marcos M. Villatoro's Romilia Chacón, Lucha Corpi's Gloria Damasco, and Carolina Garcia-Aguilera's Lupe Solano. For these critically acclaimed authors[2] and their readers, the serial format is indicative of an ongoing interest in the life experiences and perspectives of the Latina as an individual who embodies aspects of American identity in transition. Villatoro, Corpi, and Garcia-Aguilera offer different vantage points, reflecting the heterogeneous Latina experience from the perspective of the Salvadoran-American (Romilia Chacón), the Chicana (Gloria Damasco), and the Cuban-American (Lupe Solano). For the purposes of comparison, I have selected Villatoro's *Home Killings*, Corpi's *Black Widow's Wardrobe* and Garcia-Aguilera's *Havana Heat* because these novels share common narrative elements and themes. These detective novels deal with crimes that entail real and imagined border-crossings, present analyses of the colonial past as a necessary means to unravel a transcultural mystery, and reflect profound anxieties about the articulation of transnational America. In each case, the Latina detective acts as a border-crosser who calls attention to the transnational histories and cross-cultural formative processes that shaped and continue to shape "America." Her unique transcultural feminist perspective and hybrid socio-cultural methods of detection lead her to uncover and reconstitute a more comprehensive understanding of contemporary America.

The Dynamics of the Latina Detective Novel

Villatoro, Corpi, and Garcia-Aguilera did not invent the figure of the Latina detective, but they invest her character with a depth of perspective that is often lacking in stereotypical incarnations of the Latina investigator. Emerging in the 1980s and appearing frequently from the 1990s onward, the Latina detective is now a popular figure in television, film, and novels. Sexy, smart, and tough, the Latina detective often exemplifies a post-feminist Latina ideal (Holmlund 119) of glamour combined with toughness: she is the "the dick as chick with wardrobe choices" (Mizejewski 121), the woman who always gets her man, and the *femme fatale* turned detective. Appearing in the television series *Miami Vice* (1984–89), Gina Navarro Calabrese (Saundra Santiago) was perhaps the first Latina detective to capture the popular imagination. She was followed by David Lindsey's *Mercy* (1990), one of the first serial killer novels, which also features the first Latina detective to make the bestseller list. Karen Sisco, played by Jennifer Lopez, appeared in *Out of Sight* (1998) and the *Karen Sisco* TV series featuring Carla Gugino (2003–2004). More recently, Michelle Martinez's detective Melanie

---

[2] Villatorro's *Home Killings* was listed by the *Los Angeles Times Book Review* as a Best Book of 2001 and was awarded the Silver Medal from *Foreword Magazine* as well as First Prize in the Latino Literary Hall of Fame. Garcia-Aguilera won the Shamus Award for *Havana Heat*. Corpi's *Eulogy for a Brown Angel* was awarded the PEN Oakland Josephine Miles Award.

Vargas exemplifies the Latina who proudly wears her sexuality and her *tacones* (high heels).[3] In many instances, unfortunately, the Latina detective is reduced to a sexual stereotype of the "fiery Latina"; her ethnic identity serves as a marker of her seductive otherness.

More interesting are those cases in which the culture, identity, and community of the Latina detective play a role in shaping the narrative and the investigation. In America, the Hispanic proportion of the population stands at 15 percent, having outnumbered the percentage of African Americans in the past decade ("Hispanic Americans"). The increasing popularity of the Latina detective throughout the 1990s and into the new millennium reflects the shifting demographics of American society. We can see the Latina's appeal as twofold for she represents a growing target audience for advertisers and marketers as well as a subject of interest for mainstream America. Accompanying this shift, there has been and continues to be an "anxious commentary on how a Latina/o presence will change the nation" (Brady 203). The Latina detective fills a role comparable to that of the African American detectives of Chester Himes or Walter Mosley who investigate and "express African American cultural identity" (Soitos 51). These reasons help us account for the popularity of the detective stories of Villatoro, Corpi, and Garcia-Aguilera. The serial detective novel format[4] allows for a sustained, in-depth and evolving look into the experiences of a particular Latina as well as the opportunity to study "a community and its code over time" (Dilley xii). The Latina detective expresses anxieties about ethnicity in America and attests to increased cultural diversity in the United States. Individually and collectively, these novels call attention to the fact that Latino/a identity is not singular but rather reflects the plurality of Latino socio-political backgrounds, migration histories, racial/ethnic identities, religious beliefs, and other factors. By tracing the changes in the Latina detective's perspective over time or in different geographies, these novels offer a more complex investigation into the multifaceted aspects of Latino communities across America.

The Latina detective novel shares some of the generic features that characterize the feminist detective novel. Since its heyday in the 1980s (Munt 201), the feminist detective novel has offered writers and readers a chance to examine gender constructs, the role of women in society, and the impact of feminist activism in transforming society (Walton and Jones 34). Maureen Reddy notes that

---

[3] Other Latina detectives include Gloria Duran in *LA Dragnet*, Yelina Salas in *CSI Miami*, and Carmen Olivera in *NYPD Blue*.

[4] Villatoro's Romilia Chacón series includes the following novels: *Home Killings* (2001), *Minos* (2003), and *A Venom Beneath the Skin* (2005). Corpi's Gloria Damasco series includes *Eulogy for a Brown Angel* (1992), *Cactus Blood* (1995), and *Black Widow's Wardrobe* (1999). Gloria Damasco also appears in *Crimson Moon: A Brown Angel Mystery* (2004). Garcia-Aguilera's Lupe Solano series includes the following novels: *Bloody Waters* (1996), *Bloody Shame* (1997), *Bloody Secrets* (1997), *A Miracle in Paradise* (1999), *Havana Heat* (2000), and *Bitter Sugar* (2001).

the feminist detective novel is "usually related in fairly direct ways to women's continuing oppression" (Reddy 198). The history of the feminist detective novel reflects the unfolding and diverse concerns of first-wave, second-wave, and third-world feminisms. The female detective's personal narrative lends a specificity and dramatic focus to the representation of timely gender issues. In other words, the mystery story is related to a deeper unresolved enigma, that of the female detective herself. The Latina detective embodies transnational feminist concerns as well as reflects anxieties about American identity as reconstituted through Latino/a presence. What Mariana Ortega notes about "U.S. Third-World Feminists," such as Gloria Anzaldúa, Cherré Moraga, Norma Alarcón, Chéla Sandoval, and María Lugones, might be applied to Latina detectives: the "power and seductiveness of their accounts derives from the fact that they are discussing their lives, not the life of an abstract, imaginary, transcendental subject who is removed from a specific historical context" (Ortega 3).

Issues of identity play a central role in the Latina detective novel. With respect to the Latina detective, the heritage of double colonization as well as prejudicial attitudes, often prevalent in American society, figure predominantly. Latinas confront stereotyping and other forms of marginalization within both the Latino community and society at large. Latino and American constructs of gender tend to differ considerably, which can lead to a conflicted sense of femininity. The interplay of gender, ethnicity, and cultural difference plays an important role in the Latina detective's relationships to communities and contributes to her sense of self in a Latina-American vision of society. Within the "melting pot" of American society, the heterogeneous aspects of Latino identities further complicate the notion of a homogenous society. While American society is often oblivious to differences and tensions among various Latino and Hispanic communities, the Latina detective plays a powerful role in exploring the specificities of cultural difference and divergent colonial legacies. Typically, the acknowledgement of differences between Latino and Hispanic communities as well as within a given Latino community plays a role in the Latina detective's orientation to her investigation. A sense of "psychic restlessness," "cultural collision" (Anzaldúa 78) or "cultural schizophrenia" (Gaspar de Alba 106) often troubles the Latina detective; this anxious awareness of cultural difference also informs her methods of analysis and detection.

Chicana feminist Gloria Anzaldúa's concepts of borderlands and the new *mestiza* (the trans-cultural woman at the border of two or more cultures) shed light on the investigative methods of the Latina-American detective persona. In her work, Anzaldúa celebrates the new angles of vision that hybridity enables, from the location/dislocation of border-crossing women (Mack-Canty 167). The new *mestiza* "has a plural personality, she operates in a pluralistic mode" (Anzaldúa 79). What Anzaldúa observes of the new *mestiza* might also be applied to the Latina detective and her methods of detection:

> Rigidity means death. Only by remaining flexible is she able to stretch the psyche horizontally and vertically. *La mestiza* has to shift out of habitual formations; from convergent thinking, analytical reasoning that tends to use rationality to move toward a single goal (a Western mode), to divergent thinking characterized by movement away from set patterns and goals and toward a more whole perspective, one that includes rather than excludes. (79)

According to Colleen Mack-Canty, the new *mestiza* is "politically cognizant of what goes on in these different 'worlds' and therefore is capable of seeing matters from many different angles, challenging the dualistic thinking inherent in Western political thinking" (Mack-Canty 167). Her "differential consciousness," as Chéla Sandoval ("*Mestizaje*" 358) puts it becomes a method of investigation, a "movement between and among ideological positionings" ("Feminist" 217).

In terms of narrative structure, the Latina detective novel is a hybrid form, reflecting the influences of American crime fiction and Latino modes of storytelling. Just as feminists such as Anzaldúa and Moraga blend together stories and myths (*cuentos* and *mitos*), testimonial narrative (*testimonio*), and automythography (*automitografía*), the Latina detective novel relies on blended modes of narration and detection. The Latina detective's pluralistic investigative method as a witness and investigator are similarly hybrid. *Testimonio* refers to a first-person narrative told by a witness who is moved to narrate by the urgency of a situation (e.g. war, oppression, revolution, and so on) (Yúdice 4). Emphasizing popular oral discourse, the witness portrays his or her own experience as representative of a collective situation, though often the narrative presented is mediated by someone who transcribes or questions what the witness has to say because the witness is either illiterate or not a professional writer (Yúdice 4). Generally, the production of the *testimonio* involves the recording and/or transcription and editing of an oral account by an interlocutor who is a journalist, writer, or social activist (Beverley and Zimmerman 173). In the case of the Latina detective, she provides a first-person account of events as well as plays the role of the interlocutor who captures testimonies and gives voice to previously silenced minorities through her narration. By including the stories of witnesses and acting as a witness herself to the transnational experience, the detective engages in a *testimonio* that speaks to Latino concerns generally and addresses American identities as a collective.

Transcending the story of the single self, the Latina detective novel draws on *automitografía*, a narrative form that relies on border crossings as "the essential element in the formation of a radical practice of writing, a process of life writing that links communal truths and personal narrative" (Velasco 326). Quoting Gloria Anzaldúa, Juan Velasco defines *automitografía*: "I write the myths in me, the myths I am and the myths I want to become" (Anzaldúa 71; Velasco 326). Velasco notes that the "use of *mito* (myths) linked to the autobiographical act becomes a powerful way of achieving a new voice for a higher sense of the cultural 'self'" (Velasco 326). In an *automitografía*, the autobiographical act becomes "the performative agent of transformation" (Velasco 326). Though Velasco is particularly interested in the production of Chicano/a identities, one might apply his observations about pre-Columbian configurations of "self" to Latino/a identities more generally: the use of *mito* is "connected to histories of trauma linked to the loss of those cultures, and brings back into the writing the rebirth of the new consciousness" (327). The Latina detective's autoethnographic methods of detection lead her to investigate and analyze hidden and obscured relations between societies and individuals in the Americas. Often, the Latina detective finds that she needs to negotiate New World myths, (post)colonial histories, tales of migration, and varying accounts of American identities in order to solve her cases. In this sense, the Latina detective not only investigates and expresses Latino cultural identities but is also "hot on the heels" of transnational America.

I approach the intersections of gender, ethnicity, and genre in terms of the transnational perspective that the Latina detective persona brings. Her autoethnographic methods of detection focus attention on cross-border relations, flows, and exchanges among and between communities and individuals. Examining how and why she chooses to become a detective is instructive. How do her concerns about the intersections of race, ethnicity, sexuality, religion, the (post)colonial, and the transnational shape her investigative methods and questions? Postcolonial feminist theorists (including third-world feminism and Chicana feminism in particular) call attention to the "double colonization" of women through patriarchy and conquest. In her investigations of both past and present, the Latina detective explores the residual presence of the colonial in postcolonial societies. She recounts colonial interventions, examines shifting borders in the history of colonial and postcolonial America, and interrogates more recent episodes of neo-colonial intervention on the part of the United States in some Latin countries. Varying accounts of modernity, differing gender norms, and diasporic identities introduce complex pressures and possibilities for the Latina who sometimes experiences a sense of belonging to two different worlds or feels that she belongs to none at all. She pays attention to the economic, cultural, and social flows across real and imagined borders, which continue to shape the transnational identification of various Latino communities. In the process of solving her case, she identifies, explores, and maps the mythical and imagined spaces of a new-world consciousness shaped by personal migration histories and collective experiences of American transnationalism.

Translating the Latino Borderlands of America

Salvadoran-born Romilia Chacón makes her début in Marcos M. Villatoro's *Home Killings* as a rookie detective who has recently moved from Atlanta to join the Nashville police force. Psychically restless, Romilia is an ambivalent figure whose migration history and role as both outsider and insider provide the opportunity to investigate the complicated dynamics of Latino-American identities and cultural collisions. Multiple intimate histories of violence, loss, and trauma in El Salvador and the United States shape her desire to be become a detective. Romilia's family fled death squads in Central America and migrated to the United States. Romilia's husband died in an accident, leaving her to take on the role of sole economic provider for her family, including her mother and son. Romilia's older sister, Catalina, is murdered by a serial killer in Atlanta. Romilia describes herself as driven by "obsessive vengeance" (vii) to find her sister's killer; this passion plays a decisive role in her choice of profession. She says that she plays the game, follows the rules, and jumps through all of the hoops (vii), keeping her anger in check, until she can confront the killer and obtain vengeance. Following in her father's footsteps as a person who fought for justice in society, she becomes a police officer.

Numerous tensions and anxieties surface for the Latina detective who is torn between conflicting private interests and public duties and alliances. In part, Romilia becomes a police officer because (like many in the Latino community) she does not trust the police to pursue justice on behalf of her sister. The police hire her because of her ability to speak Spanish and liaise with the Latino community: "to question in that language, to gaze in and see if the suspect from the other culture was lying or being truthful" (191). As a translator and cultural interpreter for the police, Romilia becomes a kind of *La Malinche* figure (the derogatory name assigned to Malintzin Tenepal, the Aztec translator for Hernán Cortés) who embodies the ambiguities of the translator as traitor. She gains the trust of Latinos in the community because she speaks Spanish, but loses it shortly after when she breaks cultural codes, such as when she behaves like a *gringa* who departs quickly after she gets the information she needs (47) or "snitches" on the identity of an informant, *Gato Negro*. At the same time, her skills as a cultural interpreter and translator are essential to her success as a detective. For example, Romilia correctly guesses the computer password of a Latino murder victim (*pendejo* literally means "pubic hair," but is typically used to refer to someone as a complete idiot), which allows her to gain access to the victim's files. In another instance, she reads a suspect "the Miranda" (the legal rights to which someone is entitled when arrested) in Spanish (191). As an officer of the law, she experiences a double sense of alienation in relation to the Latino community and mainstream American society. Yet, her role as a detective and investigator depends on full participation in both worlds.

W.E.B. Du Bois's concept of double consciousness, which he used to describe the African American sensibility, might also apply to Romilia, who often looks at herself through the eyes of others. Her double role as an investigating subject and a subject under investigation comes to the foreground in the opening of the novel as she examines the crime scene and her own Latina image, seeking clues that will enable her to decipher the meanings of both. Heading to the scene where the corpse of a Latino journalist has been discovered, she is conscious of her position as "one of two or three women in the area" (2), causing her to hesitate in asserting her position as the chief investigating officer. As one of the police officers "gives her the once over," she recalls his comment from a few days earlier, "Check out the lady in red" (2). She reflects that her mother would not scold the man for his lewd comment but her for her appearance, which is "*Demasiado* sexy, *hija*" (3). Internally, she responds, "I was a homicide detective, not a damned debutante who waited on her fifteenth birthday at the church doors for the perfect man to come by and sweep her away. I'm a Latina, but damned if I'll be that Latina" (3). She chooses a third way, carved out of a double resistance to stereotypes of Latina femininity, namely an angry rejection of the virginal image of the Latina that her mother seems to expect and a refusal to fall into the stereotype of the hot-blooded Latina. When a police officer mispronounces the Latino name of the murder victim, she corrects him in her "clipped Salvadoran accent," which made "his very voice sound stupid" (4). The police officer responds, "Not like we need to practice our Spanish here in Nashville" (4). Romilia's anger surfaces when the police officer starts issuing orders that are "hers to give." She thinks, "It was time to show him the size of my spiked heel" (9). Through inner monologue and internalized dialogues, the reader discovers "the anxiety of Latina representation" caused by her "plight of identity" as the Latina detective constructs her identity in resistance to traditional Latin femininities as well as stereotypical, American male prejudices (Suárez 117–18).

At the same time, Romilia takes on a mediating role in the narration of transnational America and its Latino cross-border relations. She examines cultural, economic, and migrant flows to (and within) the United States and comments on the country's often fluid relations to Mexico, Central America, and South America. She acts as an interpreter who constantly traverses the borders between white, mainstream American identity and a more pluralistic vision of society. Linguistically, she switches between English- and Spanish-speaking worlds and interprets the meaning of Spanish words for an English audience. Her work as an interpreter serves to reinforce a sense of cross-border flows and relations within the United States, and draws the English reader closer to the Spanish-speaking, Latino communities of America. Moreover, through her investigation, the reader learns about migrant Latino communities in cities such as Atlanta and Nashville. In Atlanta, Romilia observes, "I had been able to lose myself in my own people, like I'd stepped over the border without having to carry a passport" (17). By contrast, Nashville has a smaller, but growing Latino community:

> In the past few years more Latinos had moved into the Nashville area, many of them migrants working on the horse farms surrounding the city. Others worked the usual crops: tomatoes, tobacco, a few corn crops. Construction crews had also brought numerous Latinos into the city. The necessary equipment for survival—*taquerías*, little Mexican markets, immigration paper selling—brought in the workers' relatives. Whole families left Guanajuato and Monterrey and Usulután and El Petén to settle down in little towns called Crossville, Carthage, Clarksville, Shelbyville. (16)

Romilia bears witness to an America where Latinos of Mexican, Guatemalan, and Salvadoran origin come together and transform culture, language, and communities. Places such as Crossville and Clarksville have been reinterpreted, socially and culturally, through Latino presence in America.

Furthermore, the identities of murder victims, witnesses, and possible suspects reflect the heterogeneous aspects of the Latino community. The first murder victim, Diego Sáenz, a bilingual journalist from Iowa who speaks English like Tom Brokaw and Spanish like he is from Mexico, writes columns in both English and Spanish because he wants to share his insights about the Hispanic community with English-speaking Americans (21). A witness, nicknamed *Gato Negro*, is a child of Mexican descent who speaks with a Southern accent (37); he overcomes his fear of the police to tell the Salvadoran-born Romilia that Tekún Umán, a.k.a. Rapahel Murillo, is setting up a drug dealing business in the area (38). Murillo is a suave, cosmopolitan figure of considerable wealth. As a philanthropist who runs shelters for the homeless and a drug dealer who is involved in trafficking cocaine from Guatemala and heroin from Haiti to the United States, he is a highly ambivalent representative of transnational America (43). The son of a Guatemalan father and American mother, this *mestizo* refers to himself as "a true Latino southerner" (55). Looking at his photo, Romilia notes that he does not appear to be Latino, but then reminds herself that Latinos come in all "shapes, sizes, and shades" (40). Similarly, a character nicknamed Pajarito is described as Tex-Mex; "his skin and his cheekbones showed his strong Mexican descent" (46). Romilia observes that there is "no real defining the look of Latinness" (40). Overall, the murder investigation offers a complex view of Latino communities in the Southern states, which are composed of peoples with varied migrant histories, hybrid identities, and often uneasy relations to mainstream American society.

As a suspect in the case and potential romantic interest, Murillo plays an important role in the investigation, directly and indirectly encouraging Romilia to explore aspects of Latino identities in relation to wider social contexts. Murillo's nickname, Tekún Umán, refers to a Quiché warrior prince in the Mayan nations of Guatemala who died during hand-to-hand combat with the colonizer Don Pedro de Alvarado in the early 1500s (55). Murillo's Guatemalan heritage, role as a drug dealer, and mythological nickname make him a suspect in the investigation because of clues that link the crime to pre-Columbian cultural history as well as more recent histories of violence in Guatemala. Jade pyramid statues, possibly from Guatemala and of Mayan origin, are found in the mouths of the murder victims. Ritual cuttings on the corpses resemble the handiwork of Guatemalan death-squad members. Internet research reveals that ex-*kaibil* (Guatemalan Special Forces) members migrated to Mexico and that some of these individuals moved on to the United States and took over gang territories by using highly specialized torture and killing techniques in order to gain power. An online article about *kaibil* attacks includes a photo of a dead body with the word *communista* carved into it. As Murillo appears to have used this same method of inscription to carve the word *soplón* (snitch) into Gato Negro's body, there appears to be a strong circumstantial case against the drug trafficker (138). A local newspaper reveals that "kaibil" is an indigenous word from Guatemala meaning "warrior" (178), which also seems to point to Murillo, who is known by the nickname of a legendary warrior figure from the region of present-day Guatemala. Articles linking mythology and transnational criminal flows cause terror among the local Nashville population, leading some citizens to call for the deportation of all Latinos or Hispanics (179). Public debates, private investigations, media reports, internet activity, and the police investigation reflect anxieties about transnational criminality. Racial divisions emerge along the lines of "white and black against brown" (182). The investigation of transnational crimes calls attention to anxieties about Latino presence in American society.

The police investigation leads Romilia to delve into personal histories of migration and violence. When Romilia takes her case photos home, her mother discovers images of what appears to be a ritual murder. Reminded of similar and more extreme acts of violence in El Salvador (69), she begs her daughter to leave the police force and distance herself from violence. However, Romilia reminds her that violence is also part of their experience in American society and cannot simply be left behind (70). Romilia's transnational connections to crime through her migrant background come to the foreground of the investigation when she tracks down what the word "kaibil" has to do with the seemingly ritualistic aspects of the murder. Romilia believes the word is associated with Central American Indians, but is not sure until she confronts one of Murillo's associates in a Chicano store while shopping with her mother. When her mother overhears the word "kaibil," she faints; when revived, she reveals that Romilia's grandparents were killed by the *kaibil*, a Guatemalan death squad unit that trained with the Salvadoran army (132–4). For the Latina detective, transnational histories and experiences of violence converge in unexpected ways. Automythographic detective methods disclose hidden facets of the Latina detective's complex transnational identity. Moreover, by investigating previously unknown aspects of her history and culture, she gains knowledge and builds skills in detection that are essential to solving the case.

Romilia's personal cross-cultural, transnational experiences teach her to resist binary interpretations and interrogate the ambiguous borderlands that shape a sense of identity, criminality, and justice. Murillo is a drug dealer, but not a ritual serial killer. Murillo carved the word *ladrón* (thief) on police officer Jerry Wilson's stomach when he discovered that Jerry had skimmed off money from his drug dealing business. Murillo is not, however, responsible for the ritualistic Latino murders under investigation. Instead, Jerry committed these crimes, killing a doctor, a nurse, a Latino journalist, and a witness; he planted the Jade pyramids and introduced other false clues of Guatemalan origin in order to frame Murillo and conceal his own criminal activities. These misleading clues take the form of a "red herring" and divert attention away from the truth about the murderer's identity. Crucially, Romilia's role as an interpreter proves essential to her success in solving the crime. During the act of translating an interrogation between Jerry and a Latino suspect, she learns that Jerry knows the Jade statue had been placed in the shattered head of one of the victims. As this is a fact that only the killer would have known, she correctly identifies Jerry as the murderer. Significantly, Romilia's success as a detective depends on her ability to investigate crime from a hybrid, multiply-situated perspective. A *mestiza* figure who occupies the borderlands of culture and identity, the Latina detective is able to see beyond the prejudices, stereotypes, myths, ethnic divisions, and anxieties about otherness that trouble American society. She scrutinizes the evidence carefully rather than relying on pre-determined notions of culpability and truth.

Just as the Latina detective gains insight through hybrid methods of investigation, the crime novel's transcultural blend of modes of detection and genres of narration enables a wide-ranging reclamation and analysis of previously hidden or unacknowledged aspects of transnational America. Autoethnographic discourses and interpretive practices reinforce the need to translate anew and negotiate continuously the multiplicities of American identities. The tendency to scapegoat the ethnic other is linked with deception and murder and, as such, comes to symbolize the moribund, even criminal, tendencies of a society where ethnic divisions and prejudices persist. At the same time, cross border drug trafficking and the migration of violence are depicted as social issues that warrant closer attention. Appropriately, the novel ends with a reminder of the transnational flows of American society. While recovering in the hospital from a near fatal wound to the neck, Romilia receives news of Murillo's escape, presumably to Guatemala. This news comes in the forms of a package containing a love letter and a diamond ring to which she responds angrily. She rails against the possibility of living in a world where crime knows no boundaries: "when the killers of another time and place had supposedly followed us to our new home" (246). For Romilia, the case highlights the fragility of American multiculturalism: a murder in the Hispanic community turns the "entire city" against "my own people" (246). Moreover, the case has thrown her mother into a "painful, unnecessary past" (246). Although Romilia observes that "it had all been a lie," the story of her investigation uncovers important truths about the transnational individual, family, community, and nation. The novel closes with a happy vision of a Latino-American family enjoying a meal of *tamales*, watching TV together, and lamenting the difficulty of finding a channel with *telenovelas*. This reference to the Latino soap opera is indicative of this novel's status as an episode in a continuous narrative, which unfolds in *Minos* and *A Venom Beneath the Skin*. Appropriately, this intimate scene serves as a reminder of the transnational flows, both positive and problematic, that shape the everyday realities of life in America.

Pre-Columbian Myths and Postcolonial Stereotypes

The third novel in the Gloria Damasco series, Lucha Corpi's *Black Widow's Wardrobe*, represents another instance of cultural and textual hybridities through the intermixed genres of the detective novel and *automitografía*. Gloria, a veteran of the Chicano civil rights movement, has a "dark gift" or the ability to glimpse the future through her dreams or nightmares, which serves her well in her work as a private investigator. When she discovers that someone wants to murder

Licia Lecuona (a.k.a. "The Black Widow"), her investigation draws her into an interrogation of colonial, patriarchal history. In many ways, the novel can be seen as a response to Anzaldúa's feminist histories of *La Llorona* (the woman who weeps for her lost or murdered children) and *La Malinche* in *Borderlands*, which seek to demonstrate the ways in which Chicanas and indigenous women were mistreated by colonizers and miscast by colonial history. From the outset of the novel, the borderland between myth and mystery proves problematic for Gloria as she seeks to explore the connections between dream and reality. Driven by visions of horror, she seeks to intervene in history and change its outcome through her investigative actions. The opening of the novel offers a number of unsettling perspectives and visions of the Black Widow, including a woman's first-person testimonial account of spousal abuse (presumably by the Widow), a fictional account of the Widow, Gloria's dream, and the story of the first encounter with the Widow herself. This plurality of viewpoints sets the stage for the investigation, which is very much concerned with the ways in which history is constructed and might be contested.

The first encounter with the Widow takes place on the Day of the Dead and establishes a mythical framework of interpretation. This Chicano celebration brings together American and Mexican symbols of nationhood as well as colonial and postcolonial cultural references. Participating in the Procession of the Dead, Gloria, her mother and her daughter see "Don Mariano Tapia and his *matachines*—dancers in Aztec dress—and Mexican *charros* on horseback, wearing death masks over their faces" (1). Two horsemen, each holding an American and Mexican flag, flank a horseman who carries a banner of the Virgin of Guadalupe. In turn, this group is framed by policemen on horseback who are there to patrol the event. Taking part in the procession is a woman whose identity becomes the subject of the mystery. Described as a "tragic Aztec princess" and a "brown murderess" (3), Licia Lecuona is also identified as *La Llorona*, "the centuries-old Mexican legend of the woman who drowned her children and whose soul had been condemned to roam the world eternally in search of them" (6). Later that evening, Gloria sees horsemen attack Lecuona, an event she describes as follows: "As the riders passed under the windows, I realized that they were not wearing San Francisco police uniforms. They were dressed as conquistadors. It was as if we had been caught in a time warp" (7). The mysterious Lecuona functions as an imaginary border crosser who traverses the divide between past and present as well as negotiates relations among Mexican, Chicano, and American identities. Later it turns out that only Gloria and the Widow have witnessed the presence of the conquistadors. Both detective and murderess/victim transgress spatial and historical borders, entering worlds of symbolic consciousness. For Gloria, this unreasoned entry into the other world is an act of clairvoyance while for the Widow it is a manifestation of her belief that she is the reincarnation of *La Malinche*. This highly symbolic and mythical presentation of Lecuona sets the stage for the later events in the novel when Lecuona literally crosses the borders in a flight to Mexico. In pursuing the investigation and the flight of the Widow across borders from California to Mexico,

Damasco comes to view history through a borderlands perspective that takes into account both present and past as well as the cross-border flows that economically, historically, and imaginatively shape the California-Mexico border region.

Myth represents a particularly powerful form of borderland narrative because it is "not synonymous with lie or untruth, but a symbolic representation of what is held to be true by the group generating the narrative" (Bruce-Novoa 106). Potentially, myth contains mysterious counter-histories and communal truths: it offers clues about the veiled past, encodes alternative ways of narrating history, and offers veiled interpretations of identities and facts. Yet, myth is not presented as a site of pure truth but instead as an opaque account of identity that requires critical interrogation. Ralph Rodriguez remarks that "Corpi's ambivalence marks a rupture with any notion of a totalizing, mythic memory that would unproblematically take recourse to the past to construct a homogenous Chicana/o identity" (165). Gloria is not content to accept myth as a submerged communal truth that need only be decoded in order to learn the truth about the past and present; she scrutinizes the contexts that lead to mythical discourses and questions the ways in which myth is both encoded and decoded.

Through her investigation into Lecuona's mythical identities and beliefs in reincarnation, Gloria uncovers a wider set of interpretations and interpretive practices linked to *mestiza* identities. Lecuona's belief that she is the reincarnation of Doña Marina is situated within a wider context of choices concerning Latina femininities. A Chicana makes the point that fantasies about reincarnation reveal deeper desires and anxieties about Latina femininities when she says, "I'd love to come back as a tall redhead with green eyes like Maureen O'Hara's, and the smarts of Gloria Steinem. Wishful thinking?" (17). As part of her investigation, Gloria consults a reincarnation specialist who speaks in Spanish, English, and Nahuatl languages, identifying in Gloria the twin presence of "*el tecolete*—the owl, whose knowing eyes see in all directions—and of *la zorra* – the fox, a crafty hunter" (55). As a detective, Gloria is assigned a predatory but beneficent role: she tracks down and seizes her prey in order to rescue the quarry and society from danger. Gloria comes to see reincarnation as a process of interpretation, self-knowledge, and transformation: "When we gain the knowledge of who we have been and what we have done, change can be effected in our present life" (51). Although she is not a believer in reincarnation, Gloria finds value in the notion of past lives as an imagined means to recover attributes of a multifarious identity. Personally and professionally, Gloria embraces automythographic methods as a means to connective inquiry, self-articulation, and symbolic rebirth.

The criminal investigation entails a quest for a new kind of postcolonial, transnational feminist hermeneutics. Postcolonial feminist perspectives emerge when Gloria uncovers the mysterious identities of Lecuona through colonial and postcolonial American, Mexican, and indigenous myths and histories. Although Gloria dismisses the superficial similarities between Tenepal (*La Malinche*) and Lecuona as women involved in loveless marriages to Spanish men who squandered their fortunes, her volunteer research assistants decide to investigate the connections between colonial experience and Chicana feminist history (72–3). This research prompts Gloria to observe "we Chicanos were proud of our heritage, but had little idea what our heritage was all about" (83). Gloria becomes a spokeswoman for *La Malinche*, referring to her as "a complex woman" and "the most maligned and misunderstood woman in the history of Mexico" (85). Solving the mystery of *La Malinche*'s disappearance and death entails the deconstruction of postcolonial femininities and serves as a linchpin to understanding the mystery of Lecuona. The word "chingada" is a term of insult applied to *La Malinche* by Octavio Paz in *Labyrinth of Solitude*. Corpi corrects this "historical distortion of Malintzin Tenepal" (Dicochea 82) in tracing the word's etymological and historic origins to the Indian woman raped by the conqueror (86). Through Gloria, Corpi critiques male colonial history, "from Bernal Díaz and other witnesses during the conquest, to López Gómara, Hernán Cortés' biographer" (97). Feminist postcolonial history is celebrated for giving "Mexicanas and Chicanas a better sense of themselves, not *las hijas de la chingada*—the Indian woman violated and subjugated by the conqueror—but as *las hijas de La Malinche*—the daughters of an intelligent woman who had exercised the options open to her and chosen her own destiny" (97). Similarly, hegemonic interpretations of *La Llorona* are contested throughout the novel. Manuel Ramos notes: "The ancient tale of the woman who murdered her children and was forced to cry forever along riverbanks […] is completely reworked in Corpi's novel: the children are the possible murderers of their mother, and it is they who must suffer the consequences" (164). Lecuona is a reincarnation of mythical femininities but in an altered, subversive form, suggesting that she is a victim of oppression, fighting to defend herself, rather than an agent of evil. Neither *la mala mujer* (the bad woman) nor *la buena mujer* (the good woman), Lecuona is a complex person whose life history and identity are shaped by the disjunctive power dynamics that inform (post)colonial femininities.

Lecuona's tale serves to open a mythical borderland space for exploring Latino, Chicano/a and mestizo/a identities. When Lecuona flees to Mexico, Gloria and an assistant Latina detective, Dora Saldaña, pursue her across the borders. This part of the narrative opens up a wider dialogue about transnational identities. For example, when asked why it is important for Chicanos to be accepted by Mexicans, Dora explains:

> We Chicanos are like the abandoned children of divorced cultures. We are forever longing to be loved by an absent neglectful parent—Mexico—and also to be truly accepted by the other parent—the United States. We want bicultural harmony. We need it to survive. We struggle to achieve it. That struggle keeps us alive. (147–8)

Similarly, Tepoztecos (indigenous people who inhabit the Tepoztlán area and have done so since pre-Columbian times) are described as "children of opposing cultures, always struggling to keep our cultural equilibrium" (149). Lecuona's history, which is tracked through space and time, calls attention to the recurring motif of the abandoned child in (post)colonial Latino history. Sold into slavery by her step-mother, *La Malinche* is abandoned; her own child is neglected and disinherited following her death (95–6). Lecuona's children are also taken from her when she goes to prison. These events take on symbolic and mythic proportions in relation to the larger contexts of Mexican and Chicano history: children are depicted as struggling to be recognized and accepted within a trans-cultural family. The investigation reveals that Latinos, Chicanos, and *mestizos* inhabit a fluid concept of home, often at odds with contemporary national borders. They inhabit places and spaces that have "been deeply affected by cultural memory and signification" (Embry 325). Through the Latina detective's investigation, shifting borderlands and cartographies throughout history are evoked, which serve to disrupt reified concepts of nationhood. Communities are defined through exchanges and flows that do not necessarily fit within legally defined borders. Simultaneously, the narrative disrupts hegemonic accounts of history as constructed according to national mythologies or colonial conquests, suggesting the need to trace and analyze people's lived relationships to territory through time.

Ultimately, Lecuona's identity is presented as enigmatic (190) and unresolved through a case that uncovers multiple ways of constructing relationships to the colonial and pre-Columbian past. As in *Home Killings*, the investigation uncovers the truth behind the appearance of pre-Columbian artifacts and myths. Just as the presence of Mayan figures turned out to be a cover for drug-related crimes in *Home Killings*, the presence of pre-Columbian goods turns out to be a cover for drug smuggling in *Black Widow's Wardrobe* (174). In both instances, the investigator accumulates knowledge about pre-colonial and colonial histories in order to get to the truth about the transnational realities of the present. Nonetheless, certain truths about identities remain entangled with myth and therefore difficult to decipher. For instance, Lecuona's double death in two places and times is unresolved. Gloria believes that Lecuona commits suicide as a result of her belief that she is the reincarnation of *La Malinche*. Some time later, witnesses testify to seeing the widow trapped inside a burning house. This second deathly apparition fulfils Gloria's dream of witnessing a woman burn to death and doing nothing to help her. The confluence of dream and reality, truth and mythology, defies a single-minded interpretation of the truth.

To solve the case, Gloria relies on the help of professional and non-professional investigators, incorporating multiple views and skills in order to see the case through to completion. This network of witnesses and investigative figures produces a pluralistic perspective that reflects the psychic landscape of the Latina detective's own new *mestiza* identity. Donna M. Bickford describes Damasco's method of investigation as an example of "epistemological parataxis": "Gloria demonstrates an ability to hold two or more potentially opposing positions in her mind at the same time, and operate as though all of them, or none of them, are true" (97). However, I see this ability as directly related to her hybrid Latina identity and postcolonial feminist interpretive praxis. In response to Chicana feminists' meditations on the figures of *La Malinche*, the Virgin Mary, and *La Llorona*, Corpi offers Damasco, a woman who shows a pragmatic readiness to pursue, investigate, and interrogate myths, histories, personal narratives, and non-rational phenomena. Relying on automythographic methods of detection, she uncovers non-violent forms of agency that enable multifarious articulations of transcultural, postcolonial identities. As in Villatoro's *Home Killings*, the Latina detective succeeds in solving her cases because she is able to track the cross-border flows of violence and offer new contexts for interpreting the hidden relations between personal narratives, myths, testimonial evidence, and communal histories.

Postcolonial Treasures meet Post-Castro Fantasies

In Carolina Garcia-Aguilera's *Havana Heat*, Lupe Solano travels from Little Havana in Miami to Havana, Cuba in a plot that focuses on the flows of peoples and commodities to and throughout the Americas. Lupe's *automitografía* takes the form of a first-person narrative investigation into the Cuban diasporic mythologies of home and exile as she seeks to recover an artwork dating to the colonial period and solve several murders. This Cuban-American detective lives in Miami and embraces her Latina femininity with a vengeance. Her first-person account of events includes references to Cuban cuisine, art, superstitions, and culture, including terms and names such as *café con leche*, *mojitos*, *arroz con pollo*, *mariquitas*, *santería*, *lavado*, Wilfredo Lam, Amelia Pelaez, Tomas Sanchez, Antonia Eiriz, and so on. Through her, the reader gains entry into various Cuban locales and areas in Miami, including the luxury area of Cocoplum she loves and the community of Hialeah ("La ciudad del progreso" or the city of progress) which she hates (198). Like Gloria and Romilia, Lupe embodies a new *mestiza* consciousness, explores borderlands and boundaries, and offers a transcultural perspective. However, her borderlands experience as a "Cuban exile" is grounded in a wealthy, elitist Cuban-American worldview that differs from Gloria's leftist, feminist perspective and Romilia's attentiveness to a wide spectrum of Latino minority issues. The child of upper middle-class parents who fled Cuba during the first wave of migration following Castro's rise to power, she has grown up as a member of a conservative family and community that are awaiting Castro's death or downfall in order to return home. Nonetheless, her success as a detective depends on her ability to engage in dialogue with a myriad of Cuban-exile perspectives and uncover explanations that often confound the ones to which she is accustomed.

Lupe's feminism reflects her position as a Cuban-American, blending elements from both parts of her hyphenated identity. She values humor and glamor, embracing a postfeminist attitude that is reminiscent of Carrie Bradshaw from *Sex and the City*. Concerned with clothing and fashion, she often makes comments such as the following: "I might be a liberated woman who wears a gun as comfortably as a handbag, but I also appreciate a compliment" (4). At the same time, Lupe is heir to what Adriana López calls the "special problem" of "Latina feminists" as she has to confront "*maríanismo*, the counterpart of *machismo*, which is still deeply embedded in our culture" (72). López asks: "Whose crazy idea was it to name all their daughters after the Virgin Mary and not expect them to grow up with some kind of sexual neurosis?" (73). *Maríanismo* plays an important role in shaping Lupe's sense of femininity, particularly as her mother has named each of the three daughters (Fatima, Lourdes, and Guadalupe) after sightings of the Virgin Mary. While Lourdes is a nun, Lupe, despite the fact that she wears religious icons pinned to her bra, seems to have appropriated machismo as a form of libratory feminism, a perspective that is evident in the opening paragraph of *Havana Heat*:

> I should have been born a man. I think like one, I act like one, I live my life like one. As a private investigator for the last eight years, I've worked in a field dominated by men. The men I've worked with, as well as the men I have been involved with, have always tried to ascertain who is the real Lupe Solano. Eventually they all discover that I have two sides: a gentle, feminine veneer that I display when I need to, and the ruthless heart and soul of a man underneath. (1)

Rather than engaging in "self-sacrifice and the rejection of pleasure"—aspects typical of the "María Paradox" according to Rosa María Gil and Carmen Inoa Vásquez—Lupe embraces hedonism, indulges her gourmand (and gourmet) appetites, and uses sexuality as a lure to acquire the favors or information she seeks (López 73). As a "macho" Latina detective, she takes center stage rather than living in the shadow of men (another aspect of *maríanismo*). The trope of the wisecracking detective serves as a vehicle for a ludic postfeminist identity as is evident when she considers asking a nun (a former teacher), "Sister, do you think that the Catholic queen and Columbus wanted to get it on, and that was why she backed him on his trips to the New World?" (33). On another occasion, when confronted with the risk of landing in a Cuban prison, she jokes that she might be able to lose weight (96). The role of detective is liberating and yet enables her to fulfill one aspect of the María Paradox: immersing herself in service to others, albeit for pay. Lupe is a "postmodern Latina feminist" with *duende* or a passion for politics, living well, enjoying her Latina inheritance, pursuing a career, enjoying multiple sexual liaisons, and still finding time for her family (López 78). Blurring traditional Latino/a gender roles is an essential, treasured, and liberating part of her identity.

Nonetheless, the opening chapter of *Havana Heat* reveals the extent to which she has internalized Cuban values in ways that are repressive to her. In an effort to impress her extended family, Lupe has corseted and girdled her body so that she can be poured into a Helmut Lang dress. Her feet are pinched inside Manolo Blahnik shoes. She worries about the image of Latina femininity she is presenting, stating: "I knew the Cuban women there would be scrutinizing me like a jeweler looking for imperfections in a stone, searching for evidence that I was letting myself go and that my sleazy profession was catching up with me" (3). The notion of femininity as a jewel is coupled for Lupe with a sense of restrictiveness—she has to be "reined in" physically and socially to conform to the ideals of Cuban beauty (3). Alvaro, her leftist Cuban-American partner of the moment, remarks that she is unusually silent because she is suffocating in her costume, telling her that she should value her own natural beauty without seeking to confine it. Lupe is not the only one who faces pressures to contain her Latina femininity. She observes that the independent-minded bride has switched from virginal white to a fashionable black dress, which clings tightly to her decidedly non-pregnant flat stomach. This change of costume is a concession to the bride's mother who wants to quiet wicked Cuban gossip (5).

As with the other Lupe Solano novels, Lupe's cases come through her connections to the Cuban-American community, whether through love interests or her network of family and friends. At the wedding, the Miranda family approaches Lupe with a case that involves the recovery of a family tapestry dating back to Columbus and now hidden in Cuba. The recovery of the art object foregrounds the intertwined themes of Cuban identity, exile, and transnational relations through Spanish-Cuban-American cultural flows. Family concerns and postcolonial history come together in the quest to recover the eighth missing tapestry from the Hunt of the Unicorn series and return it to its rightful owner. Recollecting that her (now deceased) mother admired these tapestries, Lupe speculates that she looked sad when looking at these art works because "the unicorn reminded her of her charmed life in Cuba before it was forever changed by the revolution" (14), or perhaps she compared "the imprisoned animal to the fate of the people who lived under Castro's regime" (14). When Lucia Miranda discusses the case with her, she begins by presenting a copy of a letter from Cristóbal Colón to her forefather Rogelio Miranda, which documents a gift to them (28). A letter from an expert is also provided, establishing that the eighth Unicorn tapestry is in the Miranda family possession. Lucia Miranda tells a story that entails travels from Spain to Cuba to Miami, which according to Lupe "started five centuries before with Christopher Columbus and ended in my office in Coconut Grove" (31).

At the same time, Lupe takes on two other cases that involve contemporary flows from Cuba to America, namely the traffic in stolen works of Cuban art, both authentic and forged. In one case, brothers Angel and Jesus Estrada are involved in a plot to forge and replace original works of Cuban art that have been seized by the Cuban government. Their plan is to replace the Cuban original with a forgery, which is made by their sister, Camilia, in Cuba, and then to transport the original work of art to America where it can be returned to its rightful owner or sold to another buyer. The brothers are murdered before they can carry out this plan, leaving Lupe to track down the murderer. A second case involves locating Santamaria, a missing dealer of Cuban art works. All three cases converge when Lupe goes to Havana to retrieve the tapestry and meets the art forger, Camilia Estrada. When she and Camilia attempt to transport the tapestry and artworks to Miami, Santamaria, the murderer of the Estrada brothers, confronts them and attempts to steal these treasures. In a struggle to save their lives, Lupe kills Santamaria and then knocks out and kidnaps Camilia to bring her to America, reasoning that Camilia will go to prison if she remains in Cuba. At the intersection of these multiple plots about authentic Cuban cultural commodities, the Cuban beach serves as the literal and symbolic site of multiple criminal flows, past and present, linking the Old World with the New World and Cuba with America.

The investigation tests Lupe's relationship to transnational communities past and present. Notably, her relationship with Alvaro offers the opportunity to explore the complex politics of Miami's diasporic community. Alvaro is a lawyer who advocates moderation and communication with the Cuban government, a controversial position in the Miami community. He is called a traitor, a communist, and a collaborationist on account of these views (200). Her relationship to Barbara is equally important because she represents another vantage point, that of the rural Cuban who migrated to Miami and makes a living through illegal cross-border smuggling of persons and goods from Cuba. In response to their views and experiences, Lupe negotiates her opinions about the politics of the Miami Cuban community and comes to grips with her own position on issues such as migration, the role of Castro, the functions of a democratic society, and theories of Latino/a identity. Lupe observes that "nothing between Cubans was ever simple" (63). Commenting on the 1980 wave of Cuba emigration to America, she observes, "Most had been law abiding citizens, but Castro being Castro, some of the refugees were hard-core criminals set loose from some of Cuba's worst prisons—thus making them America's problem rather than Fidel's" (46). At times, she blames Castro for all that is evil about Cuba, particularly when she emphasizes the emotional impact of migration and exile on families in terms of reunions and separations. In other instances, she is less critical of Castro's Cuba, noting that there are high rates of literacy (157). Entering Cuba, she discusses the geo-political aspects of the 90 kilometer distance from America to Cuba and the laws governing international waters. She takes a critical view of American and Cuban-American perspectives, remarking on the "ill-fated invasion by Cuban exiles at the Bay of Pigs" (157) and the 1996 law intended to "prevent Cuban exiles from launching an attack on Cuba" (239). The flows and shifting borderlands of Cuban history, geography, and identities are rendered meaningful to the reader through their connection to her personal experience or *testimonios* about various Cuban exiles she encounters in the course of her investigation.

Despite her keen awareness of political differences, Lupe posits a biological metaphor that unifies the transnational Cuban body politic: "Cubans in exile and Cubans on the island were separated by geography and politics, but I felt that our hearts beat as one" (212). Lupe observes that Cuban exiles' (she does not refer to herself as Cuban-American) "love, affection and pride for Cuba and being Cuban were not in opposition to their feelings for the United States" (213). The rhetoric of repatriation and homecoming overrides concerns about the legality of her actions as she comes to imagine the return to Cuba as a symbolic return to the womb. The "amniotic fluid that was the essence of the island" sustains and nourishes her (247). She observes that a sense of national pride or "*patria*" "was imbedded in my DNA" (247). Entering Havana, she observes: "I was seeing it. Malecon. Havana. Home" (253). Her decision to enter Cuba illegally and engage in the criminal act of smuggling persons and works of art out of Havana is justified through the rhetoric of return, repatriation, and family reunion. Lupe is on a mission to take the tapestry as well as other government-seized Cuban artworks and return them to their "rightful" owners. Furthermore, through her discussions with the Cuban forger, Irene, the novel highlights the fact that it is not only art but also real estate, sugar, farms, and all kinds of properties that ought to be returned to the "rightful" owners (205).

Nostalgia for a democratic Cuba, which never existed in the particular form Lupe envisions, is accompanied by a desire for a *patria* that might overcome its (post)colonial histories of violence and Castro-era acts of injustice. When Lupe uncovers the murdered corpse of an art appraiser next to the tapestry, she remarks that the "bones were not those of the Taino or Ciboneyes, the original inhabitants of Cuba who had been killed by Spanish colonizers" (265). Instead, this body is the result of a more recent crime committed by the Miranda family, who wanted to keep the tapestry, which was not rightfully theirs. By contrast, the forger Camilia Estrada decides to return the original paintings to the "rightful owners" (273), an act that is seen as liberating "an important part of the country's heritage" (275). Lupe confirms the view that this is an honorable, just decision (275) and as an agent of justice she follows this logic in her decision to return the missing Unicorn tapestry to Spanish authorities. When she discovers that the Miranda family had illegally obtained the tapestry, she deems that it must rightfully belong to Columbus's descendants or to Spain (297) and stages a dramatic handover of the tapestry to the Spanish ambassador.

Issues related to rightful ownership and the meaning of home extend to Lupe's view of Miami as a Cuban-American place where Caucasian Americans are being outnumbered by Latinos and would soon "have to check the box marked 'Other'" on the census (303). Barbara, Lupe's accomplice in recovering the art works, smuggles Cubans to the States and thus serves as an enabling figure in the flows of Cuban peoples and commodities between nations. Imaginatively, Lupe remaps the borders of Miami and her own identity—all the while ignoring legal, national, and territorial limits—in order to bring about justice based on principles of "original, rightful ownership." The ideal, post-Castro Havana to which she imagines returning is a mythical space: a hybrid utopia where Cuban-exile and American socio-political values are mapped onto the culture and geography of Cuba. In seeking to find and recover artifacts of Cuban culture, she investigates and remaps Latino myths of community, nationhood, and transnational identity in the Americas. Despite the fact that she engages in a sentimental rhetoric of return and reunion, her investigation uncovers political and class differences within the Cuban exile community in America, reflecting the differences among generations of migrants. Political differences often prove insurmountable as her experiences with Alvaro and her client demonstrate. Alongside dreams of unity, the realities of division and difference are visible. Lupe bears witness to the highly politicized spaces of transnational tension for Cubans at home and in exile.

To conclude, the Latina detective novel stands as a paradigmatic genre of fiction in transnational America, offering a wide-ranging examination of contested histories, shifting borderlands, and cross-border flows. Specifically, in the cases I have discussed, the presence of pre-Columbian and colonial cultural objects calls attention to the ongoing challenges of migration and transculturation in postcolonial society. Lived and imagined relations between past and present are shown to be in open, often ambiguous, dialogue. As in Dashiell Hammett's *The Maltese Falcon*, the object under investigation opens new lines of inquiry into the aspirations, dreams, and contested interpretations of a world in transition. Whereas the wandering signifier of the falcon statuette focuses attention on the perilous illusion of the American dream, particularly against the backdrop of the Great Depression, the objects and treasures associated with Latino culture call attention to the illusoriness of fixed ideas about borders and identities in America, particularly in today's multicultural society. Whatever her story, the Latina detective discovers that "the struggle to physically, spiritually, and psychologically decolonize bodies and land within the Borderlands" plays an important role in the articulation of transnational America (Hames-Garcia 120). Specifically, Latino/a identities are negotiated through research, analysis, intuition, and acts of narrative synthesis that look to the past, present, and future across borders. At the same time, the Latina detective's ability to negotiate the complexities of her own cross-border identity makes her an able witness to and investigator of American social contexts. Through her automythographic methods of investigation and her acts of gathering testimonial accounts, she discloses transcultural America or what Shelley Fisher Fishkin refers to as "the endless process of comings and goings that create familial, cultural, linguistic and economic ties across national borders" (Fisher Fishkin 24). Uncovering stories of border crossings and rewriting the histories of trans-border relations, she bears witness to a world where concepts of truth and justice are often highly contested. Through her investigations, the Latina detective uncovers the multifarious hidden histories, submerged stories, and fluid borders of transnational America. In an era of transnationalism, the Latina detective's multivalent perspectives and cross-border methods of critical inquiry attest to the complex challenges of living in and interpreting the contemporary world order.

Works Cited

Anzaldúa, Gloria. *Borderlands/La Frontera: The New Mestiza*. San Francisco: Spinsters/Aunt Lute Books, 1987.

Beverley, John and Marc Zimmerman. *Literature and Politics in the Central American Revolutions*. Austin: University of Texas Press, 1990.

Bickford, Donna M. "A Praxis of Parataxis: Epistemology and Dissonance in Luch Corpi's Detective Fiction." *Meridians: feminism, race, transnationalism* 5.2 (2005): 89–103.

Brady, Mary Pat. *Chicana Literature and the Urgency of Space*. Durham and London: Duke UP, 2002.

Bruce-Novoa, Juan. "Chicana/o Theater: Editing the Origin Myth." *Gestos: Toeria y Practica del Teatro Hispanico* 7.14 (1992): 105–16.

Corpi, Lucha. *Black Widow's Wardrobe*. Houston: Arte Público Press, 1999.

Dicochea, Perlita R. "Chicana Critical Rhetoric." *Frontiers* 25.1 (2004): 77–92.

Dilley, Kimberly J. *Busybodies, Meddlers and Snoops*. Westport: Greenwood P, 1998.

Embry, Marcus. "Chicana/o Literature and Voices of a News Chicana/o History." *CR: The New Centennial Review* 1.1 (Spring 2001): 313–31.

Fisher Fishkin, Shelley. "Crossroads of Cultures: The Transnational Turn in American Studies—Presidential Address to the American Studies Association, November 12, 2004." *American Quarterly*. 17–57.

Garcia-Aguilera, Carolina. *Havana Heat*. New York: Avon Books, 2000.

Gaspar de Alba, Alicia. "The alternative grain: Theorizing Chicano/a popular culture." *Culture and Difference: Critical Perspectives on the Bicultural Experience in the United States*. Ed. Antionia Darder. Westport: Bergin and Garvey, 1995.

Hames-Garcia, Michael. "How to tell a *Mestizo* from an Enchirito®: Colonialism and National Culture in the Borderlands." *Diacritics* 30.4 (Winter 2000): 102–22.

"Hispanic Americans by the Numbers." *Infoplease*. 2007. Pearson Education, Inc. <http://www.infoplease.com/spot/-hhmcensus1.html>.

Holmlund, Chris. "Postfeminism from A to G." *Cinema Journal* 44.2 (Winter 2005): 116–21.

James, P.D. *The Murder Room*. London: Penguin Books, 2003.

Lindsey, David. *Mercy*. New York: Bantam, 1991.

López, Adriana. "Funky Women with Duende: Feminism and Femininity." *Hopscotch: A Cultural Review* 2.2 (2000): 70–79.

Mack-Canty, Colleen. "Third-Wave Feminism and the Need to Reweave the Nature/Culture Duality." *NWSA Journal* 16.3 (Fall 2004): 154–79.

Martinez, Michele. *Most Wanted*. New York: William Morrow, 2005.

Mizejewski, Linda. "Dressed to Kill: Postfeminist Noir." *Cinema Journal* 44.2 (Winter 2005): 121–7.

Munt, Sally R. *Murder by the Book? Feminism and the Crime Novel*. London: Routledge, 1994.

Ortega, Mariana. "'New Mestizas,' 'World-Travelers,' and '*Dasein*': Phenomenology and the Multi-Voiced, Multi-Cultural Self." *Hypatia* 16.3 (Summer 2001): 1–29.

Ramos, Manuel. "The Postman and the Mex: From hard-boiled to *huevos rancheros* in detective fiction." *Hopscotch: A Cultural Review* 2.4 (2001): 160–67.

Reddy, Maureen T. "Women Detectives." Ed. Martin Priestman. *The Cambridge Companion to Crime Fiction*. Cambridge: Cambridge UP, 2003: 191–208.

Rodriguez, Ralph E. "Cultural Memory and *Chicanidad*: Detecting History, Past and Present, in Lucha Corpi's Gloria Damasco Series." *Contemporary Literature* 43.1 (2002): 138–70.

Sandoval, Chéla. "Feminist forms of agency and oppositional consciousness: U.S. third world feminist criticism." *Provoking Agents: Gender and Agency in Theory and Practice*. Ed. Judith Kegan Gardiner. Urbana: U of Illinois P, 1995.

——. "*Mestizaje* as method: Feminists-of-color challenge the canon." *Living Chicana Theory*. Ed. Carla Trujillo Berkeley: Third World Press, 1998.

Soitos, Stephen F. *The Blues Detective*. Amherst: U of Massachusetts P, 1996.

Suárez, Lucía M. "Julia Alvarez and the Anxiety of Latina Representation." *Meridians: feminism, race, transnationalism* 5.1 (2004) 117–45.

Velasco, Juan. "*Automitografías*: The Border Paradigm and Chicana/o Autobiography." *Biography* 27.2 (Spring 2004): 313–38.

Villatoro, Marcos McPeek. *Home Killings*. Houston: Art Público Press, 2001.

Walton, Priscilla and Manina Jones. *Detective Agency: Women Re-Writing the Hardboiled Tradition*. Berkeley: U of California P, 1999.

Yúdice, George. "*Testimonio* and Postmodernism." *Latin American Perspectives* 18.3 (Summer 1991): 15–31.

Chapter 10

Walter Mosley's *Devil in a Blue Dress*: The Reforming Spirit of Neo-Noir

Raphaël Lambert

Walter Mosley's debut novel, *Devil in a Blue Dress* (1990), borrows the topoi of traditional hard-boiled fiction and reformulates them through African American culture and values. Mosley's central character, Ezekiel "Easy" Rawlins, is an African American World War II veteran reluctantly drawn into the gumshoe business and repeatedly sucked into a maelstrom of murders, politics, and scandals always related to issues of race. Set in a 1948 Los Angeles steeped in racism, the novel features African American characters' responses to their hostile environment. While the virtuous Easy Rawlins uses his wits and sangfroid to subvert the city's power structure, develop his detective skills, and foster his aspirations toward an uneventful middle-class existence, his homicidal childhood friend Raymond "Mouse" Alexander is more confrontational and expresses his alienation with a devastating do-or-die approach to a system he deems unjust and racist. Strikingly, Mouse's self-justification for his violence echoes that of DeWitt Albright, the dangerous white gangster who hires Easy to track the whereabouts of Daphne Monet. Although Mouse sees the world in black and white and Albright in terms of rich and poor, they both resort to a discourse of oppression to vindicate their criminal activities and present their thirst for wealth and power as a natural outcome of the free-market economy and the corrupt society that spawned them.

At the crossroads of this flawed, dichotomous society stands Daphne, the devil in a blue dress herself. Daphne remains an enigma until Mosley reveals, at the very end of the book, that she is an African American woman passing for white. Only then, in retrospect, can the reader, along with Easy, start unraveling earlier events and information concerning Daphne. At this point, Easy's investigation leaps forward, and the reader, induced to probe his or her own prejudices about race, begins an introspective investigation. While Daphne is a stereotypical tragic mulatto (traumatized, lustful, and deceitful), she also refuses to play by the rules imposed on her by her mulatto status, suggesting that the perception we have of the tragic mulatto figure is a teleology serving the ends of a society based on racial hierarchies. Hence Mosley's tour de force is not so much to turn the reader into a detective as to make the reader discover that the issues of passing and miscegenation become vain the moment we cease to consider them as a problem and learn to see beyond them.

Black Alienation/White Racism

If the California setting in early hard-boiled fiction is, as scholar John Scaggs argues, a "direct extension of the frontier stories of the Western genre" (57), Mosley's *Devil in a Blue Dress* invites us to explore a territory largely overlooked by the pioneers of the genre: the racial frontier. In this perspective, villain DeWitt Albright's cowboy-like entrance in Joppy's bar in the opening paragraph of the novel deepens the metaphor. Joppy's patrons are not dumbstruck because a notorious outlaw has just entered their "saloon" but because the newcomer is a white man. Albright has just crossed the color line into black turf and set the novel in its defining mode: *Devil* is a story in black and white, about blacks and whites—their complex interaction, recurrent dissension, and mutual aversion. *Devil* is also a world upside down where the values and references we usually rely on are inverted. *Devil* gives us more than the picture of an era; it gives us its negative, because it both exposes the egregious nature of race relations in postwar Los Angeles and challenges our perception of the colors black and white.

If conventions have us associate everything black or dark (the night, a dark street, a poorly lit barroom and, of course, black skin) with danger, fear, violence, and any other negative feelings, Walter Mosley, in *Devil*, establishes white as the color of peril, deceit, and brutality. From the first page, the reader is conditioned to react negatively to the color white, as Dewitt Albright's off-white linen suit and shirt, bone shoes, white silk socks, and pale skin give Easy a "thrill of fear" (9). When they shake hands, Easy compares Albright's grip to "a snake coiling around my hand" (10). Albright, it is made clear, is "all white" but not "all right." He is the epitome of whiteness, down to his "big blond desk" (24), "white-leather shoulder holster" (25), "white secretary-type wallet" (28), and "white Cadillac" (63); he is also a scary, vicious, and ruthless individual who immediately awakens Easy's visceral mistrust of white people. Easy's anti-white feelings are sometimes unfounded and drive him to misjudge people, but these views underline his and other black men's alienation in a world where whites are dominant. From the racist detectives Miller and Mason, to the pedophile Matthew Teran, to the child pimp Richard McGee, to Easy's Italian foreman Benny at Champion Aircraft who is "a slaver" (72) running the place like a plantation in antebellum South, to the press that "hardly ever even reported a colored murder" (165), and to the police that "did not care about crime among Negroes" (165), white has replaced black as the color of evil.

Through *Devil in a Blue Dress*, Mosley debunks the California myth of a society free from social and racial discrimination. In postwar Los Angeles, Easy Rawlins soon discovers, blackness is a liability. The imbalance of power between whites and non-whites is as pronounced as anywhere else in the country and often impels Easy to make difficult choices. For instance, Easy is hired by white people to investigate within the black community where whites cannot blend and where they have no access. While Easy's first employer, DeWitt Albright, is a gangster, his employers in several subsequent installments of the series are the police themselves. Film scholar Ed Guerrero, in his portrayal of the Easy Rawlins character, borrows W.E.B. Du Bois's concept of double consciousness whereby the African American individual transforms the affliction of a split identity—"an American, a Negro"—into an advantage. Echoing Du Bois's notion that the African American individual is "gifted with second-sight in this American world" (3), Guerrero argues that Easy "can see deeply into both the black and white worlds and find out not only what powerful whites want to know, but also what they don't want to know, or at least what they want to deny or hide" (40).

Easy's empowerment through his liminal position, however, can turn into an embarrassing dilemma when, forced to work at the behest of the police, he is asked to snoop in his own community. In *White Butterfly* (1992), the third installment in the Easy Rawlins series, the police literally dare Easy to refuse to help them find a serial killer who operates in the black community. In effect, Easy is given *carte blanche*—literally a white card—as long as he cooperates with white authorities. Thus Easy finds himself in a catch-22 situation, as he is compelled to investigate crime in his own African American community on behalf of those who are often viewed as the prime tormentors of that community. Neither a daredevil nor an aspiring lawman, Easy still displays all the qualities Raymond Chandler, in his seminal essay "The Simple Art of Murder" (1944), ascribes to his ideal private eye: "He must be a complete man and a common man and yet an unusual man. He must be […] a man of honor, by instinct, by inevitability" (992). But Easy, for all his integrity, still has to negotiate a very fine line between serving his community and the police in a world where not all citizens are equal before the law. In order not to become the police's stooge inside the ghetto, Easy, more so than his white counterparts, is bound to work by his own rules and, in some cases, become morally compromised.

The deterministic environment that compels Easy to exercise his PI profession in a nondescript zone between crime and legality also affects his ambition to live the life of a modest middle-class American. In *Little Scarlet* (2004), the eighth Easy Rawlins mystery, Easy has managed to create a semblance of a family with his girlfriend Bonnie and their two adopted children Jesus and Feather. Easy's janitorial job at Sojourner Truth High School comforts him in his self-created image of a family man, but it is also a perfect cover to exercise his sleuth trade as well as run his real estate business. This real estate business lies at the heart of *A Little Yellow Dog* (1996) and *Bad Boy Brawly Brown* (2002), respectively the fifth and seventh Easy Rawlins novels set in the early and mid-1960s. In a white-dominated society that will not let a young, up-and-coming African American man achieve social respectability, Easy manages his properties through his frontman Mofass—a dapper, smooth-talking, cigar-chomping, older black man who passes for the man in charge while Easy plays the handyman.

Over the 20 years spanning the Easy Rawlins series—the latest volume, *Blonde Faith* (2007), is set in post-Watts riots 1967—Easy has achieved a certain stability without ever giving in to the irrational response his absurd environment has been relentlessly calling forth.[1] However, each and every Easy Rawlins mystery has borne witness to a distorted social order in which ethnic minorities inevitably lag behind the dominant group and resort to all kinds of expediencies to survive. The frustration that such a flawed system produces is always on the verge of degenerating into deviant behaviors, and Easy's capacity to manage his anger is more an exception than a rule, as the case of Raymond "Mouse" Alexander, Easy's trigger-happy childhood friend, illustrates.

Mouse is an alienated psychopath who is aware of his condition and makes no apology for it. As he tries to coax Easy into teaming up with him as in the past, Mouse declares:

> Nigger can't pull his way out of the swamp wit'out no help, Easy. You wanna hole on to this house and get some money and have some white girls callin' on the phone? Alright. That's alright. But Easy, you gotta have somebody at yo' back, man. That's just a lie them white men give 'bout makin' it they own. They always got they backs covered. (158)

Mouse explodes the founding myth of the American self-made man. The widespread belief that a hard-working individual will eventually be rewarded ("heaven helps those who help themselves" goes the maxim) does not fool Mouse because it does not apply to all, and especially not to African Americans. In his polarized view of the world, Mouse also holds whites responsible for the vicious circle of violence and poverty that plagues his community and individuals like himself. To Easy, who finally yields and takes Mouse in on the condition that Mouse will follow his orders to the letter (i.e., he won't go gun crazy), Mouse sneers: "Whatever you say, Easy. Maybe you gonna show me how a poor man can live wit'out blood" (159). With these words, Mouse justifies, coldly and remorselessly, his own violence. As shocking as Mouse's self-justification is, the remainder of the story proves him right. When Mouse tells Easy, at the end of *Devil*, "a nigger ain't never gonna be happy 'less he accept what he is" (209), Mouse dismisses Easy's aspiration to a middle-class existence because he believes the average African American is never given access to such a way of life. Prefiguring the social pariah and ex-convict Socrates Fortlow—the protagonist of Mosley's latter-day protest novel *Always Outnumbered, Always Outgunned* (1998)—the colorful but dangerous Mouse is Mosley's vehicle to locate the origins of African American crime and violence within American racial and social disparities. From Mouse's point of view, a poor, uneducated black man from the Deep South cannot escape his destiny as a misfit

---

[1] Easy's stability must be qualified. While the latest of the Easy Rawlins mysteries, *Blonde Faith* (2007), suggests that Easy's professional life is in order, his love life is in disarray. Easy is 47 and estranged from his lover Bonnie Shay, who cheated on him with an African Prince, Joguye Cham. To complicate matters, Cham is also the man who saved the life of Easy's 11-year-old adopted daughter Feather by paying for her hospitalization in an exclusive clinic in Switzerland (see *Cinnamon Kiss*, 2005).

and outlaw, and must live accordingly—that is, in Mouse's mind, with one gun in both hands. Mouse's implacable logic is disheartening and cynical, and in a way, Mouse is what Easy is afraid he might become if he yields to a similar anger.

Mouse's impulsive, confrontational response to his hostile environment will never win Easy over. Yet, it is revealing that the impulse to subvert the dominant social order has dawned on Easy not from his experience as a private eye but from his experience as a black man with ambition and talent. It is Easy's experience as a clandestine, yet legal property-owner that has hastened a loss of innocence and helped forge the conviction that there is little hope in a society based on racial prejudice. Easy has to fake poverty and humility, endure verbal and sometimes physical abuse, in order to preserve what he has. Mouse, after all, is not entirely wrong: in a racist society, a black man must learn to stay in his place, and if he does not, he must either fight or lie. By virtue of his blackness, Easy is closer to his friend Mouse than he dares to admit. Easy and Mouse have reached the same conclusions about the society they live in: the black community is discriminated against, kept in abject indigence, and beset with crime. Easy and Mouse only differ in the methods they choose to face their plight. In the end, Easy's dream seems to prevail over Mouse's destructive, nihilistic views since Mouse's assertion that there is no such a thing as a black self-made-man is disproved by Easy who, over time and not without hurdles, has become his own boss both as a private investigator and an undercover entrepreneur. Easy has paid for this success with a relative loss of trust in human nature.

But he has also learned valuable lessons from people, including those he does not trust. In the concluding chapter of *Devil*, Easy confesses to his friend Odell that he is now doing private investigations. When Odell comments that it "sounds like a dangerous business," Easy replies: "I guess. But you know, a man could end up dead just crossin' the street. Least this way I say I earned it" (218). The remark would be casual if Easy's words did not reproduce the words arch-villain DeWitt Albright had used to dismiss Easy's apprehension about the possible dangers of tracking the whereabouts of Daphne: "Easy, walk out your door in the morning and you're mixed up in something. The only thing you can really worry about is if you get mixed up to the top or not" (27).

As a Southern white male, Albright starts with a handicap in his endeavor to convince Easy, a Southern black male, to work for him. The long history of racial strife in the South, added to Albright's thuggish demeanor, raises an instinctual distrust in Easy's mind. To overcome Easy's suspicion, Albright appeals to a common hatred of corporations, banks, police, and the law: "The law [...] is made by the rich people so that the poor people can't get ahead. You don't want to get mixed up with the law and neither do I" (27). Albright lures Easy on not only with good Bourbon and money, but also with rhetoric finely tuned to Easy's sensibility. And Albright polishes off his seduction game as he brings Easy back down South and literally speaks the same language as Easy's: "He [Albright] told me a few stories, the kind of tales that we called 'lies' back home in Texas" (28).

However, more than Easy's language, it is Mouse's language Albright speaks. Earlier, during his job interview with Albright, Easy, for the second time in the story, compares Albright to Mouse: "The way he smiled when he sat back in his chair reminded me of Mouse again. I thought of how Mouse was always smiling, especially when misfortune happened to someone else" (28). Albright and Mouse's similarity, however, reaches beyond their brutal nature and cynicism. On the one hand, Albright and Mouse seem to share a strong concern with social injustice, but while Albright interprets social injustice along class lines (rich vs. poor), Mouse does so along racial lines (white vs. black). In the context of the novel, where whiteness is associated with money and power and blackness with their opposites, Albright and Mouse's respective discourses are essentially the same. But even more striking is how both use social injustice as a justification for their criminal activities. Albright, once a lawyer in Louisiana, tells Easy how he bullied a prosecutor into dropping charges against his client, "a shit-kicker who was charged with burning down a banker's house" (28). Seeing that the client, Leon, was certain to lose his case, Albright went down to the house of the prosecutor, the honorable Randolph Corey, and pulled out his pistol: "All I did was talk about the weather we'd been having, and while I did that I cleaned my gun" (29). And Albright goes on to justify his intimidation with blood-curdling logic: "Shit! Leon was trash. But Randy had been riding pretty high for a couple' a years and I had it in mind that it was time for him to lose a case" (29). Albright concludes with a sense of poetic justice that positions him somewhere between frightening deviousness and insanity: "You have to have a sense of balance when it comes to the law, Easy. Everything has to come out just right" (29).

It will be too late when Easy realizes he was not hired but purchased by Albright, who made him his retainer: "You take my money and you belong to me" (108), Albright says when Easy wants to quit and return the money after Albright and his henchmen have broken into his house. The bond Albright established earlier with Easy is also abruptly severed as Albright, to make clear that he will not be denied nor even challenged, drops the heretofore gentlemanly "Mr. Rawlins" for "nigger" and "boy" as he gets angry at Easy. The plantation patter, meant to debase Easy, turns almost effortlessly to capitalist phraseology: "We all owe out something, Easy. When you owe out then you're in debt and when you're in debt then you can't be your own man. That's capitalism" (109). Albright's definition of capitalism is a gross simplification but it also reveals the limits of capitalist ideology as its Darwinian logic can lead to excesses and generate monsters like Albright and Mouse. Capitalism as understood by Albright is not very different from the one practiced by those at "the top." The only difference, already pointed out to Easy by Mouse, is that those at the top devised a set of rules that has made their power, their money, and their social position lawful and enduring.

Easy never embraces Albright's all-or-nothing vision of the world, but he learns to become independent from those in power, and when he defines what he does at the beginning of *A Red Death* (1991), the follow-up to *Devil*, Easy says he is "in the business of favors" (5), a convenient phrase he borrowed from Albright, who had described his job to Easy thus: "I'm just another fella who does favors for friends, and for friends of friends" (*Devil* 12).

Seeing Beyond and Tearing Down The Veil: The Case of Daphne Monet

Easy's capacity to assume various personalities secures his invisibility and allows him to navigate the treacherous waters of a racist society. He is, to borrow Henry Louis Gates Jr.'s famous terminology, "signifyin(g)" as he resorts to the masking technique favored by the African American trickster figure to outsmart his enemies (Gates 74–7). Yet Easy is not the most protean character of the novel, as Daphne Monet, by virtue of her inherent duality, tricks both Easy and the reader. Through its creation of the Daphne character, the novel itself "signifies," not so much to outwit the reader as to guide them to lucid reflection of what W.E.B. Du Bois called, more than a century ago, "the problem of the color line" in America.

When Easy Rawlins first meets Daphne Monet, he notices her beauty and immediately feels tenderness for her. He finds her vulnerable and wants to put his "arms around her—to protect her" (96). This is the first in a series of misconceptions about Daphne Monet as the seemingly fragile ingénue turns out to be a tough-minded woman who steals money, manipulates strangers, friends, and lovers alike, and unflinchingly resorts to murder when she deems it necessary. By the end of the novel Easy, who has had a torrid affair with Daphne, still has strong feelings for her, but he concludes, "Daphne was death herself" (208). Indeed, Daphne, the devil in a blue dress, brings about mayhem, and in her trail corpses are piling up.

Easy regards Daphne as the devil incarnate as he never really manages either to control or to understand her. Easy first sees Daphne on a photograph Dewitt Albright shows him: "The picture had been black and white originally," Easy notices, "but it was touched up for color like the photos of jazz singers that they put out in front of nightclubs. She had light hair coming down over her bare shoulders and high cheekbones and eyes that might have been blue if the artist got it right" (25). Easy, who narrates the story, is usually keen on minute physical descriptions (especially hair, eyes, and skin color), but when it comes to describing Daphne, he uses a very cautious "might," and this cautious verbal auxiliary still sticks to his description when he meets Daphne for real: "Her face was beautiful […] Wavy hair so light brown that you *might* have called it blond from a distance, and eyes that were either green or blue depending on how she held her head" (96; emphasis added). Later, Daphne's color-changing eyes still puzzle Easy when the two become lovers. Yet these eyes, which Easy can never definitively categorize or fix in a reassuring color, are the most tangible expression of Daphne's complex individuality.

Daphne is a good illustration of the African god Esu-Elegbara, whom Gates describes as the "classic figure of mediation and of the unity of opposed forces" (6) and whose power resides in his mutability. While Easy is able to drop his favored black vernacular for standard English when circumstances demand it, Daphne jumps from one mode of language to the next almost without transition, following her mercurial personality. Between her first phone call to Easy and a visit to the house of her ex-boyfriend, Richard McGee, Daphne switches from a French accent to local street lingo to polished, standard English, whether she intends to seduce, convey anger, or wield authority. Later in the novel, Daphne develops a typically southern "light drawl" (194) as she starts to reminisce about her early teen years in Louisiana. Daphne, Easy finds out, is a chameleon-woman who knows how to adapt to very different milieus and situations. She is strong, resilient, and enterprising, and Easy soon discovers the full-range of her power when she decides, after she bathes and nurses him back to health, to make love to him. She seems to literally metamorphose into a man in front of Easy's eyes: "she sat on the toilet and urinated so loud that it reminded me more of a man" (186). She then stands over the tub and signifies to Easy her role of domination in very crude terms: "If my pussy was like a man's thing it'd be as big as your head, Easy" (186). Coddled in the womb-like ceramic tub of a motel room by a caring, motherly Daphne, Easy, the *homme foetal*, is suddenly thrust in the arms of a *femme fatale* who controls him completely: "I stood out of the tub and let her hold me around the testicles" (186). Although Easy presents himself as the agent of these verbs, his remark leaves very little doubt as to who holds phallic power in this scene.

Daphne remains an enigma for most of the novel. Everything revolves around her, but information about her is too contradictory and scarce for the reader to figure things out. The key to the novel is that Daphne, who looks white, happens to be part African American. She is a mulatto passing for white, the absolute in-between. She looks white but her black ancestry suffices to make her an outcast in a race-based society. In the past, passing mulattos were especially liable to white rage as their whiteness and the subsequent privileges they could enjoy exposed the phoniness of pseudoscientific theories whereby blackness, even in the slightest trace, lowered an individual's status.

After Mouse casually reveals Daphne's mixed heritage, the reader starts piecing together some of the puzzling information about her, starting with her baffling intimacy with the very dark-complexioned Frank Green, a notorious gangster known as "Knifehand" in the underworld. The reader also understands how Matthew Teran, a major contender in the upcoming mayoral election, and Richard McGee, Daphne's former boyfriend, could blackmail Daphne's new boyfriend, wealthy philanthropist Todd Carter, and force him out of the mayoral race: Daphne's blackness, if made public, would ruin Carter's political career. Finally, Daphne's paradoxical explanation for leaving Carter starts making sense: "I do love him and because of that I can't ever see him" (190). Drawing on reader-response theory, scholar Andrew Pepper contends that neo-noir novels "deliberately embrace anxieties and discontinuities in order to open up and draw attention to wider social, economic and political tensions in American society as a whole, and force readers into an active, interpretive role, since meanings are not secured or legitimized within texts themselves" (32). In *Devil*, the hero's quest for truth has become the reader's. The configuration whereby detective fiction not only challenges the readers' imagination but also draws them into a form of detection harkens back to Edgar Allan Poe's "The Murders in the Rue Morgue" (1841) and probably accounts for the genre's popular success ever since.

Devil's originality, however, is that it suddenly compels readers to read the story backward not because their new knowledge of Daphne's biracial identity alters elements of the plot, but because this knowledge urges them to ponder their own moral views and the significance of racial identity in the United States.

The myth of the tragic mulatto is as old as slavery and Mosley engages with it in a way that is clichéd and innovative at the same time. The reader's first reaction after inadvertently learning from Mouse that Daphne is not a white woman is to look back at earlier events in which Daphne's whiteness is particularly significant. In this regard, Daphne's love affair with Easy immediately comes to mind. Part of Easy's infatuation with Daphne is her whiteness (she is a forbidden fruit), and considering the novel's polarization along the axis of white authority and black submissiveness, it is safe to assume that Daphne's phallic authority over Easy comes from her whiteness as well.[2] In retrospect, the revelation underscores Easy's scornful views of interracial relationships since he once suspected Daphne of simply being a white girl who wanted to get "a little nigger-love out back" (191). Daphne herself is affected by the sudden exposure of her secret as she angrily spurns Easy, who still loves her and is ready for a long-term commitment regardless of her mixed heritage. A black man involved with a white woman is a rare occurrence in post-World War II America; 1948, the year the story takes place, was also the year of the landmark case *Perez v. Lippold* in which the California Supreme Court challenged general public opinion and declared unconstitutional a ban on interracial marriage.[3] Mosley, readers realize, has been toying with their own preconceived ideas about miscegenation and has forced them to reconsider

---

2 Examples of the novel's rather Manichean view of race relations abound. Thus, the color white can be an omen: "Big white clouds sailed eastward toward the San Bernardino mountain range" (51) at the very moment Coretta James is being murdered. White is also the portent of death: "Frank's black face cracked into a white grin" (152) when he is about to thrust his knife in Easy's throat. Whiteness is also associated with wealth: "I decided to milk all those white people for all the money they'd let go of" (127), Easy reflects when he realizes people like Carter and Albright throw money his way for a little information about Daphne. And finally, whiteness is synonymous with power: arguing that workers in factories are treated like children by their bosses and that "everyone knows how lazy children are" (69), Easy explains that such infantilization is harder on black than white workers because the latter "didn't come from a place where men were always called boys" (69).

3 In *Perez v. Lippold* (32 Cal. 2d 711, 1948), Peggy Pascoe explains, lawyer Daniel Marshall substituted an issue of religious rights for the expected issue of miscegenation. Since both Andrea Perez (a white female) and Sylvester Davis (a black male) were Catholics, and since "the Catholic Church did not prohibit interracial marriage, California miscegenation law was, he argued, an arbitrary and unreasonable restraint on their freedom of religion" (19). The race debate, however, was not absent from the proceedings, and Marshall even compared the then-widespread eugenicist argument to Adolf Hitler's *Mein Kampf*. Marshall won, thus invalidating the miscegenation law of the state of California. Needless to say, the decision was controversial in a country where 38 states still forbade interracial marriage, six of which did so by state constitutional provision.

many points in the novel, such as Daphne's account of her teenage years some ten pages prior to Mouse's revelation.

A careful study of Daphne's past, although narrated to Easy by the very unreliable Daphne, sheds light on the sociological issues raised in the novel. Recounting a day at the zoo with her father, Daphne reminisces about how her "daddy" kissed her on the lips "like lovers do" (194) right after they watched a male zebra mounting a female. It is not mere coincidence that Daphne draws a parallel between her incestuous relationship with her father and the vision of this intercourse between wild equines whose distinctive characteristic is a black and white striped coat. Like the zebras, Daphne is black and white, but her "bi-coloredness" is not conspicuous. It is concealed, indecipherable, and yet traumatizing because what is perfectly acceptable in nature is taboo and forbidden in Daphne's society. Daphne claims that her father's inappropriate kissing is not the source of the trauma. She actually evokes her relationship with her "daddy" with nostalgia and deplores that he left her and her "Momma" the following year when she was 14. What Daphne cannot cope with is being demonized and even ostracized because she "passes." Daphne trespasses the color line and is perceived as a threat by a bigoted society whose foundations lie on a strict division of skin color.

It is essential, if not vital, for Daphne to mask her minute percentage of black blood. In this perspective, Daphne plays up her whiteness in her banter to Easy: "Too bad we won't have a chance to get to know each other, Easy. Otherwise, I'd let you eat this little white girl up" (101). Daphne's Caucasian features such as her light hair and her blue eyes are emphasized before the investigation even starts, in the picture Dewitt Albright shows Easy: it has been touched up with colors. Modifying the black and white photograph also dissimulates Daphne's black and white identity. More than concealment, the re-coloring of Daphne in the photograph erases and therefore denies her African ancestry. This process of dissimulation/deletion is furthered by Todd Carter's insistence, after Easy queries him on Daphne's origins, that Daphne is from "New Orleans and that her family was an old French family that traced their heritage to Napoleon" (125).[4] By asserting Daphne's illustrious lineage, Carter intends to dismiss any notion that Daphne could be a non-white person.

The reader can never fully determine Daphne's origins, a task further complicated by her psychological maladjustment and split personality. Once

---

4 Carter's reference to Napoleon Bonaparte is particularly interesting because of the confusion surrounding Napoleon's wife Joséphine de Beauharnais, whom people, to this day, have been mistaking for a person of mixed ancestry. Born in the West Indies in a family of planters, Joséphine was called a Creole after the so-called Louisiana usage of the term, which designates an individual of pure French or Spanish rather than mixed lineage. Whether Mosley intended, with such a hint, to foreshadow subsequent questions around the racial origins of the Daphne character is debatable, but there is no doubt that some readers, upon learning of Daphne's mixed heritage at the end of the novel, pondered Carter's remark about Daphne's origins in a different light.

Daphne is identified by Mouse as Ruby, an African American woman passing for white, she rejects Easy's extended hand and bitterly snaps:

> I'm not Daphne. My given name is Ruby Hanks and I was born in Lake Charles, Louisiana. I'm different than you because I'm two people. I'm her *and* I'm me. I never went to that zoo, she did. She was there and that's where she lost her father. I had a different father. He came home and fell in my bed about as many times as he fell in my mother's. He did that until one night Frank killed him. (208)

In this verbal salvo, Daphne speaks in the first person as Ruby Hanks, the African American country girl from Lake Charles, Louisiana, and dissociates herself from her public persona, Daphne Monet, the white girl of pure French lineage to whom she refers in the third person. The mystery surrounding Daphne's family history is never fully solved, but what is relevant is that the split of identity (the distinction between Ruby and Daphne) coincides with the change of father.[5] Daphne's African American identity emerges when she narrates her victimization by that incestuous father: in other words, Daphne sees herself as Ruby Hanks, a tragic mulatto, as soon as she becomes the object of men's lust.

Daphne's differentiation of fathers also suggests that she has internalized the stereotypes about the mulatto woman as a sexual pervert, a seducer whose irresistible beauty white men can not resist. Racist ideology has it that white men do not rape mulatto women but offer them, in exchange for sexual gratification, the opportunity to enjoy a comfortable lifestyle—i.e., the lifestyle of a white lady. This interpretation, in turn, raises questions about the nature of Daphne's relationship with her white lovers, Richard McGee and Todd Carter. Daphne's affairs with McGee and Carter may appear as a way of either reenacting or confronting her past in a desperate attempt to make normal an act (sex with a white father figure) that was abnormal in the first place. The novel provides no detail about McGee and Daphne's relationship, but it presents Todd Carter as a genuine romantic who loves Daphne regardless of her racial heritage. This may explain why Daphne associates her "daddy" from the zoo—for whose kisses she is nostalgic—with Todd Carter. As she tells Easy: "He [Daphne's 'Daddy'] knew me, the real me, and whenever you

---

[5] Daphne, speaking as Ruby, makes a clear distinction between the man who kissed her at the zoo and the one who raped her at home. In fact, Daphne is not very clear about how far her relationship with her father from the zoo went. He would kiss Daphne "like a father and his little girl but then we'd get alone some place and *act* like real lovers" (196; emphasis mine). Whether the verb *to act* implies kissing or something more is unclear. Yet Daphne's overall discourse seeks to exculpate her father from the zoo on the ground that his sexual misconduct did not go beyond kissing and drove him to abandon mother and child, allegedly as a form of *mea culpa*. Since Daphne turns out to be a mythomaniac, it is hard to give credence to any piece of information she provides and it is fair to believe that in fact, the father from the zoo never left her but became, in her distorted perception, another man once he started to have sex with her.

know somebody that well you just have to leave" (196). Although this is another of Daphne's utterances that remains too obscure to interpret, we may venture that "the real me" in Daphne's mind is someone who is appreciated or loved not solely on account of her race but rather as an individual in all her complexity. This is precisely, Easy accurately guesses, "what she had with Carter" (196). Carter, the story makes clear, is not with Daphne because it embodies a fantasy—namely the light skinned mulatto mistress. He has genuine feelings for Daphne and his color-blindness is emphasized when Easy, who has a pathological distrust of white men, is actually baffled by Carter, who seems to betray none of the "fear or contempt that most white people showed" (126) toward African Americans like him.[6]

The Daphne character is so ambiguous that she seems to have unsettled the author himself. Through Daphne, Mosley simultaneously fuels and debunks stereotypes of mulattoes. On the one hand, Mosley has Daphne steal thirty thousand dollars from Carter's foundation before she leaves Carter, allegedly out of love and consideration for his political career, and sleep with another man (Easy) within a few weeks of her purportedly painful but necessary separation. The myth that mulattoes are dishonest, sly, and duplicitous philanderers is here reinforced. On the other hand, Mosley debunks the stereotype of the opportunistic mulatto who tries to conceal her blackness at any price so that she can enjoy the comfortable lifestyle of a white woman. On the contrary, Daphne does not hesitate to be seen in black neighborhoods and bars in the company of her half-brother Frank, even if the condition remains that their kinship and her African American lineage be kept a secret. Unlike other passing mulattoes of Daphne's era, such as screen characters Pinky in Elia Kazan's *Pinky* (1949), Peola in John Stahl's *Imitation of Life* (1949), and the Carter family in Alfred L. Werker's *Lost Boundaries* (1949), who consent to severing their ties to their black community in order to make it in the white world, Daphne resolutely navigates both worlds simultaneously, until her mixed heritage is discovered and brings about trouble. Daphne challenges the unwritten rule of the tragic mulatto, and she and those around her end up paying dearly for it.

Conclusion

As Mosley deceives his reader until the end of the novel as to Daphne's biracial heritage, the reader will probably use that new piece of information in order to solve all previous enigmas about Daphne, including key elements of the plot such as Daphne's separation from Todd Carter, but also some of Daphne's more disturbing behaviors such as her unbounded libido: indeed, the prejudiced but convenient association of racial hybridity with concupiscence is likely to satisfy

[6] On the other hand, Easy attributes this lack of fear to Carter's wealth and power: "Mr. Todd Carter was so rich that he didn't even consider me in human terms. […] It was the worst kind of racism. The fact that he didn't even recognize our difference showed that he didn't care one damn about me" (126).

a thirst for comprehension. It is at this junction between the raw, indeterminate text and the reader's active participation that fiction, as Wolfgang Iser argues, "suddenly take[s] on the shape of an 'enduring form of life'" (106). This creation of meaning is particularly significant in *Devil* as Mosley leaves to the reader the responsibility of making sense of Daphne and all related events in the novel, thus forcing the reader to a moral introspection.

I have suggested above that Mosley seems to be flirting with racial prejudices and misogyny, but it is also fair to argue that Mosley inverts the racist representation of mulattoes as Daphne, in the logic of the novel that makes whiteness the root of all evil, appears as a profligate, deceptive, and even murderous individual when she masquerades as a white person. Her African American alter ego, Ruby Hanks, is not a paragon of virtue, but the novel implies that Daphne's heart is tainted by her whiteness rather than by her blackness. The unmasking of Daphne's double identity is painful, not so much because she cannot deceive people any longer, but because it forces her unconditionally to assume her black personality. The fact that Daphne slept with both white and black men may be interpreted as examples of her indiscretion, but it may also participate in her refusal to comply with the demands of a society that compels her to remain black even though she is proportionally much more white. Unlike a typical tragic mulatto, Daphne does not find it natural to go back to her black roots and accept her fate as a black person with equanimity. Her seemingly sincere feelings for Todd Carter (although tarnished by the thirty thousand dollars she stole from his investment company), her public relationship with her brother, and her fling with Easy suggest that Daphne grants herself the right to live on her own terms rather than on the terms of a racist society. The law whereby the infinitesimal percentage of black blood running through her veins makes her biologically black and demands that she naturally assume her status as a black person is not acceptable to Daphne. It is not that Daphne "wanna be white" (209) as Mouse has it, but rather that she won't let this one portion of her ancestry dictate her way of life.

Implicit in Daphne's behavior and passing status is the transcendence of the black/white dichotomy in American culture: "Embodied in the passing figure," scholar John Sheehy argues, "is the possibility of a discourse of racial identity which moves beyond the terms of both our racial antipathies and our racial sympathies" (414). The passing figure, Sheehy suggests, challenges Du Bois's metaphor of the veil that posits an indefinite separation between blacks and whites in America.[7] Of course, the life of the Daphne character is much too hectic and trapped in its historical framework in postwar Los Angeles for readers to imagine that Daphne's existential choices constitute a political agenda. However, as the majority of Mosley's prose fiction (whether it is detective stories,

---

[7] In *The Souls of Black Folk*, W.E.B. Du Bois writes: "Leaving, then, the white world, I have stepped within the Veil, raising it that you may view faintly its deeper recesses—the meaning of its religion, the passion of its human sorrow, and the struggles of its greatest souls" (qtd. in Sheehy 412).

protest literature, science fiction, or a blues novel) has been entrenched in identity politics and the idiosyncrasies of the African American experience, we might interpret Daphne Monet as Mosley's attempt to address the delicate issues of racial separation and enmity in the United States, perhaps even to point the way toward a post-racial American society proud of its racial diversity but freed from its obsession with racial difference.

Works Cited

Chandler, Raymond. "The Simple Art of Murder." 1944. *Later Novels and Other Writings*. New York: Library of America, 1995. 977–92.

Du Bois, W.E.B. *The Souls of Black Folk: Essays and Sketches*. 1905. Early Modern African American Writers, Volume IX. Tokyo: Hon-No-Tomosha, 1997.

Gates, Henry Louis Jr. *The Signifying Monkey: A Theory of African American Literary Criticism*. London: Oxford UP, 1989.

Guerrero, Ed. "*Devil in a Blue Dress*." *Cinéaste* 22:1 (1996): 38–40.

Iser, Wolfgang. "The Reading Process." 1972. *Issues in Contemporary Critical Theory: A Casebook*. Ed. Peter Barry. London: McMillan Education, 1987. 105–19.

Mosley, Walter. *Devil in a Blue Dress*. 1990. London: Serpent's Tail, 2001.

Pascoe, Peggy. "Miscegenation Law, Court Cases, and Ideologies of 'Race' in Twentieth-Century America." *The Journal of American History* 83:1 (1996): 44–69.

Pepper, Andrew. *The Contemporary American Crime Novel: Race, Ethnicity, Gender, Class*. Edinburgh: Edinburgh UP, 2000.

Scaggs, John. *Crime Fiction*. London: Routledge, 2005.

Sheehy, John. "The Mirror and the Veil: The Passing Novel and the Quest for American Racial Identity." *African American Review* 33.3 (1999): 401–15.

Chapter 11
Lost in Translation: The Multicultural Interpreter as Metaphysical Detective in Suki Kim's *The Interpreter*

Soo Yeon Kim

> [P]ostmodernist discourses appeal primarily to the winners in the processes of globalization and fundamentalist discourses to the losers. In other words, the current global tendencies toward increased mobility, indeterminacy, and hybridity are experienced by some as a kind of liberation but by others as an exacerbation of their suffering [...] The losers in the processes of globalization might indeed be the ones who give us the strongest indication of the transformation in progress.
>
> —Michael Hardt and Antonio Negri, *Empire*

Globalization, used reciprocally with multinationalism, implies the breakdown of national boundaries while multiculturalism often connotes the endorsement of distinctive identities of racialized cultures. Deploying a plethora of multicultural and multinational references, Suki Kim's *The Interpreter* follows a 29-year-old Korean American woman's sumptuous yet inexplicably hollow life in New York City, where racial and global references are mingled in the commodified landscape of the city and its heterogeneous residents. In Kim's novel, both globalization and multiculturalism espouse what Michael Hardt and Antonio Negri note as postmodern qualities: namely, "mobility" as represented by the ability to move across national boundaries and cultural geographies; "difference" that privileges heterogeneity over homogenization; and "hybridity," a synergetic merging of disparate identities. A vivid illustration of the cosmopolitan life, *The Interpreter* traverses the streets of Manhattan, from busy 32nd street across from Penn Station, where exotic Korean restaurants and pubs line up, to Columbia University uptown, where students from all over the world discuss their "usual suspects" (51): Jacques Derrida, Vladimir Nabokov, Edward Said, and Akira Kurosawa, to name a few. Fancy multinational brand names such as Prada, Ralph Lauren, and Starbucks embody the globalized city as well and appear in the daily language of the novel's protagonist—a court interpreter named Suzy Park. What establishes *The Interpreter* as a compelling work on American multiculturalism and globalization, however, is neither these ample "multi-" references nor the fact that the novel was written by a Korean American author who, one interviewer points out, still has "a lingering Korean accent" (McGee). In portraying the postmodern America that upholds the auspicious prospect of a multicultural society, *The Interpreter* makes a unique contribution by revealing the painful story of "losers in the process of globalization" (Hardt and Negri 150) and intervenes in the liberatory discourse of globalization and its platitudes of mobility, difference, and hybridity. For example, the Parks, Suzy's parents, run a crammed grocery store in Manhattan, barely speaking English and suffering from "the claustrophobia of immigrant life" (122). Damian and Tamiko, an eminent scholar-couple of East Asian studies and Comparative literature at Columbia, are viewed as "the perfect union between East and West" (49). Yet the couple's hybridity, which conjoins a white male and a Japanese female, turns out to be falsely founded upon Damian's "xenophilia," an "uncritical embrace of the Other" (Adler 497), which results from his hatred of his own race rather than from a genuine understanding of his Asian wife. Above all, Suzy is haunted by loneliness and hollowness despite her ability to understand two languages and cultures. Insofar as Suzy feels "stuck in a vacuum" (166) rather than culturally enriched by her multicultural knowledge, Suzy's life testifies to the downside of multiculturalism. These examples illuminate the blind spots of such global "virtues"—mobility, difference, and hybridity—which can cause dislocation and uprootedness as well as liberation.[1]

Suzy's failure to mediate between two cultures and peoples is aptly disclosed through the skeptical frame of the metaphysical detective story, a postmodernist form of the detective story characterized by its replacement of the conventional "whodunit" question with an epistemological question on the detection of the truth as such.[2] *The Interpreter* opens with Suzy's recollection that she dropped out of

[1] My essay assumes that since the 1980s, neoliberal policies of unfettered globalization have dominated world economy and politics, and have fostered the exclusively liberatory discourse of economic/cultural globalization. For anarco-capitalists' argument on the inopportuneness of national boundaries and State-forms, see the works of Murray Rothbard and Hans Hermann-Hoppe: in particular, the latter's "On Free Immigration and Forced Integration" (1999). Since the beginning of the millennium, the studies that tackle the negativities of globalization and cultural imperialism have emerged in various disciplines. For the best synthesizing analysis of the postmodern, global form of sovereignty, see Hardt and Negri's *Empire* (2000). While Hardt and Negri advocate the Deleuzean nomad as the agent of the revolution against the postmodern empire, they also argue the need to account for the stories of "the losers"—legal and illegal guest workers and immigrants, for instance—whose stability of life is endangered in the United States. For further studies on limits and possibilities of the migrant identity from the postcolonial and/or feminist perspective, refer to the latest works of Gayatri Chakravorty Spivak and Rosi Braidotti, such as *Who Sings the Nation-State?: Language, Politics, Belonging* (2007) and *Transpositions: Of Nomadic Ethics* (2006), respectively; Spivak and Braidotti introduce the notion of cultural "belongings" in place of fixed identity. For general critical works on global capitalism and multiculturalism, see Leslie Sklair's *Globalization: Capitalism and Its Alternatives* (2002); and Martin Gannon's *Paradoxes of Culture and Globalization* (2007).

[2] In *Detecting Texts: The Metaphysical Detective Story from Poe to Postmodern* (1999), Merivale and Sweeney define the metaphysical detective story as a text that "parodies or subverts traditional detective-story conventions—such as narrative closure and

Columbia University to live with a married American professor, Damian. Four years after Suzy was bitterly disowned by her father because of the shame she caused her family, her parents were shot to death by a seemingly random attacker in their grocery store. From the beginning of the novel, Suzy is traumatized by guilt and grief, and solving the mystery of her parents' murder becomes an ontological imperative for her to remove her guilt and go on with her life. The perturbing secrets of Suzy's parents and her sister Grace, however, which Suzy learns in her detection in the latter part of the novel, complicate rather than resolve the situation. Suzy's discovery that no one is innocent—that is, that Suzy, Grace, and her parents are all more or less responsible for the murder—calls into question the validity and the finality of "truth," a crucial theme of metaphysical detective fiction. Suzy's "[r]eturning to the scene of the crime" (264) at the end of the novel, an element of conventional detective fiction, is derided in Kim's novel and does not lead to a disentanglement. Kim's twist does little but enhance a sense of the stalemate of immigrant existence, because in the offices of the INS, the scene of Suzy's father's crime, Suzy finds out that the crimes committed by illegal immigrants are ongoing regardless of her father's punishment by death; he ratted out other illegal Korean immigrants in return for citizenship and financial security and was shot by an ex-Korean gang member. In translating Mrs Choi's confession that she stabbed a black girl who attempted to steal fruit from her store, Suzy witnesses the continuing grief, guilt, and "collective paranoia" (240) of the majority of immigrants who have lost the battle of globalization. By taking issue with the notions of guilt, truth, and narrative closure, the metaphysical detective plot of *The Interpreter* exposes the protagonist's deadlocked situation between two cultures and challenges the uncritical celebration of multiculturalism.

As Hardt and Negri cogently indicate, "certainly from the standpoint of many around the world, hybridity, mobility, and difference do not immediately appear as liberatory in themselves" (154). Drawing on Hardt and Negri's critique of the exclusively liberatory discourse of globalization, the first part of this essay discusses the ways in which *The Interpreter* reworks the conventional detective plot in order

---

the detective's role as surrogate reader—with the intention, or at least the effect, of asking questions about mysteries of being and knowing which transcend the mere machinations of the mystery plot" (2). A felicitous example of the metaphysical detective story, *The Interpreter* features five of the six characteristic themes of this genre: "the defeated sleuth"; "the world, city, or text as labyrinth"; "the ambiguity, ubiquity, eerie meaningfulness, or sheer meaninglessness of clues and evidences"; "the missing person, the double, and the lost, stolen, or exchanged identity"; "absence, falseness, circularity, or self-defeating nature of any kind of closure to the investigation" (ibid. 8). For more works on the intersection of postmodernism and metaphysical detective fiction, see Michael Holquist's "Whodunit and Other Questions: Metaphysical Detective Stories in Post-War Fiction" (1983); Jon Thompson, *Fiction, Crime, and Empire: Clues to Modernity and Postmodernism* (1993); John Irwin, *The Mystery to a Solution: Poe, Borges, and the Analytic Detective* (1994); and the last chapter on postmodernist uses of the detective form in *The Cambridge Companion to Crime Fiction* (2003).

to reveal that hybridity, mobility, and difference can invoke a devastating sense of homelessness in those who cannot readily break down boundaries and acculturate themselves. The term "interpreter" carries multiple meanings in this novel. Suzy's investigation of her parents' murder, for instance, reveals that interpretation refers not only to the disinterested translation between words but also to a way of understanding the self and others. This revelation transforms the novel into a metaphysical detective story that seeks an answer to the ontological question of Suzy's identity. Suzy's profession as an interpreter is inseparable from her role as a metaphysical detective who must "interpret" the clues and solve the mysterious death of her parents in order to make sense of her current self. By focusing on the relationship between detection and interpretation, the latter part of the essay examines the "final" truth—or the lack thereof—of the interpreter/detective in Kim's novel, who struggles to find her own place but is destined to remain "lost in translation" between different cultures in a globalized world.

The Other Side of Paradise: Multiculturalism in the United States

The acute divisiveness of Suzy's life as a Korean American in New York City is apparent from the beginning of the novel. On the one hand, Suzy is a competent court interpreter and leads a stylish cosmopolitan life. Sharing an Upper East Side flat with the young, gay artist-to-be Caleb, Suzy's life, if only on the surface, demonstrates mobility and hybridity through her interpreting job and the worldwide products that she consumes on a daily basis. On the other hand, Jen, Suzy's friend from Columbia University, refers to Suzy's chic life shrouded in "power colors" (4) as "so nineties" (13), because Suzy refuses to commit herself to anything except inanimate commodities.[3] After Caleb moves out, Suzy's growing detachment from real people and lives presents itself via a bouquet of dead irises in a cut Evian bottle (flowers sent from an unidentified sender), a small TV set airing *All My Children* for hours, and a telephone, all of which occupy her spacious apartment. The intermittent phone calls from European airports that convey only the voice of Michael, Suzy's married American businessman lover following her break-up with Damian, add to the global dimension in her life. Yet, more significantly, the invisible lover and his buzzing voice on the phone from the other side of the world underscore her isolation. This sense of detachment and alienation transforms into fear and suspense when Suzy starts to get eerie calls that always stop after the fourth ring. Her detachment is exemplified by her "career phobia" (13) as well.

---

[3] Consumerism and the alienation of the individual caused by it have been indicated by many postmodernist thinkers as a fundamental feature of postmodernization. For seminal works on "hypercommodity," cultural materialism, and the apathy it breeds, refer to Jean Baudrillard's *The Consumer Society: Myths and Structures* ([1970] 1998) and *Simulacra and Simulation* ([1981] 1995). For a follow-up study, see David Clarke's *The Consumer Society and the Postmodern City* (2003).

Unable to tolerate desk jobs, Suzy finds the irregular interpreting jobs bearable, because she believes that an interpreter, invisible and anonymous, belongs with neither side: "one of the job requirements was no involvement. Shut up and get the work done. That's fine with her" (15).

Suzy's "no involvement" rule shows that, under the surface of her carefree metropolitan life, a traumatic sense of loneliness, hollowness, and grief prevails. For all her interpreting skills Suzy cannot connect to either culture: "Being bilingual, being multicultural should have brought two worlds into one heart, and yet for Suzy, it meant a persistent hollowness [...]. She was stuck in a vacuum where neither culture moved nor owned her. Deep inside, she felt no connection" (166). Insofar as Suzy's interpreting skills and multicultural knowledge leave her utterly vacuous rather than enriching her life with a better understanding of both cultures, Suzy remains a "loser" in a global city rather than becoming a cosmopolitan hybrid. Suzy's failure to connect to either culture is illustrated by her painful situation between two equally difficult (im)possibilities in the novel. On one hand, her father's dated Korean patriarchal values are no longer tenable in the United States, but impossible for her to violate without feeling the enormous guilt of a traitor to her father and fatherland. On the other, American values assume "the impossibility of desire" (160), to borrow Suzy Park's words, inasmuch as they are embodied in illegitimate affairs with married American men. Hence, "the immigrant goal of becoming American without becoming Americanized" (Filbin 558) that the Parks desperately pursue proves an impossible project.

Broaching an investigation into her parents' murder means for Suzy an exploration of her own inertia. Suzy gradually breaks her coolness and begins to trace clues, getting on a train to Montauk impulsively and running across dark raining alleys in order to lose a mysterious follower. Via this amateur sleuthing, Suzy learns her family secrets one by one, which prove more important than the name of the shooter, who has been long dead; she discovers the shocking truth of her parents' treacherous past and her model sister Grace's hidden identity as Marianna—user of marijuana—and her romantic connection to the Korean gang "the Fearsome Four." Suzy's investigation as a metaphysical detective opens up an epiphany for her that successful interpretation requires the interpreter's involvement and that it can bring about a new understanding of others, no matter how uncomfortable the new learning turns out to be. To use the metaphor constructed by Hans-Georg Gadamer, a German philosopher of hermeneutics, interpreting and understanding the other calls for "the fusion of horizons" (Taylor 287), a process in which two different terms meet on the same plane, engage themselves in an active conversation with each other, and accept each other's terms without abandoning the self. Gadamer's theory on interpreting and understanding the other without sacrificing one's own integrity, however, proves difficult to practice. In a series of interviews, Suki Kim observes that, while working as a court interpreter to research for the novel, she was struck by the tension and the hardships of the interpreter, who must confront her split identity despite her control of the courtroom due to her knowledge of both languages and cultures. Kim chose an interpreter as the main character of her debut novel so as to assert the fact that "[t]here's a gigantic amount of success among Asian Americans, but also pain, isolation, loneliness, failure and heartache" (McGee). A self-proclaimed lover of Alain Robbe-Grillet, the inventor of French *nouveau roman*, Kim adopted the noirish detective angle and turned the interpreter into a metaphysical detective, whose interpretation of the clues of a crime generates deeper existential questions. Suzy's metamorphosis from interpreter to detective is fundamental to revealing her past misinterpretation of her family and her current stalemate as an Asian American who is torn between two cultures.

Kim's use of the detective figure is instrumental to disclosing the most disturbing truth of the novel as well. In the interviews with Adam Langer and Cindy Yoon, Kim clarifies that she "really wanted to write an American book," rather than an "immigrant fiction." What America is about, according to Kim, is "killing your parents." By making Suzy's father an informer on illegal Korean immigrants for the INS and by having both parents brutally murdered, *The Interpreter* breaks away from traditional Asian American stories in which strong family ties are glorified and often sentimentalized.[4] Until Suzy's father's secret is brought to light, the immigrant life of Suzy's parents, filled with humiliation and frustration, provides the embittering example of the "losers of globalization." Whereas Suzy suffers from hollowness in spite of her bilingual and multicultural knowledge, Suzy's parents, having neither of these knowledges, hold on to a fundamentalist principle that Hardt and Negri indicate as "a powerful refusal of the contemporary passage" (147) toward globalization. Observing that "postmodernism's primary site of application is within an elite segment of the U.S. intelligentsia" (154), Hardt and Negri elaborate on various types of fundamentalist reactions to globalization that occur outside this elite group. Among others, the fundamentalist response centers on the "return to 'the traditional family'" (Hardt and Negri 48). Rooted in the groundless nostalgia for the past, however, this yearning for the traditional family remains an implausible slogan in a contemporary multicultural society. Suzy's father serves as a good example of fundamentalist thinking. Rejecting everything that is American as "the Western conspiracy" (211), Mr. Park brainwashes Suzy and Grace to believe that "[y]ou must never forget your language; once you do, you no longer have a home" (45). Suzy's father's notion of home, however, signifies little more than the futile attempt of a fundamentalist who wishes for the irretrievable past: the girls left Korea when they were five and six and hardly remember the country. Pointing to a hybrid dog, Suzy's father viciously remarks: "See what happens when you mix blood? Even dogs turn out a mess, stupid and ugly!" (53).

---

4 In the interview with Celia McGee, Kim notes that traditional Asian American fiction often portrays sentimental characters because "intrinsic in their set-up is memory [sic]." To use Kim's example, Amy Tan's *The Joy Luck Club* (1989) is representative of this tradition. Kim remarks that she adopted a detective angle in order to show the different ways of dealing with family memories that are often painful yet true to the reality of many Asian Americans.

Mr Park's fundamentalist assertion of "racial purity" (Hardt and Negri 148) and vain attempt at parental authority paradoxically expose "his own powerlessness [that resulted from] the ordeal of having to rely on his young daughter for such basic functions" like communicating in English (109). Yet, by renovating the story of a victimized Asian American immigrant worker through what I call a rebellion of the loser, Kim's novel recreates Asian American immigrant life as a site of tragic confrontation between fidelity to fatherland and the American dream. In creating her protagonist as a detached detective at odds with her parents' values and her hyphenated identity, Kim also demystifies the myth of the young Asian American model citizen, whose accomplishments have been presumed to derive from the successful mediation between acculturating American values at school and work and cherishing Asian values, bequeathed by her parents, at home.[5]

Suzy's "purgatorial suspension of guilt" (75) caused by her elopement with Damian and her parents' murder haunts her with the thorough meaninglessness of life, a life that "she, at twenty-five, had already given up" (23). Suzy's guilt is also noteworthy in relation to the sense of the illegitimacy that she has as a Korean American woman. Enraged at Suzy's affair, her father expels her and calls her "Yang-gal-bo" (32), a derogatory Korean word that Elaine Kim translates into the "whore of the West" (7). Given that her father's dated Korean values have no currency in multicultural America and that her father commits a no less immoral crime than Suzy (that is, betraying his fellow immigrants), Suzy's "betrayal" of her father, if not entirely justifiable, does not appear as perfidious as her father

---

5 I do not discuss Damian and Tamiko's relationship in detail in this essay because their case has little bearing upon the detective theme of Kim's novel. Nonetheless, Damian and Tamiko's marriage is noteworthy for the subtler peril of multiculturalism it presents. While Suzy's parents remain largely locked up in a "subculture of immigrants [that] had nothing much to do with the rest of America" (165), Damian and his Japanese-American wife Tamiko display the difficulty of gaining true understanding of another culture even in a highly educated multicultural society. Their relationship is presumed to be based on Damian's profound knowledge of East Asian culture and the academic achievements of Tamiko, whose elegance and passion mesmerize students during her lectures at Columbia University. Suzy's secluded life with Damian for four years, however, illustrates that his love of Asian women derives less from an understanding of Asian culture than from his abhorrence of American culture, which he believes to be "the gutter, worse than drugs" (35), and from which he struggles to escape throughout his life: "His whole life had been about running from his whiteness. His purpose was searching the other. He couldn't even love his own kind. She [Suzy] was the antidote for his inability to love" (288). Thus, Damian's love for the East and East Asian women proves to be no more than "xenophilia," which is as ruinous as xenophobia. In spite of Tamiko's seeming ability to bridge East and West, demonstrated in the scene where she discusses Kurosawa's *King Lear*, her discussion ends up polarizing "us" and "them" (82), betraying her dichotomization between races and sexes. Listening to Tamiko warn her that Damian "cannot love an Asian woman" (139), Suzy learns that Tamiko is as xenophobic and claustrophobic as her father, who also divides "us" and "them."

condemns it to be. Nevertheless, Suzy fully acknowledges her "betrayal" and defines herself as "a bona fide mistress" (29) of married men: "she betrayed [her parents], *so she might live*" (212; original italics); "She even sacrificed her own parents to be [a mistress], so she had better be damn good at it" (29). Suzy's self-sarcasm and guilt that rise from her extramarital and interracial relationships with Damian and Michael would explain Elaine Kim's analogy between Korean American women and Korean sex workers for the United States military stationed in South Korea: both are marginalized and suspected as traitors to Korea. The metaphor of the "whore of the West" not only indicates Suzy's choice of married Americans as her lovers but also means her violation of her father's—and fatherland's—values: hence, the illegitimacy of her life as a Korean American woman. Similarly, inasmuch as Suzy belongs to both sexual and racial minorities, she makes a doubly "illegitimate" female detective, a felicitous example of the non-professional detective that the postmodern metaphysical detective story often chooses as its protagonist-sleuth. Suzy's sense of guilt that springs from her doubly othered status renders her better aware of the dark side of globalization, thus making her a "better" metaphysical detective.

Detection as Interpretation: The Metaphysical Detective in Postmodern America

Suzy's guilt is a driving force that changes *The Interpreter* into a metaphysical detective story. Since Suzy is obsessed with guilt, "still hoping for the third bullet, which was surely fired [with the two bullets that killed her parents], which will reach her heart with dead certainty" (77), the need to investigate the murder mystery becomes imperative for her to continue to live. In *Detecting Texts*, Patricia Merivale and Susan Elizabeth Sweeney argue that in the metaphysical detective story, the detective's search for another often closes with an "unsuccessful search for himself" (10). Oftentimes, the detective turns out to be the missing person or the murderer whom he or she has been seeking, thereby challenging the epistemology of subjectivity and "final" truth that is conventionalized in the structure of the detective narrative. *The Interpreter* adapts this crux of the metaphysical detective plot in order to reveal the unpredictable "truth": neither Suzy's parents nor her sister Grace are without responsibility for the murder. Suzy's father was a longtime snitch for the INS and the shooter was Grace's Korean gang-member boyfriend, DJ, who could not stand witnessing Grace's misery in her family any longer; Grace was forced to become an accomplice to her father's treachery by interpreting for her father for the INS during her adolescent years. Although Grace and Suzy did not pull the trigger, the sisters share the guilt through their hatred towards their parents and their "betrayal" in the form of their affairs with American men. The truth about their parents' death, far from bringing peace of mind to the sisters, devastates Suzy and Grace, causing Suzy to feel completely hollow with shock and Grace to drown her lover when she learns he was the shooter, then disappear. In the end, Suzy's discovery that her father was not blameless does not relieve her of her guilt. To the reader's bafflement, the novel concludes—rather, opens anew—with the new mystery of the missing Grace. The puzzling ending of *The Interpreter* illustrates the core of the metaphysical detective story in which the distinctions between murderer and victim, truth and lie, and resolution and complication are blurred and problematized.

Suzy's profession as an interpreter furnishes a fitting metaphor for the detective because the postmodern detective story often tells a self-reflexive story of "textual interpreters" (Black 78). The protagonist's principal activity in postmodernist detective fiction is no longer detection, which seeks answers to the traditional "whodunit" question, but the reading and interpretation of texts. In the sense that the persons engaged in the "quest of truth" are not professional detectives in this genre, they are investigators only in a metaphorical and metaphysical sense: Jorge Louis Borges's librarian, Umberto Eco's friar, and Thomas Pynchon's housewife sleuth can represent these postmodern metaphysical investigators. Joe Black's view of the detective as a "postmodernist cryptographer" (94) helps us understand the multi-layered meanings of interpretation that Kim successfully interweaves in *The Interpreter*. The interpretation refers not only to translation between Korean and English, a mechanical word-by-word transference, but also to the interpretation of the clues of a murder mystery, such as bouquets of irises from an unknown sender, the calls that stop ringing on the fourth ring, and a missing member of "the Fearsome Four." The "correct" interpretation of each clue, that is, the successful deciphering of each text, guides Suzy to the next site of investigation until she reaches the underground world of the Korean gang in Manhattan's Koreatown. Thus, the interpreter is a synonym for the detective in Kim's novel. In a *New York Times* review of *The Interpreter*, Katherine Dieckmann condemns Kim's use of a "Big Mystery," stating that "Kim's ability to build and sustain tension" is "next to nil." Dieckmann's dismissal of the mystery plot as the "playing [of] [a] girl detective," however, fails to recognize the entire point of such an ineffective and unprofessional detective as Suzy. Like Oedipa Maas in Pynchon's *The Crying of Lot 49*, the postmodern detective, who is led to—almost forced to—interpret clues through a series of accidents and who stumbles toward the "truth" with a worried obsession rather than with the masculine confidence of an owner of the truth, often finds an apt portrayal in female (or feminine) characters.

A well-qualified interpreter, a "bear[er] [of] the truth" (12) and "the most astute listener in the world" (99), Suzy is expected to be a successful detective. In contrast, Suzy's experience as an amateur sleuth unveils her past misunderstanding of her sister and ignorance about her parents. Suzy's bitter question to herself at the end of the novel succinctly characterizes the postmodern detective who, lost in clues and texts, always finds the truth too late: "what the hell's an interpreter if she can't even interpret her own sister?" (293). The ontology of the postmodern metaphysical detective is instrumental to understanding Suzy's failure as a multicultural interpreter. While the metaphysical detective tries to interpret the mystery of a crime and grapple with the mystery of the self and the world, what he or she finally confronts is not the truth of "who is guilty" but a new, unnerving question of "who is not guilty." This is because, in the postmodern world, one's identity remains ungraspable due to its inseparability from a larger web in which numerable factors, such as one's race, gender, sexuality, nationality, and class, intersect, clash, and influence each other.[6] Similarly, the final knowledge that the metaphysical detective reaches is that "'reality' is ultimately unknowable or at least ineffable" (Merivale and Sweeney 4). The ineffableness of subjectivity, that is, the difficulty of shaping one's own identity in an unknowable reality, leaves the postmodern metaphysical detective with a sense of frustration and scepticism. Like a metaphysical detective who is doomed to be frustrated by an incomprehensible reality, Suzy, a multicultural interpreter, is fated for loneliness and aloofness from both cultures for all her applauded translation skills. Suzy's investigation appears successful when she "solves" her parents' murder mystery by identifying the killer. Yet the name of the killer, who is already dead, is by no means as significant as the other family secrets that lead Suzy to realize that she has entirely failed to "interpret" and understand her closest relatives until now. Ironically, Suzy's successful discovery of the killer and her final sense of failure are coterminous in Kim's postmodern metaphysical detective novel.

The ironic effect of the final "truth," the coexistent senses of success and failure, is one of the major features that other metaphysical detective stories share, from Edgar Allan Poe's seminal works in the late nineteenth century to the works of Borges, Pynchon, Paul Auster, Kazuo Ishiguro, and Julian Barnes.[7] Among others, the ending of Ishiguro's *When We Were Orphans* (2000) remarkably resembles that of *The Interpreter*. Ishiguro's novel follows the investigation of Christopher Banks, renowned detective in London circa the 1930s, into his parents, who were allegedly kidnapped for their political beliefs in Shanghai in the 1910s. The penultimate chapter of the novel reveals the disruptive truth: his father was not kidnapped for

---

6 A metaphysical detective's realization of one's inseparability from the other is strikingly evocative of Levinasian ethics, inasmuch as it brings to my mind the great thinker's favorite quotation from Fyodor Dostoyevsky's *The Brothers Karamazov*: "We are all responsible for everyone else—but I am more responsible than all the others" (qtd. in Levinas 1). While further development of the topic is beyond the scope of this chapter, I would argue that Kim's metaphysical detective story (and many other stories of the same genre) asserts an ethical obligation to the Other in a globalized society. *The Interpreter* illuminates the steps whereby a detached Asian American female sleuth, through her metaphysical detection/interpretation, learns the need to "face" (Levinasian term) and understand the Other, the two cultures that are alien to her, so as to become a truly caring metropolitan.

7 For a discussion of Poe as an inventor of classical detective fiction, the metaphysical detective story, and the "kind of playfully self-reflexive storytelling that we now call 'postmodernist'" (6), see Merivale and Sweeney's introduction to *Detecting Texts*. In addition to the titles mentioned in the chapter by Pynchon and Ishiguro, Borges' "Death and the Compass" (1942), Auster's *The New York Trilogy* (1987), and Julian Barnes' *Arthur and George* (2005) aptly exemplify the postmodernist metaphysical detective story.

political reasons but ran off with his mistress; his mother, after being threatened by a Chinese warlord, agreed to a life as his concubine in exchange for an inheritance that would secure her son's future in London. The final truth of Ishiguro's novel fills the protagonist with disillusionment from his "enchanted world" (315) and enormous frustration as a detective, radically undermining the epistemology of the "truth quest" of the detective story. Nevertheless, no matter how disappointing the truth remains, the last chapter of *When We Were Orphans* reaffirms the validity of truth as it ends with Banks' newfound bond with his long-lost mother, who, as if embodying the truth coming too late, does not recognize her son because of her old age and mental trauma. Inasmuch as late is better than never, the dark truth is still worth detecting and results in Banks's better perception of himself, his family, and the world around him. Banks, a formerly proud detective who believed in the accountability of reality, now understands its ultimate ineffableness. Matured, Banks learns how to "face the world as orphans" (335) and concludes that "There is nothing for it but to try and see through our missions to the end, as best we can" (336). This is the moment when the defeated detective becomes a metaphysical detective who can meditate upon the upsetting truth that opens up more profound questions about the self and the world.

Similarly, Suzy's final knowledge that she has failed to understand herself and her family still constitutes valuable knowledge, however unsettling and belated it is. The hopeful last sentence of *The Interpreter* offers the ironic catharsis of the metaphysical detective novel that is also evident in Ishiguro's novel. Kim's affirmation of the rebirth of Suzy and Grace as "Two girls with no parents, such fine American beauties" (294), appears contradictory to the sense of deadlock and isolation that pervades the novel. Yet, Kim's last sentence does not nullify the mysterious richness of the novel. Rather, the "emotional" reunion of the sad but beautiful Korean American sisters, although one of them is missing, offers an ironic catharsis at the heart of an unresolved grief. Grace, by keeping Suzy from interpreting for their father and by undertaking the interpretation for the INS all by herself, protected her little sister from becoming a part of their father's crime. Suzy's discovery of family secrets, as painful as they are, is better than ignorance. Suzy, if too late, now understands Grace's grief and shares it. This irony is the accursed privilege of the metaphysical detective, who is endowed with the ability to interpret reality only to apprehend a number of metaphysical questions that go beyond her capability of resolving. Yet she is more blessed than those who are unaware of the existence of these questions.

In postmodern America, difference, mobility, and hybridity are enthusiastically advertised and uncritically imposed on everybody, without regard to one's particularities, in the name of globalization and multiculturalism. By reworking an Asian American story in the framework of the metaphysical detective story and by featuring an interpreter as a metaphysical detective, *The Interpreter* poses a compelling question about the struggle to communicate between languages, cultures, and people(s) in contemporary America. Kim does not valorize either culture. While Suzy keenly wishes to acculturate in America, a large portion of Korean culture, including her father's outdated Korean values—attached to her like an "ugly tattoo" (122)—is unavoidably a part of her. Kim's vivid depictions of Korean restaurants and billiards clubs in Manhattan and Korean church communities in New Jersey are very much alive and engaging, while mingled with sarcasm and belittlement. American culture, while painted as desirable and superior, is neither necessarily attractive, if embodied in the masculinist relationships with Damian and Michael, nor possible to imitate, if represented by Caleb and Jen, Suzy's rich white friends who have "a sense of entitlement, the certainty of belonging" (161) from the start. *The Interpreter* is a powerful testimony to the difficulty of cultural interpretation in the age of globalization, where a multicultural interpreter as metaphysical detective is destined to remain lost in his or her "divided soul" (McGee).

Works Cited

Adler, Franklin Hugh. "Antiracism, Difference and Xenologica." *Cultural Values* 3.4 (1999): 492–502.

Auster, Paul. *The New York Trilogy*. Los Angeles: Sun & Moon Press, 1994.

Barnes, Julian. *Arthur and George*. London: Jonathan Cape, 2005.

Baudrillard, Jean. *Simulacra and Simulation*. Ann Arbor: U of Michigan P, 1995.

——. *The Consumer Society: Myths and Structures*. London: Sage, 1998.

Black, Joe. "(De)feats of Detection: The Spurious Key Text from Poe to Eco." Eds Patricia Merivale and Susan Elizabeth Sweeney. *Detecting Texts: the Metaphysical detective Story from Poe to Postmodernism*. Philadelphia: U of Pennsylvania P, 1999. 75–98.

Borges, Jorge Luis. *Ficciones*. New York: Grove, 1962.

Braidotti, Rosi. *Transpositions: Of Nomadic Ethics*. Cambridge: Polity Press, 2006.

Clarke, David. *The Consumer Society and the Postmodern City*. New York: Routledge, 2003.

Dieckmann, Katherine. "Found in Translation." *The New York Times Book Review* 108.4 (2003): 22.

Filbin, Thomas. "Modernism Without Dogmas." *Hudson Review* 56.3 (August 2003): 557–62.

Gannon, Martin. *Paradoxes of Culture and Globalization*. Los Angeles: Sage, 2007.

Hardt, Michael and Antonio Negri. *Empire*. Cambridge: Harvard UP, 2000.

Hermann-Hoppe, Hans. "On Free Immigration and Forced Integration (1999)." <http://www.lewrockwell.com/-hoppe/hoppe-arch.html>.

Holquist, Michael. "Whodunit and Other Questions: Metaphysical Detective Stories in Post-War Fiction." *The Poetics of Murder: Detective Fiction and Literary Theory*. Eds Glenn Most and William Stowe. New York: Hartcourt, 1983.

Irwin, John. *The Mystery to a Solution: Poe, Borges, and the Analytic Detective*. Baltimore: Johns Hopkins UP, 1994.

Ishiguro, Kazuo. *When We Were Orphans*. New York: Vintage, 2000.

Kim, Elaine. "Dangerous Affinities: Korean American Feminisms (En)Counter Gendered Korean and Racialized U.S. Nationalist Narratives." *Hitting Critical Mass* 6.1 (Fall 1999): 1–12.

Kim, Suki. *The Interpreter*. New York: Farrar, 2003.

Langer, Adam. "Ten to Watch in 2003, Suki Kim: The New Electra." *Book Magazine* Jan/Feb 2003. <http://www.sukikim.com/reviews.html#4>.

Lévinas, Emmanuel. *The Levinas Reader*. Ed. Seán Hand. Oxford: Blackwell, 1989.

McGee, Celia. "New Yorkorean Translator: Novelist Suki Kim Plumbs a Divided Soul in *The Interpreter*." *Daily News* 3 February 2003. <http://www.nydailynews.com/entertainment/story/58755p-55023c.html>.

Merivale, Patricia and Susan Elizabeth Sweeney. "The Game's Afoot: On the Trail of the Metaphysical Detective Story." *Detecting Texts: the Metaphysical Detective Story from Poe to Postmodernism*. Philadelphia: U of Pennsylvania P, 1999. 1–26.

Priestman, Martin. *The Cambridge Companion to Crime Fiction*. Cambridge: Cambridge UP. 2003.

Pynchon. Thomas. *The Crying of Lot 49*. New York: Perenial [1966] 1986.

Sklair, Leslie. *Globalization: Capitalism and Its Alternatives*. Oxford: Oxford UP, 2002.

Spivak, Gayatri. *Who Sings the Nation-State?: Language, Politics, Belonging*. New York: Seagull Books, 2007.

Tan, Amy. *The Joy Luck Club*. New York: Putnam's, 1989.

Taylor, Charles. "Understanding the Other: A Gadamerian View on Conceptual Schemes." *Gadamer's Century: Essays in Honor of Hans-Georg Gadamer*. Ed. Jeff Malpas et al. Cambridge: The MIT Press, 2002. 279–97.

Thompson, Jon. *Fiction, Crime, and Empire: Clues to Modernity and Postmodernism*. Urbana: U of Illinois P, 1993.

Yoon, Cindy. "Interview with Suki Kim: Author of *The Interpreter*." *Asia Source* 24 (March 2003). <http://www.asiasource.org/arts/sukikim.cfm>.

Index